Memoirs of a Coarse Zoo Keeper

Memoirs
of a
Coarse Zoo Keeper

George Jacobs
as told to
Franklyn Wood

Frederick Muller Limited
London

First published in Great Britain in 1982 by Frederick Muller Limited,
Dataday House, Alexandra Road, London SW19 7JZ

British Library Cataloguing in Publication Data

Jacobs, George
  Memoirs of a coarse zoo keeper.
  1. Jacobs, George   2. Zoologists—Biography
  I. Title   II. Wood, Franklyn
  591'.092'4   QL31.J/

  ISBN 0 584 11025 1

Phototypeset by Input Typesetting Ltd, London SW19 8DR
Printed in Great Britain by
Butler & Tanner Ltd, Frome and London

Contents

Introduction

From Gordon Mills and Tom Jones

I laughed outright and long when I read this book of George Jacobs's life story and I laughed particularly because it is so close to me. Tom Jones and I have known Tiger George for a long time and many hilarious things happened when he worked for me.

George has written a lot about Tom and me, but let *me* tell you a few things about George which he hasn't said about himself.

I can tell you about the time that I went to his room and found him with ten crates of hard boiled eggs. 'What the hell are you doing, George?' I asked.

He replied: 'Well, sir, I'm trying to break the *Guinness Book of Records* for eating the most boiled eggs in a minute.' Nor has he told you about the time when I bought Ollie, a full-grown gorilla, and George pleaded: 'Let me go in with him, it's always been my ambition to go in a cage with a fully-grown gorilla'.

I told him: 'All right, George, as long as I can have the exclusive rights to this'.

Ollie took no notice at all at first until George started to jump about to attract his attention. Then Ollie became interested, a bit too interested and he began mauling George. To cut a long story short, it resulted in Ollie stripping George of every remnant of clothing he was wearing. Then he was trapped in a corner and yelling, 'Please help me, sir'.

The only weapon I could find to defend us with was a heavy, long-handled shovel so I went into the cage with that and I whacked it across Ollie's face as hard as I could to get him off George.

Ollie didn't even blink, it was as if I'd hit him with a

feather. I said, '. . . you, George, sorry, but I'm off'. And I got out of that cage as fast as I could.

Oh yes, Tom Jones and I could tell a few tales about Tiger George if we chose to. But we wish him every success with this hilarious book.

Gordon Mills
Tom Jones

About George Jacobs

GEORGE JACOBS – Big George – is an elephant man, and elephants, by some natural intuition, know it. So wherever the great beasts are – circus, zoo or safari park – he is likely to be around. No matter what their size, a twelve foot giant or a 42-inch baby, they will take to him and do as he says. He knows their moods, their likes and foibles so well that each one has an individual relationship with him and he cares intensely about their welfare; more intensely still about their survival in the wild and the appalling prospect of them becoming extinct outside zoos in our lifetime.

But, like many of the genuine breed of zoo keepers who dedicate their lives to animals, all animals are his province from tiny marmosets, tropical birds, deer, orang-utans, and gorillas to big cats.

He won distinction and made national headlines in the newspapers when he walked into the cage, after a tiger had gone berserk at Gordon Mills's zoo, in Weybridge, to rescue his friend, Nick Marx, who was being severely savaged.

The power of wild animals is not lost on him: his associates and close friends, Bob Wilson and Brian Stocks, were both killed by tigers within weeks of each other in 1980.

'Every keeper always thinks that other people's animals are always more dangerous than his own; you see yours as friends who you know and love,' he says.

Animals have been the mainstay of his life but there is more to it than that: he has been circus act, singer, seaman, ship's cook and rolling-stone in his time. He lives life with an animal zest and vitality, which often means

3

that trouble is just around the corner. This is the story of George and his friends, tame and wild, animal and human.

Illustrations by
Richard Johnstone Scott

RICHARD JOHNSTONE SCOTT is recognised as one of the best gorilla men in the country; if there were a league table he would be rated among the top five in the world.

Which is why he has the distinction of being *Gerald Durrell's* gorilla keeper at the famous zoo on the island of Jersey, The Jersey Wildlife Preservation Trust.

Since Durrell introduced his gorillas, N'Pongo and Nandi, to the male Jambo and persuaded them to breed, they have been a vital part of his unqiue collection marking a breakthrough in conservation and captive breeding techniques. Durrell and Johnstone Scott were pioneers in the field.

But Richard's own successes in breeding captive animals have been just as distinguished: ten gorillas, two of them hand-reared; the first captive breeding of the African honey badgers and the hand-rearing of the tricky Saki monkeys, plus remarkable results with chimpanzees.

Durrell argued and eventually proved that to breed wild animals in captivity, first you had to make them feel happy; which meant not only good but proper housing, conditions, diet and environment and the security of a good relationship of trust and confidence with their keepers; which, in turn, meant *understanding* the complex natures of the animals. It requires special gifts and attitudes to be able to do that and Richard's is a natural talent brought about by a deep affinity with animals.

Just how natural are his talents is best illustrated by recalling the fact that he began his working life as a bricklayer and he went into zoo keeping, with no training and a substantial drop in earnings, because of the compelling attraction he felt for wild creatures. His intense appreciation in the most minute detail of observation and understanding shows clearly in his remarkable drawings of them, another natural talent that has expressed itself. He is often implored to give up the punishingly hard slog of practical zoo keeping to concentrate on his illustrations. But the answer is always no, he cannot bear to give up a living, close relationship with his charges.

Chapter 1

The Lord Mayor's Show

Half the fun of life is in knowing that it is a shambles. It may look all right from the sidelines, all neat, tidy and well-organised, but from where we are watching the game we know that it is chaos. We watch Government ministers, with an air of unreality about them, presiding over disaster; we observe remote top management, with an aura of executive sanctity surrounding them, restructuring themselves and their industries out of existence and proclaiming it a triumph; we listen to politicians, economists and experts, with the sounds of dissemblance thick in their mouths, tell us the one day that things are getting good and tell us the next that things have never been blacker. We have heard it all so many times, we have seen it all so often that, sensible people that we are, we laugh at them with tolerant indulgence and, in the vein of George Orwell, think that all people are lunatic but some are more lunatic than others.

Animals arrange things better. They know what they are for, what they are about and they have their priorities right: food, a place to sleep, space to play and peace in our time if others keep the peace. Animals are good to watch and live with – only humans mess them about.

But it isn't quite as simple as that . . .

Were you there on Jubilee day for the big parade? If you weren't, the rest of the world seemed to have flocked to London to celebrate the Queen's twenty-five years of rule.

I was there right in the middle of it with Rani, Rebecca, Gita and Vicky – tricky, underhanded Vicky, the naughty girl of the troupe of elephants.

The organisation was fantastic, marshals and stewards

by the hundred with everything planned as a precise military operation; a sense of pulsating excitement and high drama – but somebody cocked it up. They made a mistake by not understanding the simple facts of animal nature, and when you are handling two and three ton elephants it is best to know a little bit about them.

We were there in place led by the band of the Brigade of Guards, their buttons and instruments glistening in the warm summer sunshine, and followed by a band of baton-twirling, high-stepping drum majorettes gorgeously arrayed in their finery.

They needed to be high-stepping and agile. When an elephant walks, with that rolling, lumbering gait, swaying from side to side and lurching about, the action churns up her guts and her digestion works overtime; the logistics of elephants are very simple, you shovel one-and-a-half hundredweight of hay, 30 to 40 pounds of bread and vegetables and 40 gallons of water in at the front and it comes out, fully processed, at the rear. It drops in half-hundredweight consignments the size of footballs.

The guards in their metalled marching boots might have been all right though the shine on their polished toecaps would have dimmed a bit, but the girls in their white socks and patent leather shoes had to nip about somewhat causing ripples in their immaculate ranks and a flood of language that turned hardened Guardsmen's faces as scarlet as their tunics.

Vicky, of course, was being her usual bitchy self. She had a mean squint in her evil little eyes and, at every opportunity, she lunged into the crowd, they thought it all tremendous fun and part of the act, but we knew that her idea was to pick up a couple of bystanders and chuck them through a plate glass window just for the heck of it.

You could learn to love Vicky but you had to work damned hard at it. Seventeen miles we walked with Vicky making a lunge every couple of hundred yards or so; I have never been so battered, bruised and hoarse in all my life with elephants.

Behind the girls' band they had put the Whitbread Brewery dray horses, magnificent creatures dressed in their cockades and horse-brasses, which was a good and a bad thing: good for us because a limitless supply of bottles of pale ale made its way forward, bad for the following procession because the horses picked up the elephants' bad habits and made it even rougher underfoot for the marchers.

Bad, it turned out, for us as well because Carlos McManus who was leading Rani, the lead elephant, felt a desperate need to relieve himself and nipped through the crowd to go behind a bush; Rani could not bear the thought of life without him, so she followed – and so did Rebecca, Gita and Vicky.

The Guards marched off to the right, we shambled off to the left, the girls with their eyes fixed on our elephants' bottoms as a precaution followed us and a marshal blew a gut blowing his whistle. Vicky thought it was a marvellous opportunity to try and kneel on a few collected heads.

What I haven't explained is that when an elephant goes to the loo, she stops dead in her tracks. Which caused not a little confusion down the line. The Colonel Bogey boys in front steamed off into the distance and the rest piled up behind the piles.

Following the dray horses were a group of Turkish Cypriot acrobatic dancers and tumblers who always seemed to be in the middle of one of their more exotic tumbles at the moment one of our elephants felt the urge, so they cannoned into each other. The crowd thought it was very clever. The less wary of the Turks made some highly unorthodox landings when they touched ground on a pile of elephant droppings.

Meanwhile the Queen and the Queen Mother smiled their radiant smiles at the passing cavalcade.

We were not the only cause of trouble. Somebody had put Divvy Peter – he didn't have another name, just Divvy because he didn't have all his marbles at home – in charge of the camel. That was because Alfie or I usually looked after her but we were tied up with the elephants. Alfie was another without a name, a lot of circus and zoo men don't have names and it is better not to enquire too closely into the matter.

Sahara, the camel, objected to having her harness and fancy canopy put on, she was another awkward customer; since we were pushed for time, Alfie had walloped her to bring her into line.

9

So, at Battersea Park, when she was unloaded from the transporter box, she was in a vile mood. She kept curling back her lips and blowing foul breath at Alfie, camels are notorious for their halitosis, the foulest smelling breath of all beasts.

Though in this case it was difficult to know who smelled the sweeter, Divvy or Sahara, because Divvy had only one suit of clothes which he worked in, mucked out the stables in, emptied the Elsans in and slept in; it looked as if it was welded to him.

The procession had just moved off along Battersea Park Road when Sahara realised that Alfie and I had left and only Divvy was about, so she threw a 'wobbler' kicking out in all directions; camels have a hell of a kick, backwards, sideways or forwards with all legs. Pandemonium broke out among the other animals and Sahara decided to take off. A posh-voiced marshal called out: 'Hey there, you fellow, keep that camel in line'.

But Sahara was in full flight by this time with Divvy strung out horizontally behind her hanging on for grim death; dumb he was, but very conscientious. The pair of them shot past us like a rocket. 'Christ,' said Alfie, 'there goes the Red Shadow'.

They were really travelling, through red lights, through crowd barriers, through scattering crowds, and they kept going and half of London had its own little one-man Jubilee show. That was ten o'clock in the morning and at nine o'clock in the evening a solitary, lonely transporter was still awaiting their return to Battersea Park.

It was no use asking Divvy where they had been, he didn't even know what day it was.

A wonderful day, a triumph, a glorious exhibition of love and loyalty the press and television proclaimed. But one ice-cream seller was not happy about it.

At the beginning of the day we had been issued with tickets for a packed lunch to be collected at one of the many rest points. They needed rest points, people were keeling over everywhere, Chelsea Pensioners, poor old souls, had just about walked their legs off.

Our point was by a park and we thought we would rest the elephants under the trees. That was a mistake because it was instantly up-trunks and rip down the leafy branches for a munch, the park keeper was beginning to niggle about it.

There was a queue half-a-mile long and one old dear dishing out the grub. Two of us stood in the queue and the others kept watch on the animals.

Soon a crowd collected round the elephants and a passing ice-cream seller, attracted by the thought of a quick profit from the crowd, screeched to a halt. But business wasn't brisk enough for him so he turned on his electric musical box and the chimes rang out loud and clear. That did it. The elephants were shocked to attention, then they trumpeted back and charged.

There must have been fifty people round the van and they were just flung on one side as ten-odd ton of elephant crashed into its side. There was a great discordant clamour from the chimes, cornets flew into the air to splosh white in the road, choc-ices skidded along the pavement and wafers crumbled to dust. They toppled the van over like pushing over a pack of cards and the ice-cream drums emptied themselves over the hapless owner. He stood on the inside side of his van with his head protruding through his serving hatch screaming: 'I'll sue you for 60 gallons of ice-cream'.

Vicky looked well pleased with herself, it made her day, she was as good as gold afterwards.

That is one for the elephant keeper's book, never take an elephant near a musical ice-cream van, they're tone deaf.

But all is not high days and holidays, fun though they are. There is a glamour about wild animals and a fascination with them, but the public usually only sees them in their front-of-the-house role in the circus, safari park or zoo.

To state the absolutely obvious, an animal is a 24-hours-a-day creature, living, breathing and needing constant attention. The men who tend them are often as wild as their charges because it takes a very special breed to do the work. They do not do it for the money because there isn't any; they do it for the love of the beasts, without that it would be an impossible task. You must make a friend of the animal, winning its confidence and trust – even its respect.

Forget the idea that a wild animal can be tamed. It is not in the nature of the beast for that to happen. You can break it as you break a horse, you can make it manageable and train it to perform certain functions and routines; you can even induce the semblance of tameness, but under the skin there will always be its essential wildness, though wild is a wrong word, it is simply the nature of the creature behaving in its natural way.

Getting to know an animal is a matter of patience, getting the animal to know you needs even more patience. Take Shebe, a calf African elephant captured in the wild, crated and shipped by air through Amsterdam to Howletts Zoo in Kent. There is no way that creature is not going to be terrified when it arrives at its new home. Until that time it has probably never seen men at close quarters, now it will be among them, deprived of its mother, in a cold, inhospitable environment.

So there is the crate, six foot by eight foot by four foot: Shebe is a baby but a big baby with astonishing power in her limbs. The problem is how to get her out of that prison. The crate was fitted with a sliding door at the front. We dare not open it, she would just run wild and wreak havoc; she had to be chained round the legs so she could be eased out. To reach her legs holes were cut in the sides of the crate and the chains passed through by hand; it is as easy a way as any to break or even lose an arm.

She was going frantic inside the box, rearing, turning over, standing on her head; we did a little at a time then left her to calm down. It took a day-and-a-half to fix the chains before the door could be opened. Then, when she saw the light of day, she came out at a thundering rush.

Nine strong men were holding on to one chain, she dragged them round the shed like so much chaff; anybody who got in her way was butted or trunked, heavy men were being flung ten yards or more; the mayhem went on until she exhausted herself and the chains were slipped through retaining rings in the floor of the shed. Secured by back and front legs, she was manageable.

But she tugged at the chains and they chafed. So they had to be changed to alternative legs every other day. Doing the back legs was comparatively easy, slip one new

12

chain round the free leg then knock out the bolt from the other. But to do the front legs was something different – an experience. Right under her head and within easy reach of her lashing trunk, more men were hurled across the floor, but you just had to get in and do the job.

It was my job to break her. I sat in front of her, out of trunk reach, with a box of grapes and fed her one at a time. At the right moment I moved in an inch or two and fed her another batch of single grapes. She could not be left alone in case she fell over or tangled herself up. So we slept in the shed, and all the time I fed her and gave her milk and water. In a week she allowed me to go round behind her without lunging. We were winning.

Somewhere along the line since her capture (she was a victim of an elephant cull in her native area), she had developed an abcess on her side. It was pouring puss. The day of triumph came when she let me clean it.

That was only part of the process, the next stage was to integrate her with the rest of the herd. Elephants are choosy about that.

Shebe – a zoo man's joke name springing from the ruckus when she arrived. 'She be a right little bastard,' exclaimed one sprawling victim, picking himself up from the dust. Shebe is safe. But there is a terrible sadness about her of which she knows nothing. She was one of twenty elephants saved from the cull which destroyed 700; soon there will be no wild African elephants left. That is a statement of fact, they will become extinct in their own habitat and be found only in European and American zoos. Protection and conservation is a myth because there are no honourable men watching their interests in home territory; ivory smuggling goes on unabated, a few pounds buys as many capture or slaughter permits as you require. There is no way to impose Western ethics and standards upon a native African population – and we ourselves have only just learned the lesson ourselves – almost certainly too late.

Those of us who, in our time, have plundered the wild-life areas of the world and shipped a veritable Noah's Ark of specimens back to 'civilisation' for medical research or experiment as well as to zoos, know just how late it is for a thousand species.

13

By way of warning – this is an account of *coarse* zoo-keeping; that is because though animals have grace and powerful elegance of movement, they seldom have good manners and are never house trained. There are blood, guts and horrors behind the be-flowered faces of all zoos; carnivores eat *meat* and it has to be found in vast quantities from somewhere.

In one episode of the television series *All Creatures Great and Small* young Tristan, the lovely, gentle James Herriot's buffoon assistant attended a cow chronically sick with colic; he used the standard veterinary technique of piercing a knife through the rib cage to puncture the stomach and release the noxious gases. He was smoking a cigarette at the time and when the stinking, highly explosive vapour gushed out, it caught fire and burned down the barn.

When I worked at Gerald Durrell's zoo on the Island of Jersey, the Jersey Wildlife Preservation Trust, one of the finest of zoos I have ever been in, an old shire horse was brought in for slaughter. Meat was not much of a problem on the island, nearly all bull calves born to the vast Island Jersey herds are slaughtered. But putting down a huge shire horse is a different proposition from dealing with tiny calves. It was trouble from the beginning. First I hitched the old fellow to a balcony inside the shed, upstairs were the vet's office and the zoo's quarantine quarters. The powerful old brute pulled down the balcony and half the ceiling and lay among the dust and rubble with marmosets, tropical birds, and small mammals leaping around. But put the old boy down I did, all 16·2 hands of him. It is one of the unhappy jobs which has to be done.

A couple of days later I went to butcher the carcass for distribution. I was very green in those days and, at the height of a Jersey summer, the dead horse was also very green. Like Tristan, I too was smoking as I plunged in the knife. . . . The resulting explosion shook three baboon cages and a solid oak door. Carcasses produce many gases: methane, the deadly fire-damp, which, when synthesised, is used in high-explosive bombs.

It is a mad job, appallingly paid with, more often than not, sub-human living conditions with the dregs of humanity. Zoos take on the otherwise unemployable to do

14

the manual graft, nobody else would consider doing the work.

My mother gave me a good public school education, she struggled to pay my boarding school fees and I think she visualised me being a high court judge or doctor – something respectable, at least.

For twenty years she has hung her head in shame at the thought of me shovelling elephant, tiger, monkey – any old kind of animal – dung and hoping for a promotion that might raise my standard of living to the level of the gutters of Calcutta.

It all really began in Calcutta, so I'll begin at the beginning. . . .

High steppers – of necessity – in the big parade.

Chapter 2

Animal farms, town and country

All Darwinian theory is proved QED *in five minutes in a London comprehensive school, only the fittest can survive: not the brightest, not the kindest, not the brainiest, not the hardest working and most conscientious – only the fittest. Know the ways of a London comprehensive and you will learn to love the gentility of nature of the snarling tiger, rogue bull elephant and lethal hamadryad. Wild-eyed and bared-fanged, a London comprehensive school teacher is the wildest animal you will ever encounter. A loving mother took me out of this environment into that of an exclusive upper-class school. But it wasn't as simple as all that . . .*

The seeds of my passion for animals and zoos were probably sown at Holland Park Secondary School, the London educational establishment which attracted a lot of comment, fame or notoriety, depending on your views of progressive education in the 1960s. It had a distinctly zoo-like quality: the assembled pupil body of the school could generate the tensions of a tiger compound and the staff were there as much in the role of keepers as teachers.

It was full-frontal nature in the raw and the curator-headmaster had an unwavering belief in the torment and chastisement of the flesh as a way to academic enlightenment; so there were public beatings on the stage at morning assembly when one member of staff held the victim and another practised his golf swing on him.

What Regents Park is to members of the London Zoological Society, Holland Park could be to members of a London Educational Sociologists Society, if such a body existed: a large collection of rare species under one roof available for scientific study – except that Holland Park specimens would probably eat the investigators. At least they would have done in my time.

The curator was an ordained minister in one of the off-licence non-conformist churches and he convinced me of the truth that a true Christian must suffer if he is to achieve life everlasting – though what the bonus would be in that if it was anything like life at Holland Park, I never discovered. He made a deep impression on me and I think of him often, particularly when I am working in the gorilla cages when they are behaving a bit uppity.

On reflection, there must be some sympathy for the staff; I was a very big lad and fully aware of my own strength, and there were others like me in the school. It cannot have been easy or fun keeping us in order. Once I threatened to wrestle and wallop the headmaster if he tried to lay hands on me. The awful thing is that I could have done it and caused a lot of damage.

Ah well, animals are nicer and safer than human beings.

Then my mother decided that she would try to turn her increasingly rough rough-diamond into a polished City Gent and sent me away to boarding school at Seaford College, Worthing: chapel in the morning, chapel in the evening and unmitigated purgatory in between. No place for the likes of me.

But Mum could never grasp the fact that she had spawned a misfit. When she dies she will go murmuring: 'I wanted him to be a doctor'. And on her poor old heart will be inscribed: '. . . or a high court judge would have done'. She insisted on blowing the profits from the family guest house in Earls Court on a fruitless quest for a higher education and a public school old boys' tie to ease my way into the genteel, polite world she craved.

Seaford is, of course, a great and famous school of high academic standards. Apart from the set curriculum, pupils are encouraged to study any specialist subject of their choice: Serbo-Croat – no problem; Chinese metaphysics – the tutor will call three times a week. But they drew the line at all-in wrestling. It was all I wanted to do at that time. I worshipped all those gruesome hulks on television;

17

they were my heroes. I wondered at their agility and the crashing falls they bounced back from.

A raised eyebrow and a certain glint in the eye and you could virtually hear the staff thinking the public school equivalent of 'We've got a right one 'ere, Charlie'.

They wouldn't, couldn't take me seriously but the big difference between Seaford College and Holland Park Secondary was that whereas Alan Clark would have exploded about 'cheek and gross impertinence', here they muttered something along the lines of 'original, shows spirit' and they wrote glowing reports of my progress to Mum who kissed the letters in delight and murmured ecstatically: 'He's going to be a doctor, yet . . . or maybe a High Court judge'.

The rule at Seaford in those days was that nobody under 18 could wear long trousers or shave. When mother took me to Corringes to be kitted out with my baggy shorts and straw boater, the salesman all but split his gut laughing, but he looked at the size of me, the evil expression on my face, listened to Mum admonishingly telling me, 'Now George, behave,' and decided to choke on his smirk. The result of the shaving ban was that my five o'clock shadow lasted a term, and I looked permanently unwashed; I went to school all scrubbed clean, smart and sharp only to come home looking like Wurzel Gummidge. All that effort, all that money, the sustained agony to produce not a single simple O-level. Nothing!

In the background there were always animals. Like a fully grown sooty mangabey, a large African monkey which I bought for £8. The only place to keep it was my Great Aunt Gertrude's box room, so I left her with instructions to clean it out, feed and water it while I was away at school. Poor old Great Aunt Gertie, she was topping 70 then, a remnant of Victorian prudery.

Vladimir, the monkey, would sit scratching his great dangling testicles while occasionally breaking down the door and ripping her entire wardrobe to shreds; in her panic and frustration she called the local police, so half of Kensington police station force were on permanent duty detailed to make regular calls to keep Vladimir in order.

There were other little charmers like a pet fox whose name was abbreviated to Bast. He could emit a pungently acrid stream of piss which scorched the nostrils and stripped the paintwork and he couldn't be housetrained.

Saddest of all was little Honker, a gorgeous tame toucan who played football. He was called Honker because he honked incessantly and drove the neighbours to distraction with his honking until there came the time when either we all had to move or I had to part with him. Heartbreaking for me, heaven for them.

Naturally, I had gone through all the standard domestic stuff like white mice, rats, rabbits, hamsters and suchlike; I wanted bigger animals and birds who would do interesting things like take somebody's finger off or maim the unwary, things you had to know something about in order to keep them alive. The wild ones always attracted and fascinated me.

In the holidays I used to work for Charlie Palmer, the Camden Town animal dealer, who, in his time, was one of the biggest dealers in England. The front of his premises was just an ordinary pet shop, but the back was a teeming menagerie of thousands of creatures; they arrived by the crateload, by day and by night, every known species in the world; it was in the days before controls and conservation laws; £20 would buy you the rarest specimen known to man, if it was carryable, you could walk out of the shop with it under your arm.

Thousands upon thousands of creatures: small mammals, large mammals, reptiles, birds . . . in every sense, *all creatures great and small*: creatures so rare that they will never be seen again, the beautiful, the grotesque and downright ugly. And all of us involved were ignorant of the irreparable damage we were doing, but so too were governments, zoo curators, veterinary surgeons, zoologists – experts and simple animal lovers alike.

Nobody honestly believed that two short decades could lead to the virtual extermination of whole species of fantastic animals then in profuse population in their habitats. Like the plentiful, common fishes of the sea around the shores, and the massive armadas of whales in their Antarctic breeding grounds, it seemed laughably impossible that man could ever devise the physical means to catch his prey and denude his environment to the extent of utter barrenness.

19

Yet it was all happening behind the facade of that friendly pet shop in Camden Town. Do not blame Charlie Palmer, he was doing the job that he knew best and he was doing it well. He was supplying a need, a need created by public demand and business was BOOMING. He was a big cog in the international wheel, but there were dozens of others in the wildlife trade.

At Charlie Palmer's I learned the self-evident, obvious – but then not immediately apparent to a gauche teenage lad – fact that animals are a twenty-four hour job just to keep them alive. And dealers like living stock since carcasses do not make a profit. So as fast as the stock rolled in they were uncrated, fed, watered, bedded-down and made comfortable to ensure that they thrived. Those that were alive when they arrived, that is.

I took a permanent job with Charlie when I finished school. Animal magic! Oh, drop dead Johnny Morris and Walt Disney, only the idiot classes go in for looking after animals and suffer the rough end of other people's pleasure; along with zoo keepers are convent-educated middle-class riding school stable girls who do it because they like the feel of ponies under their bottoms, and emaciated stable lads who keep alive by dreaming of the big break which will turn them overnight into a Lester Piggot or Steve Cauthen.

We do it because we are daft, there can be no other reason.

Chapter 3

Camden Town and other faraway places

Being by inclination and achievement a natural born problem for the Job Centre, I didn't bother them to help me find work. I let my part-time weekend work with Charlie Palmer operate under Parkinson's Law and expand into a full-time job. But tinkering about in your teens is all very well until the dreadful thought strikes: 'I can't keep doing this for the rest of my life'. And the fear sets in that your life will be over before you have done anything positive. 'Hell! I'll be eighteen in two years time.' The sea, that was the answer; see the world and do a useful constructive job at the same time, a good, stable life. But it wasn't as simple as all that . . .

Goodbye to my straw boater, baggy shorts, natty blazer, school tie, chapel in the morning, chapel in the evening, chapel nearly all the time . . . at last, freedom. Goodbye too to Mum's cherished dreams of a white-coated career under the Hippocratic Oath, or even a pin-striped suited career under the oath of 'I swear by Almighty God to tell the truth etc. etc.,' as a lawyer. The only oaths I was to become fully acquainted with were those of a fruitier variety.

My interests were in animals, so what more natural than that I should start work with animal dealer pal, Charlie Palmer. But, of course, that statement isn't the whole truth of the matter, there was nothing else I could do; not a whisper of academic achievement had graced my school career and Mum lamented in stunned disbelief: 'Such a good school, not a single O-level'. In cases like mine a 'good' school is a distinct drawback; expectations are raised too high and prospective employers, hearing the illustrious name of the school, think: 'Splendid, he must be a good lad'. When they see a total blank on the results sheet their opinion is rapidly changed to: 'Good God! What have we here? Must be a total lunatic'. End of interview.

So it had to be Charlie Palmer's.

London is a city full of unexpected surprises, particularly commercial surprises. Enterprise lurks behind the most unlikely facades: the public would never have dreamed that behind the homely facade of that friendly pet shop there was an international organisation with connections in India, Thailand, Borneo, the Cameroons, all parts of Africa, South America, the United States, Middle East, Europe . . . everywhere where animals lived and bred.

Pet-shop Charlie's tentacles encompassed the world to provide livestock for domestic pets, commercial entertainment and zoological education.

Had they but known the facts, anti-vivisectionists could have learned more about the trade than they ever dreamed possible and laid permanent siege to the place.

It does no good to soul or conscience to recall that, in the callowness of youth, you served a trade that was ultimately to be shown as disreputably, culpably, dishonestly destructive to LIFE and inimical to all the things you would grow to hold most treasured. But even such a very short time ago we were all guilty through ignorance: medical men, scientists, zoologists, fur traders, fashion houses, farmers, agriculturalists, perfumiers, jewellery designers, milliners, shoe makers, handbag manufacturers – in some way, there is hardly a trade or profession which has not in its time been responsible for denuding the world's animal life.

And the public in the street is just as blameworthy; all those super-sexy ones of you who like the feel of leather next to your skin and love to cut a dash in your crocodile skin coat with matching handbag; all the thousands who take exotic pets without any idea how to care for them and shed a crocodile tear when they die, as die they must; a million tortoises perish through neglect every year.

It is often said with a hint of chauvinistic pride that an

22

Englishman cares more for his animals than for his children and critics claim significance in the fact that, of the two great national caring charities, it is The *Royal* Society for the Prevention of Cruelty to Animals whereas it is only the *National* Society for the Prevention of Cruelty to Children, the latter being denied the accolade of worthiness implied by the royal prefix.

But R.S.P.C.A. inspectors and zoo keepers would question the assertion having experienced at first hand the horrors the public can inflict on captive animals. Unwitting cruelty is disgusting enough, like the appalling damage done to ducks, geese and wading birds by micro-thin fishing line, wickedly lethal fish hooks and lead weights strewn along all our waterways by careless, callous fishermen. If only they would stop to think that the casually discarded length of hook, line and sinker can mean almost certain death by slow starvation for the bird entangled in it, death by choking or internal bleeding for the bird which swallows a hook, death by poisoning from a gizzard full of lead weights; and remember, it is a lonely death, with no help at hand from any creature other than a bird or game warden happening to chance by, and such people are very thin on the ground.

Gerald Durrell records how he nearly lost his whole stock of water fowl, including some exceptionally rare species, by lead poisoning when a cache of twelve bore cartridges, hidden during the Nazi occupation of Jersey, disintegrated in his lake and spewed the deadly lead pellets into the water.

He also tells of razor blades and lighted cigarettes being fed to monkeys and apes – unbelievable, by any civilised standards; and he tells the story of the fat lady who actually sat on his macaw, Captain Koe, and squashed it to death. He remarks in wonderment how anybody could sit on a bird the size of a macaw and not notice it, but she walked away apparently completely unaware.

So I started my life with animals in the bedlam of the dealers' market and learned the facts of animal life the hard way, loving it all until a sense of conscience caught up with me as I gained experience and respect for the creatures I tended.

There is no way you can be mealy-mouthed about the

animal world when you live in it. Death, disease, blood and mess are an intrinsic element of nature; killing is the instinct of predators to be exercised at every available opportunity: carnivora crave fresh, newly killed meat and consequently kill for it; the herbivora will fight to kill to preserve their patch of lush grazing. These simple, incontrovertible facts you must learn to live with if you wish to enjoy the animal kingdom.

But an anti-animal disease afflicts the human species. It is called *anthropomorphism*; it is far more dangerous than man's craving to shoot animals because it destroys by minimising them. Anthropomorphism is attributing human qualities to wild animals. Apart from being insulting to the animals it is a threat to species including the human one. Walt Disney has a great deal to answer for in this field: millions of people look upon animals in a completely distorted way because of his work, for them the caricature becomes more real than the reality. The disease is astonishingly widespread ranging from Teddy bears to tigers in the tank. Consider the slanders perpetrated against just a few wild creatures:

BEARS: *the fiction:* stupid, goofy-voiced rollicking creatures, good for a laugh but essentially cuddlesome and good-natured.
The fact: not friendly and benign beasts, they are aggressive and utterly unpredictable.
TIGERS: *the fiction:* also soppy-voiced, affable four-legged friends ever ready with a nudge and a wink; comedians, rascals but cuddly lovable creatures.
The fact: animals of immense dignity and reserve without an ungraceful movement in them; intelligent with a complex, sophisticated communications system between themselves; ruthless killers.
FOXES: *the fiction:* sly, wily, unscrupulous and selfish; the epitome of evil and cunning – very nasty pieces of work.
The fact: strong family animals, brilliant providers for their brood; keen, alert and extremely beautiful; resourceful enough to survive in conditions from the Arctic to the desert.

Why do we kid ourselves? Why do we let advertising

manipulators distort our views? If a city-bred child of the 1980s were to meet a grizzly or a polar bear, or a tiger, in its natural habitat, the truth would be shock enough to kill – if the media-admass weaned infant hadn't been disembowelled and dismembered first.

As a species we have inflicted indignity and hardship on most animals in the world, not only by eating them but by wearing them, usurping their grazing and feeding grounds, processing their innards to make ourselves smell sweeter, making them work for us and catching them and keeping them for our amusement. We call ourselves animal lovers: as a lover an animal needs us like a hole in the pelt.

Let us face it, most animals would never seek our company. Given the chance most of them would run a hundred miles, climb the highest mountain and swim the deepest river to avoid us, and, once we have them in our loving care, most will take the earliest opportunity to escape from our kindliest of intentions.

Cruelty is, sadly, very often involved in keeping animals in captivity. But not usually, you may be surprised to hear, at the hands of dealers like Charlie Palmer. Dealers need their stock in prime condition, gleaming with health and looking happy if they are going to sell them for a good price, so animals are well kept. But some diabolical strokes are occasionally pulled on the gullible public.

In animal conservation, twenty years ago is a very long time away. To think now of the livestock which was being shunted, unthinkingly, round the world of animal dealers in those days is a chastening experience: the rarest of species which were being brought to the brink of extinction by the trade were handled in an almost cavalier fashion.

It seems a very lame excuse to say that nobody knew any better, but it was true. On the other side of the coin, if those wily dealers could lay hands on one-hundredth of the stock they had then and sell it today, they would be rich men indeed on rarity value alone.

The whole business was a very casual affair. You wouldn't think you were dealing with living, breathing creatures each of which, as we are now too well aware, needed its own special diet and treatment; in those days they were bunged into a crate, a note stuck on the side saying: 'Please give water,' put on a ship or airplane and sent. Deaths in transit were formidable, but it was remarkable how many did survive.

It is truly remarkable that you can take a wild animal, which in most cases has never known mankind, tear it from its natural habitat, remove it from family and companions, deprive it of its food supply, incarcerate it in a space so confined that it has hardly the room to turn, place it in a roaring, throbbing machine of which it can have no possible conception, despatch it to a different climate, put it into a hostile environment, in fact, subject it to a terror which the hardiest members of the human race would be hard put to to survive, and it will come out chirpy and bright-eyed and almost always hungry, when all good sense says it should have died of fright.

One day a shipping agent's clerk telephoned the shop and told us: 'I've got a consignment of tortoises for you at the docks, can you collect?'

We visualised a couple of crates of infant cigarette packet-sized chelonians which would scramble and tumble over each other in the pet shop window until eventually they were bought and all were lost in the gardens of Camden Town, Islington and Hampstead, like they are every year.

But, cautiously, we asked: 'What are they like? How many? Where are they from?'

'Big 'uns,' said the clerk, 'big buggers. How the hell should I know how many? Count 'em when you collect. All it says on the manifest is "Livestock, bloody abracadabra bleedin' tortoises," and the crates bust open and they're all over the bleedin' shop, so get down bloody quick, they're 'oldin the job up.'

Down on the dockside we found a dozen Aldabra Giant Tortoises, each the size of a large labrador dog and, even in those days, not a common-or-garden everyday shipment.

They come from the Aldabra atoll in the Seychelles and the *Encyclopaedia Britannica* states: 'In 1955 the islands were leased for commercial exploitation of mangrove timber and fishing, under stringent safeguards for the rare flora

26

and fauna. South Island has been declared a nature reserve with absolute protection for wildlife. Rarities include a rail, an ibis and a dove. The giant land tortoise (*Testudo Elephantina*) occurs and the lagoon teems with hawksbill and edible turtles.'

Somebody had not read the rules about them and, clearly, they had suffered a hell of a voyage in the hold of that pitching, rolling tramp ship, tossed around like dice in a shaker. Whether they had ever been fed or watered during that torrid eleven-week voyage from the Indian Ocean, via Singapore, was questionable. Maybe somebody had chucked in a few green vegetables and some water when the hatches were opened at ports of call . . . maybe, but highly unlikely. We could get no sense out of the Sepoy deck-hands and the foreign officers looked such an evil lot as would have slit your throat for a tot of rum, that we didn't dare press the point. Definitely not the types to be kind to animals or grandmothers; with that crew the miracle was that the tortoises had not arrived as a job-lot of assorted fancy tortoise-shell hair combs and fashion frames for spectacles.

Magnificent creatures that they were, they looked, indeed, a sorry sight, covered in grease and dust, their shells cracked with holes the size of a Bramley cooking apple punched into them; they must have been flung against the sides of that crate with the force of cannonballs from a cannon.

Can there be a creature less able to look after itself in stormy conditions at sea? The poor thing is virtually unstable on a billiard table top; in a rolling, pitching, yawing ship it can only go wherever the tempest tosses it; no effective limbs to hold or push against a support, no balance, no adhesion to a solid surface. It knows fear, as we can tell by its instant retraction within its shell when it senses danger; that voyage must have inflicted terror into the creatures.

We did what we could for them; immediate food, water, fresh, clean straw, a wash down to remove the vile smelling grease – but how can you tell if you've made a tortoise happy?

Yet these unfortunate creatures were destined to become zoological firsts, pioneers in their own way.

Charlie Palmer was destroyed when he set eyes upon them. He raged against idiot, mercenary Asiatic dealers, uncaring shipping lines, callous crews and cruel mankind in general. In that condition they weren't worth a light to him. Such is the fickleness of the British public – to be fair, all publics – that they wish to see only pretty animals in prime conditon: maimed and crippled animals upset and offend them. Zoos are well aware of this and will buy only good-looking stock for public display.

Nobody, nobody at all, was ever going to buy a bunch of knocked-about tortoises, no matter how rare or unusual. The public relates to tortoises: they've kept them in boxes in the garden, they've fed them lettuce leaves, they've wrapped them in straw when they hibernate if they haven't lost them before then, and they have been thrilled when they have come out of hibernation in the spring – and if not, well, a hibernating tortoise is a pretty inanimate thing so the sadness is minimised. In a giant tortoise at a zoo, they like to see a bigger, more magnificent version of Tommy, their own pet, and they love to gasp in wonderment when they learn the great age of the zoo specimen.

Charlie was an extremely resourceful man: this was the period of the great fibreglass boom when people were patching up old bangers in the garage; boats were coming on to the market in increasing numbers manufactured entirely from fibre glass; incredibly tough, rustproof, flexible, resilient stuff, the advertisements claimed.

The caller asked to see Mr. Palmer. 'Tell him it's the sculptor,' he instructed. What the hell did Charlie want with an arty, crafty sculptor? Was he going to have his ugly old features chiselled in marble for posterity? Had he actually kept an animal long enough to grow to love it so much that he wanted a permanent reminder of it?

'Lift one of the tortoises on to the bench,' Charlie said. It was rested astride a block on the bench, its fat little legs waving in the air until it grew tired of that exercise and retreated for a nap in its shell.

The sculptor got out his pack of Isopon fibreglass, paste, mixing rod, tube of hardener, piece of glass-tissue plus assorted tinctures and dyes. He first filled a small crack in the shell, moulded and rubbed it to an astonishingly perfect fit and announced: 'Yes, it will work, it has bonded perfectly.'

Little by little each segment of the shell was filled. He worked with immense patience to achieve perfect colour matches. He moulded the lines in the shell and copied each and every pattern in the texture until there was a tortoise shining new and in a perfect, gleaming shell. A month later it was still intact; it is still intact today.

It was I think probably the first cosmetic surgery performed upon an animal, or to be precise, a reptile. And from that developed a booming trade in restoring damaged birds' beaks, other shells and most horny protuberences. They seem to like it: most of them buck up considerably when their damaged parts are artificially restored – perhaps they too have a streak of vanity and feel good, like we do when a tooth is filled.

I must confess that I took quite a pride in working the odd trick on Charlie's gullible customers. I would romp and play with tiny bear cubs, let them nibble and suck at my fingers, tickle their tummies and extol their virtues as lovable, charming, unusual little pets, marvellous for the children. It was the same technique with assorted monkeys: wonderful, playful pets, we said but we did not explain how quickly they would grow. When the distracted Mum reappeared a few months later pleading to know what she could do with the four foot monster which was now wrecking house and home, and would we *please* take it back, we sympathised while explaining that, unfortunately, the bottom had just fallen out of the market for her particular pet and nobody was buying bears or monkeys.

With deeper sympathy we asked: 'Do you find it expensive to feed?' She did. 'That's the problem,' we commiserated, 'you see how much it will cost us if we take it back, we will have to keep it for a long time since it was most unlikely that we would be able to sell it quickly. We'd have to advertise it to the trade and that would cost us money.' So she could see how difficult it was for us poor animal dealers though we would dearly love to help. In the finish she would be at the stage of offering us money to take it off her hands and apologising for the trouble she was causing. 'We'll look after it, love,' we

29

promised, 'here, have a hamster in exchange, or a couple of white mice. Lovely – oh, err, that's a fiver for the cage, the animals are free.'

One pet craze reached serious proportions and caused an alarming public nuisance. It became fashionable to keep a crocodile or alligator in the house (crocs from the Nile, alligators, with broader snouts, different teeth and other slight differences, from America; some from Australasia, but in a muddy river on a murky night, they are all the same to the man who gets his leg bitten off). Thousands of caimans were imported from South America and sold as 'pets' when they were a teeny one or two foot long. It all began after a series of articles about unusual pets appeared in various glossy, way-out magazines and fashion photographers thought it sexy to show a long, thin model holding a wicked looking croc. The trouble is that in four or five years a tiddling toy pet becomes a sizable monster with jaws that can inflict considerable damage, like biting off and swallowing the hand that feeds it. Moreover it can never be domesticated like a cat or dog.

The craze died as quickly as it had begun and London Zoo, among many other zoos, was inundated with offers of secondhand crocs of varying sizes. The zoos could not cope: they did not have the room to house them all, and they would have had more crocs than paying customers.

In America, as is usually the case, the craze went to greater extremes and the problems of disposing of the creatures were so much the greater when the fashion waned. Many a New Yorker solved the dilemma by flushing his 'pet' down the lavatory, but they didn't all die when that happened. Anybody who has walked the streets of New York city cannot have failed to notice the unique New York phenomenon of steam issuing from every crack in the sidewalks, vents, pipes and grids. Ever since central heating was invented, New Yorkers have been slowly cooking themselves in steamed-jam-pudding temperatures and the waste from that excessive heat has naturally percolated to the sewers below the city which has made them very cosy, hospitable places for orphaned crocs and, by all reports, a number of them survived. It was not many years before New York sewage workers going about their vital but unappealing duties in the murky caverns of the city's bowels observed, to their shock and horror, the occasional fully grown crocodile – one man claimed a ten footer – slithering away into the steamy gloom . . . the stuff of horror sci-fi movies which could be entitled *The Monster from the Inner Sewers*.

Moving any wild animal from its natural habitat to another, even a continent away, can, and so often does, have unexpected and disastrous results: even in England's monster-free, green and pleasant land such follies have reaped devastating rewards. The zoologists who imported the pretty grey squirrel to Regents Park, in 1925, did not foresee that they were bringing a plague to the land, now that they have bred to pestilential proportions, nor did the Suffolk landowner who brought home as mementoes a pair of Indian collared-doves anticipate that they would proliferate to become a national curse to farmers; similarly with mink and coypu.

' 'Tis flyin' in the face o' nature,' said Grandma in *Cold Comfort Farm*, Stella Gibbon's hilarious classic, and Grandma had seen 'something nasty in the woodshed'. The warning should be that by 'flyin' in the face of nature' you might unwittingly let that nasty something out of the woodshed and live to regret it.

Talk of tens of thousands of wild animals captured, transported and sold to satisfy a passing craze seems, to people outside the animal world, to be totally unreal; it is difficult for the average city dweller to conceive such numbers and they are entitled to be sceptical. At the same time they should pay some heed to the doomwatchers who, in the case of conservation, are not protecting vested interests and profits; on the contrary, their findings frequently go against commercial interests.

There is little disagreement among the experts who study the subject that by the end of the 1980 decade one species will disappear from the face of the earth for ever every hour; that, of course, includes flora as well as fauna and covers everything from invertebrates to whales. Species would disappear anyway, but the awful worry is that man is accelerating the process so rapidly that it really is 'flyin' in the face o' nature'.

Dr. Malcolm Coe, of the Department of Zoology at Oxford University, points out that rarity is much commoner in nature than commonness, so the danger is that with every acre of rain forest destroyed by man in South America there is the probability that some rare species will also be eliminated . . . and we will probably never know.

What we do know is disturbing enough: the whales of the sea, decimated; the tigers of India reduced to a few hundreds where once were thousands; closer home, our own birds of prey killed in such numbers by chemicals that they have almost ceased to exist.

Consider one official fact: the World Wildlife resident observer stationed in Uganda reported 14,000 elephants and 3,000 rhino slaughtered in that sad country in one year, 1980. My own little lovely, Shebe, came from one of those culls, but our man in Uganda reported 22,000 elephants destroyed that year, not 14,000. And that was to satisfy a comparatively small but highly lucrative market in ivory, in the first case, and aphrodisiac powder made from ground rhino horn, in the other.

The year 1980 is a significant year to quote, a new decade of enlightenment, so-called; a concensus of opinion that wild life must be protected and saved; the Greenpeace movement winning a major success with the Russians finally agreeing to desist from the mass destruction of the world's whale population. Yet out in the field, where the endangered animals are, the implementing of brave words and ideals was proving an impossible task and the mindless slaughter continuing unabated.

Observation of attitudes to animals often gives an insight into human nature; to the native population of Uganda, animals are there for killing and profit. A 'kill' of a good specimen of big game is still regarded as an initiation into manhood, but if the native population holds rare animal life cheap, they hold their fellow mankind equally cheaply and kill each other with the same lack of understanding and compassion.

When whole urban populations fall for some fad or fashion, the damage to the animal world can be devastating. In the Victorian age no self-respecting city gent would be seen without his tall beaver hat, the stovepipe headgear shown in Dickensian illustrations. Londoners, New Yorkers, Mancunians, Milwaukeeans, all over the world it was a social obligation for any male with pretensions to being a gentleman to sport a beaver pelt on his head; it became one of the widest international fashions of all time surpassed only by the universal blue jeans compulsion of recent years. The fashion nearly denuded the whole North American continent of its beaver population. Massive fortunes were made from the trade and the foundations of great American and British commercial dynasties were laid by trappers pillaging the simple, lovable beaver's lodge. If beavers hadn't been just as busy breeding as well as building boring old dams across mountain streams, the whole American species could easily have become extinct.

Like they do, the fashion collapsed and the beaver was saved to be left to go about his business of civil engineering on the American and Canadian rivers, scoffing great quantities of trout and salmon and generally living the good life. Actually, the sheer thrill and pleasure of watching a colony of beaver at quicksilver work and play by their dam is worth a couple of plates of smoked salmon or a trout with almonds, lemon and the butter poured over it, any time – well, nearly worth it.

Talking about Uganda and North America may seem a digression from my story but it isn't really. I spent most of my time in Charlie Palmer's service digressing from the mundane daily routine. I watched with awe and wonder the strange exotic creatures: Wanderoo monkeys from Sri Lanka – (then called Ceylon), very rare marmosets, ten other species of monkey at any given time, Indian otters, eagles, falcons, birds in wild, brilliant profusion, snakes of such precise, vivid colour and design they looked as if they had been hand-painted. The smells excited my nostrils, fustiness intermingled with sharp, acidic tangs; the noise and the clamour suggested a wider, more stimulating environment.

I tried to imagine them free, swinging in the trees, slinking through the undergrowth, fully extended in acrobatic exercise. I asked a gnarled, old assistant who had been everywhere, seen everything, if they were really commonplace and everyday where they came from. ' 'farsan's of 'em abart,' he assured me, 'trip over the bleeders in the street, knock yer 'at off in the jungle, so many of

33

'em. Where the sun's out, the 'ole bleedin' world's alive wiv 'em.'

The names on the crates intoxicated me: Sarawak, Borneo, Calcutta, Mombassa – names from deep in the heart of the rain forests of South America, the jungles of Africa and India, remote islands in the South Pacific and Indian Oceans, faraway places with strange sounding names. . . . 'Some lucky bastard has been out to those places, caught the creatures and sent them back here,' I reasoned, bringing the full weight of my so-called classical education to bear upon the problem. There were problems: problem one, no money. Solution: dead easy, join the merchant navy and sail away to mysterious Eastern ports, palm-fringed islands and fetid rivers in steamy jungles where nights were made terrifying with strange shrieks, screams and roars. Great!

I signed on in the Norwegian merchant navy and joined this Norwegian ship which the agent assured me sailed exclusively under hot tropical suns calling only at romantic places where Trevor Howard, George Sanders, Humphrey Bogart and Somerset Maugham lounged in wicker chairs, a chota-peg in hand and a dusky maiden in tow. It didn't.

The *S. S. Ravnfell* plowed a weary furrow from Glasgow to Montreal and all points west to Chicago; the only wild creatures to be observed being Glaswegian dockers and Chicago longshoremen and Teamsters. We sailed not like a stately Spanish galleon with a cargo of diamonds, emeralds, amethysts, topazes, and cinnamon, and gold moidores; not even like a dirty British coaster with a salt-caked smoke stack and a cargo of Tyne coal, road-rail, pig-lead, firewood, iron-ware and cheap tin trays. No, we sailed with a cargo of Teachers, Glen Grant, Livet, Dimple Haig and Booths Dry Gin – 10,000 tons of fine Scotch whisky and gin destined to add an extra glow to the Great American Dream.

The sea is a hard taskmaster, first things must come first, the basics of survival are the great priority. 'Listen good,' said the bosun, 'they allow one per cent of the cargo for pilferage, remember that.' 'Listen,' said the deckhands on the mess desk, 'they allow one per cent of the cargo for pilferage, remember that.' 'Listen,' said the third mate . . . but by this time I'd got the message.

Again the classical education was brought into play. Depending on what those hard-drinking Glasgow dockies had left, and each and every one of them had a thirst like the Sahara and Gobi deserts combined, there should be the residue of 100 tons; how many bottles to the ton? At 26.4 fluid ounces per bottle . . . remember the weight of the bottle . . . oh, what the heck, there is enough for a hell of a party, it could be a very interesting voyage.

Not much happened on those voyages – not much that I can remember very clearly. Only one thing sticks in my memory, the other part of the cargo was bars of chocolate, I never could figure that out.

Then came the break I had waited for, the *S.S. Count Bernadotte* was sailing under the Norwegian flag bound for Calcutta. That sounded more my cup of Indian tea. There was no problem moving from one Norwegian ship to another, so I signed on with her.

I never seem to have the good sense to sign on a completely sober ship, or perhaps they don't make them. The mate on the *Count Bernadotte* was slightly eccentric, a very dedicated and sincere man who was awe-struck by the character and achievement of the great and distinguished Swedish international statesman the ship was named after. The Count had no more ardent supporter, fan, advocate and admirer than our mate who would burst dramatically and noisily on to the mess deck screaming: 'Layabouts – drunkards – worthless swine, you should be *honoured*, honoured, to serve in a ship bearing so great a name. There is no greater name than Bernadotte – and he died for scum like you.' He had a curious way of trying to underline and enforce the strength and validity of his views and we would say quickly and with urgent sincerity in our voices: 'We are honoured, Chief, very, very honoured – now will you put the meat cleaver down, please'. The mate would then be overcome with remorse and grief at the memory of his hero and would collapse in sobs at the nearest table until we could persuade him to go to bed, or drive the ship or do anything except sob and swing the meat cleaver about on our mess deck.

In Calcutta, *Count Bernadotte*, the ship, that is, got a

terrible gut-ache and required urgent attention to her boilers and engines which, so we gleaned from visiting engineers, agents and shipwrights, would require parts being shipped from Europe and would take weeks possibly running into months. The idea did not appeal so I decided to forgo the honour of serving any longer on *Count Bernadotte* and jumped ship.

Chapter 4

Oh, Calcutta!

At last I'd found the difference – and it was quite as exciting as discovering the opposite sex. It caused the same rushes of blood to the head, the same nervous tingling, the same breathless anticipation. There was the same sweet smell of mystery in the air and a longing to touch. This was the world I'd run away to see; this was India and, before setting foot on her shores, I was in love with her. The rest of the world I'd seen had been Hilton-ised; concrete, plastic Milwaukee is a replica of Manchester with a different accent; Chicago repeats Cardiff; being in Toronto is like being in Tilbury Docks with a drawl. Now here was the great, babbling, sweltering subcontinent: I knew that this was what I was looking for.

But it wasn't as simple as that . . .

I was ashore on the great, magical subcontinent, feet firmly in the red dust, boats burned and seeking gainful employment.

Calcutta does not awaken in the morning, it shimmers into life. In the same way a reclining woman will rise, shaking the creases from a spangled dress and swirling the skirt, the city shakes the folds of night and swirls away the purple mists of morning from its palace towers and gilded cupolas. The mists from the Hooghly River are thicker, more solid and purple than those European eyes are accustomed to, and the air feels more substantial, sufficient to support the great weight of the cumbersome scavenging birds which stagger on their massive wings into the lightening sky to flap and flounder until they find

37

a rising thermal current to lift them to their natural soaring element.

The 'City of Palaces' they call it; palaces of a magnificence unequalled anywhere in the world, but matched by a squalor also unequalled. Because there are no fixed trading or shop opening hours, there is no preamble to morning, no dawn chorus of milkmen, postmen, paperboys and commuters travelling to begin the day. The new day begins instantly with the same hectic haggle with which the previous evening ended. In a city of a million homeless sleeping on the streets there are as many people there in the morning as were there the day before; they come to garrulous life at first light. For a few fleeting moments, the tropical light is thin and the city is painted in subdued pastel shades until the sun asserts itself and a more vivid palette of richer oils blocks in the watercolour sketch. Then Calcutta is alive and concerned only with the clamorous business of living. Then the smells come through: burning charcoal, cooked-meats, spices, decay and animals.

Beasts of burden have disappeared from Western cities. We can no longer accept them as an integral part of everyday life; our domestic animals have been relegated to an ornamental role, not essential to the actual continuance and living of life, like they are in India. So the jingle of harness, the clang and tinkle of cattle bells has gone from the streets. We no longer hear the satisfying squeak of leather against leather and wood, or the gasp of quickly snatched breath and blubbering exhalations of blowing pack animals, no farts and grunts, no gush of piss, nor a whiff of dung to excite the nostrils; no bran, no oats, no sweetly musty smell of hay.

Western cities have gone antiseptic, metallic and filled with synthetic din, isolated from the country and sanitised against nature. But in great Eastern cities like Calcutta, the country and nature arrive in a daily tide of peasants, creaking manure-splattered carts, livestock – horses, donkeys, asses, oxen, camels, goats, squealing pigs, cackling poultry – flies, fleas and filth. All with the fodder-munching, groaning, indignantly squealing sounds of living, breathing, suffering creatures and the stink of basic existence.

In Calcutta, the centre of it all is the Hogg Market. The West has its hypermarkets, this is the ultra-hyper-bazaar of the subcontinent. In an age of superlatives, quite the biggest market in all creation and literally the place to buy an emerald and an elephant to ride on while you are wearing it; Japanese micro-chip wizardry squatted alongside the titbits cook with his charcoal brazier, the market trader haggled over the price of Western drugs while the silversmith tapped his precious metal into intricate shapes.

On the corner stood a one-eyed, one-legged peasant peddling American and British cigarettes from a tray suspended round his neck with more negotiating skills over a packet of Marlboro than a conference-full of trades unions secretaries over a wage deal.

A primitive society based upon the most ancient of lifestyles, fundamental bargaining and bartering, yet with more status symbols than you could find in a Madison Avenue advertising executive's New England home.

I had been brought up in the post-raj era when the sahibs and memsahibs had retreated, grumbling, to the Isle of Wight, Cheltenham or Bournemouth, and Kipling's books had been discreetly lifted to top shelves in libraries until the anti-colonial hubbubs died down, so I had no *Tales of the Raj* to draw upon. I had not even read the book or seen the film of *The Lives of a Bengal Lancer*, so I was dumb. I looked at Calcutta through incredulous eyes. I could not believe the sheer force of life burgeoning in the dusty streets, even hollow-eyed beggars looked glamorous to me. You think like that at 19, and the pleasure of memory often lies in recalling dazzling first impressions. So compound them in your memory before the facts of life tarnish them for ever – as surely they must in India. For India is neither a fun nor happy place to live.

In the heart of the Hogg Market's teeming bedlam is the famous establishment of Mr. Rajinda Singh, a name to conjure with in animals, a purveyor to the world of rare animals, large mammals, exotic and ornamental birds, reptilia and aquatic reptilia. Cables: IMPEX, Calcutta. If it walked, slithered, flew or swam, Singh would have it in stock by the hundred; if not, word would go out on the grapevine and an army of appallingly badly paid minions would go out to snare, trap, coax or catch it by hand into captivity.

Civilised governments, in their solicitous concern for the unemployed and the social welfare of their citizens, make it desperately difficult for people to get jobs – people like me, that is: they want Social Security numbers, health cards, insurance cards, they think of our well-being and forget our natures.

Personally, I like the easy life, a solid, hard day's back-breaking graft, a few quid in my pocket and thank you very much; official documents induce a state of torpor in me and I require at least a fortnight on the 'Social' to recover from the shock of being presented with them.

In Britain, there are ways round the problem which means that all the naughty, hard-working, two-job, moon-lighting, document and tax-shy yobbos have established the thriving 'black economy'. There are ways in India of getting round regulations which would boggle the minds of Britain's most adept tax dodgers; the lovely thing about it is that Indians give illegality a semi-official status; the gun-toting policemen will smile and tell you: 'Oh, no, Sahib, that which you require is a forbidden article and you will not be able to buy it in the proper bazaar, you must go to the Smugglers' Bazaar and my cousin will drive you there in his taxi'.

I could see no great difficulties in finding a job paying enough to sustain myself with some left over for a few pints of whatever was available, and there were always ships in the river with well-stocked bars.

Outside Mr. Singh's emporium (nothing so common as a shop for so well-established a concern) was a crowd of buyers including many Europeans. It was a stroke of luck for me, we could talk animals at length and with enthusiasm.

Mr. Singh's mobile Indian features, which could reflect the status of whoever he was talking to with a series of quick-change instant expressions to suit every occasion, beamed with appreciation at the earnest conversations being carried on outside his doorway: talk meant the pos-sibility of profit, the more intense the talk, the greater the possible profit. He was clearly impressed with my appar-ent knowledge – so was I. I discovered that I knew a bit

40

more than I thought I did and the years of hanging around animals, picking up titbits of information were beginning to pay off. I caught him out completely when I asked for a job, he hadn't a facial expression to fit the circumstance, or if he had, he'd left it at home that day. But the Indian formalities had, of course, to be completed fully in proper accordance with time-honoured Indian ritual which, in order of priorities, runs to a ten-point schedule:

1. A cup of tea.
2. A lengthy philosophical discourse on the nature of the business the prospective employer is engaged in.
3. An even longer philosophical discourse on the honourable part the prospective employer plays in such business.
4. A detailed inventory of the rogues, vagabonds, cheats, corrupt government officials and wicked relatives on his wife's side whose sole objectives in life are to deviate him from the course of righteousness and dispossess him of his meagre possessions.
5. A cup of tea.
6. An exchange of confidential intimacies such as the fact that God has a personal binding convenant with him to strike dead or turn into a pillar of camel dung any miscreant who should as much *point* a finger at his till let alone put one *into* it.
7. An agonised appraisal of the impending financial doom hanging over his poor, afflicted business with the only possible result suicide or the gutter.
8. An exercise in logic to prove – Q.E.D. – that by offering one quarter of what you are asking he is a man of disproportionate generosity and utterly selfless demeanour.
9. An act of friendship and compassion in that he will offer one half of your asking price, less breakages, cups of tea, wear and tear and may God forgive him for his profligate foolishness.
10. A cup of tea and you can start now sweeping up the shop and despatching the day's orders written in proper English as spoken by her Gracious Majesty the Queen of England.

41

'You will be good to talk to these white buyers and show them how little they are trying to pay me, you can tell them they are robbing me, and should be thankful for so honest and genuine a person to do business with and that they should not take advantage of a simple Indian person like myself who has no great education at a famous university. And you can stand at the front of the premises to show other rascally dealers that I am not a person to be trifled with.'

A white sahib on the staff was as great a status symbol as a Rolls at the door, Gucci shoes on the desk and a key to his own private loo for a white tycoon. I lived up to the part.

Five hundred different species of tropical birds under one roof: a Joseph's coat of ornithological colour, a rainbow of incandescent hues concentrated within the scope of a single glance. It was the whole bird house of any major zoo collected in one aviary, a sight you will never see in any zoological gardens.

Then the range of Mr. Singh's activities and the brilliance of his business acumen became startingly apparent. He had 500 or so mynah birds – apart from the other species – in separate sheds. In each shed was a tape recorder playing incessantly night and day repeating a few stock phrases along the lines of: Pretty Polly; Who's a pretty bird, then?; Good morning; Good night; Lovely day. But in each individual shed they played in a different language, German, French, Japanese and English. Another first, the world's first ornithological language laboratory.

The only trouble was that the buffoons he employed, or illiterate peasants unloading them at Calcutta Airport, would keep putting the wrong consignments of mynahs on to the wrong flights with the result that Japanese speaking mynahs destined for Tokyo were arriving in Paris and vice versa occasioning cables demanding to know: 'What language are these bloody birds squawking in?'

We sold non-poisonous snakes by the foot and poisonous varieties by the head: so we would uncoil a python, measure it, if it would stop its wriggling, and invoice the customer: One 16 ft. python at X dollars a foot, total XX

42

dollars. Anything above 15 foot came a bit pricey. So if the reptile grew an inch or two from 14 ft. 11 inches to 15ft. 1 inch in flight or at sea, the buyer got a bonus.

Monkeys came and monkeys went. There were fine specimens of langur and wanderoo species, nearly all babies because few zoos wanted to take on fully grown adults, and they required pairs which were much more difficult to come by as adults. But overwhelmingly it was rhesus monkeys, they arrived by the crateload numbering up to thousands a week.

The catchers were usually more pathetic than the poor, scared animals themselves; emaciated country boys with matchstick arms and legs, thin cheeks with the bones protruding, they brought in their catches in lashed-up bamboo cages cobbled together with a few sticks of bamboo and inferior twine, having carried them for a couple of days to make a sale in the big city. And their efforts were worth the price of a couple of bowls of rice or so, pathetically miserable payments to pathetically miserable peasants.

Often the cages fell to pieces when left in the store, the monkeys jumped, the string broke and the cage fell apart. Away went the monkeys like quicksilver on to roofs, up telephone and electricity poles, on to the tops of passing vehicles. It created pandemonium, fruit sellers screamed abuse at us, anybody with foodstuffs for sale saw an imminent risk of losing the lot.

But we had bought them in so cheaply that it wasn't worth the effort to catch them, if we could have caught them in that seething cauldron of Indian panic and ineptitude. In the commotion beggars and street boys made the most of it and raided the food stalls so everybody ended up chasing everybody else and the monkeys sat high in their vantage points watching the follies of mankind with rapt, solemn attention.

This was the era of the monkey. Or, seen from the standpoint of the monkey, the age of annihilation.

Whatever the cause, and it was probably the increased ease of access through air travel, science suddenly discovered the monkey as an indispensable aid to research. There is nothing remarkable in that fact in itself, animals had been used for experimentation for decades. I had often met people, through the Camden Town pet shop, who had such way-out sounding jobs as laboratory rat attendants, all species of animals used in experimental establishments needed attendants.

What was astounding, and what could only be seen at the despatching end of the business in such places as Calcutta, was the sheer volume of the trade, the huge numbers of animals being shipped to all parts of the world. In my ignorance I had always thought of research as a pretty limited field in comparison with the rest of industry, commerce and medicine; how could they possibly need tens of thousands of rhesus monkeys? How could they use them? Yet the evidence was there plain for everybody to see, tens of thousands of monkeys being shipped weekly.

Rajinda Singh played his part in the business. He was a big dealer not afflicted with European or American scruples about the treatment of animals or even Western hypocritical attitudes. He fulfilled orders and, to him, it was good business.

But the biggest dealer by far was Monkey Paterson who specialised in the trade and gained the reputation of being the only man ever to make a million out of monkeys.

How the trade grew was fascinating. It sort of crept in unobtrusively like water seeping under the door, suddenly turning into a flash flood. Nobody seemed to know what was going on and the public was completely unaware until stories of mass deaths in transit began to appear in newspapers; by the time that animal protection societies' protests had pushed governments into action, the Indian Government was shocked to find that its jungles had been stripped and depleted to an alarming extent. They moved quickly to stem the trade and limit exports of live animals but nobody knows how many millions of rhesus monkeys were plundered in the name of science and progress during the infamous Years of the Monkey.

Not that anybody apparently acted out of compassion for the poor old rhesus monkey itself, the whole affair only served to make people think of the monkey in a new light, as a commercial asset; restrictions were put on primarily to preserve stocks and increase the animal's value by limitation of supplies.

One good result of the outcry is that nowadays monkeys do travel in greater comfort and with sufficient food and water to enable them to survive the journey, not that many survive the arriving.

Life can be comfortable in a sub-subsistence level, poverty stricken, corruption riddled society providing you join it and never attempt to fight it; nothing annoys a starving peasant more than being handed 50 rupees 'aid' by a well-intentioned Western relief worker who, at the same time, is depriving him of his traditional 5 rupees backsheesh. Though some sense has, at last, crept into the scene: Western aid and relief officials are no longer scandalised by the amount of relief goods which arrive in the smugglers' markets. The official line has now become: a good thing that this does happen, it means that the original recipient of the aid has sold it for money to provide for his more immediate and personal needs – so he has still received aid. And in practice, on the ground, that is the system that works and allows people to survive. Not that those of us who live our lives at, or just below, the official survival level of income can often afford to be over-concerned with moral and ethical considerations, we are too deeply concerned with where the next pint of ale is coming from – first things first.

My job with Rajinda Singh made me the envy of Calcutta; it enabled me to invent a whole new dimension of backsheesh: visiting dealers were often confused by the system and befuddled by the din, and they were not unaccustomed to buying a clutch of resplendently fine-feathered birds of brilliant plumage in Calcutta only to open the crate at home and have a gaggle of cross-eyed, bow-legged, bedraggled chickens stagger out.

The European and American dealers bought me expensive dinners. I naturally made a list of all the very finest restaurants, drinking dens and bawdy houses; their proprietors gave me a 'consideration' for taking our clients there, the clients gave me a 'consideration' for showing them the town, they gave me another 'consideration' for finding the best stock for them and another 'consideration' for making sure that it got on to the aircraft; Rajinda gave

45

me a small 'consideration' for getting him far better prices than he would have made; my trump card was that I knew the European prices, I knew what was being paid over there and it took only a minimal adjustment to bump up the Calcutta price to a level to make Rajinda's eyes gleam.

The great Eastern Hotel runs hard on the pocket of a Calcutta worker, even a comparatively wealthy one like me who was paid much above the average pittance. Prices there were geared to multi-national company expense accounts, not at European rates by any standards, but high in India.

The Raj has gone but remnants of splendour remain: great winged fans in the ceilings which used to be rotated by poker-faced punka-wallahs, pulling their strings; the marble isn't quite as polished as it once was and the taps are tarnished, but the gloomy caverns of long-lost British dignity are there as reminders of past days of glory.

There is an impression of antiquity and permanence, which are both false. Calcutta looks as if it has been there since God invented the first apple, but on any international time-scale it is a newcomer which wasn't founded until 1690; August 24, to be exact, when Job Charnock, of the English East India Company, set it up and built a fort to subdue the dusky natives across the river.

In 1931 it had a population of 1·1 million, in 1951 it had risen to 2·6 million, in 1971 it was past counting; but, plant a seed in India and, if the conditions come right, you can have a jungle in five minutes; then when you've got your jungle the sun won't stop shining double hot until it burns it to shrivelled stumps in an arid desert; if that doesn't happen, then an excessive monsoon drenches it under ten foot of muddy water with ten thousand corpses floating by. How Calcutta survived 270 years of such tribulations is a mystery of the East; in its present jammed-packed state it could die of suffocation because all the air has been used up.

Just off the Chowringhee road is a flea-pit, a classic piece of Indian seediness which would automatically attract a preservation order in England. And it is inhabited by equally seedy people who are natural drop-outs from the pages of John Masters, Maugham and E. M. Forster

46

– the ones the printer's ink never quite covered and who were left on the overmatter random as just too awful.

It was a comedown after the Great Eastern, but for two quid a month, what could you expect? What you could expect were shifty Europeans who had run out of cash and were perpetually waiting for cheques to arrive, drunken matelots who had missed ship, Indian salesmen who were all high-speed talk but no business.

Lizards pranced noisily on the roof, fine-mesh netting kept the flies in and fresh air – such as it was, slightly used air would be more accurate – out; I thought of calling it Invertebrates Palace and running package tours for entymologists. And, of course, it was suffused with the pungent aroma of the Orient, even my socks smelled of stale curry.

There was only one thing to do in such circumstances, play the game, keep a stiff upper lip, show the flag, let 'em know we're British and act the way generations of British Tommies and Jolly Jack Tars had done for two centuries . . . behave abominably.

The dealers were in town and twenty dollar bills were flashing around: 'When you pack the birds, George, see that I get the best. OK? Good lad.' Even in those cheap, inflationless days Scotch was 17 rupees (30 rupees to the £1) but the local brew, Bee Hive Gin, known to the drinking public as 'send-you-blind', came at the equivalent of pennies; so getting hooched could cost very little in hard currency and total oblivion was only a little extra. Quite a few of those 20 dollar bills, plus Deutschmarks, Swiss Francs and other colourful crispies had, naturally, flashed their way into my pocket, so every night was party night.

Outside the Great Eastern Hotel is a gharry rank – for the uninitiated, a horse-drawn carriage with two six-foot diameter back wheels, the driver perched high on a bench over the front steering wheels and passengers sitting face to face in the middle, two looking forward, two looking backwards, motive power is a decrepit nag. The drivers sleep under their vehicles at night.

We fell out of the hotel early one morning and hijacked one. The nag in the shafts looked like a skeletal exhibit from the Natural History Museum with a coloured sheet flung over it; it was so thin that it was nearly transparent, you could see every part of the poor creature working. But, surprise, surprise, it had the turn of foot of a 2,000 Guineas winner.

We took off down Chowringhee road like a bat-out-of-hell, cornering on two wheels, sliding across the road at each junction, completely out of control but, amazingly, still upright.

At full gallop we entered into the square where the embassies were located. Embassy cars are parked boot to the kerb, bonnet pointing out into the road. A back wheel hooked round the bumper of a black, Russian Embassy limousine and bumper, lights, grill, embassy badges and CD plates bounced down the street with a deafening clamour.

Calcutta police do not breathalyse you, they anaesthe-tise with the thick end of a machine-gun butt and once inside an Indian nick, there are difficulties, to put it mildly, in getting out again; soppy British do-gooders say that prison isn't a deterrent, the thought of it deterred us that night: we abandoned ship a bit quickish and scar-pered through the bazaars even more quickly.

Work began at five o'clock in the morning. The throng of peasants who had been in the country all night brought in their catches, squabbled vociferously to be first to sell and argued about the price; the birds and animals arrived in every ramshackle box and temporary crate imaginable; a box of fabulous exotic birds . . . a few pennies. The stealth, patience and skill that must have gone into catch-ing them – undamaged – with only the bare hands as implements was, clearly, quite considerable and such re-wards seemed sadly inadequate. There were centuries of tradition behind the catching skills: Indian princes and rajahs have kept menageries, often huge collections, as a sign of their wealth and omnipotence throughout time.

Away from the city, the countryside teemed with wild-life. But how long could it last? Every week we sent 400 crates of assorted birds to destinations all over the world: softbills, hoopoes, flycatchers, babblers and a staggering 10,000 mynahs. It was plunder on such a scale that the Indian Government eventually had to step in and control it, but by the time they did whole native species were endangered.

Then there were moments of high excitement which you could hear beginning a long way down the market and approaching until it reached a crescendo outside the yard. Somebody had captured a Bengal tiger and the awesome beast was being carried in its rickety cage through the city streets to the market. The evening before it had been free as the wind with men as passing shadows on the horizon. Now it was in the midst of turmoil, strange sounds, smells, a terrifying new world: great sinews and muscles flex, restless eyes glint anger, the pent-up tension within those fragile-looking bamboos is almost tangible, an explosion of devastating rage seems imminent. How these frail, underfed villagers can have contained such sheer power is a matter for wonderment. Everybody breathes a little easier when it is poked, prodded, pushed into more substantial quarters.

A man rings to say that he has some very fine bears for sale, Himalayans and sloth bears so Mr. Singh arranges an appointment for him the following day. Bears are notoriously difficult to sell because they are notoriously difficult and expensive to keep and house. They can climb, jump, break bars and generally be a bloody nuisance; the only absolutely secure compound is a pit which has got to be wide and deep, taking up a lot of space and costing huge sums of money to excavate. To be worth handling, from a dealer's point of view, they have to be bought in very cheaply.

Now the wily Mr. Singh sends his minions running to all quarters of the city asking every known bear catcher to bring his stock along tomorrow. They all turned up, the original caller included.

'The market is flooded with dam' bears,' Mr. Singh bewailed, 'everywhere all the time are dam' bears, people are trying to give them away and can't succeed, they are a nuisance and a drag on the market.'

Crestfallen, the poor little bear catcher is given a miserly, paltry handout counting himself lucky to get anything with trade so bad.

They caught crocodiles as well, again with apparently no specialised equipment; the Hooghly river crocodiles are North Indian gharials which are noted for very long pointed snouts and tails. And the big salt water crocs are

49

plentiful all round the estuaries of Bengal. I have distinct recollections of handling false gharials as well. The difference is that one is worth quite a few bob and the other comes cheap. The textbooks say that false gharials come from Borneo and Sumatra, so how they wound up in Calcutta's Hogg Market, I am not at all sure. I really thought they were from the Hooghly river. The way to tell a gharial from a false gharial is to count its teeth. Just say: 'Come along, croc, open sesame,' and if it has 27–29 teeth in its upper jaw, it is a genuine gharial, if it has only 20–22 it's a falsie . . . I could never get that interested to be bothered to find out – no thank you.

The Hogg Market is, I think, an essential zoological experience, well worth seeing and studying, it is fifty zoos rolled into one.

But it isn't all that pleasant living in India. Well, certainly not living there as an Indian does. It isn't bad for television and pressmen or multi-national company representatives who, no matter how well they get to know the country, are there essentially as observers with help, support and rescue a telephone or telex link away.

But living and working at ground roots level, you soon become overwhelmed with the absolute hopelessness of the situation; the population continues to explode; talk of improvements is just talk because anything the government does is immediately swallowed up and negated by the ever increasing millions of hungry mouths. You step over sleeping beggars on the doorstep of your digs; the nights are made miserable by the tubercular coughs of beggars sleeping on the pavements; rats crawl and leap over them, no proper sanitation, water supply and power cuts all the time. A feeling of hopelessness becomes absolutely debilitating and you can feel yourself being dragged down by it.

Without in any way intending to diminish her work, I think it is reasonable to say that very few of us are born with the compassion and selfless love of Mother Teresa and what she does in the circumstances of Indian poverty is quite the opposite of how the rest of us lesser mortals react; too often we cannot stomach it and we feel that there is no way we can help, joining in their despair merely adds to it. Then it is time to move on.

All things taken into consideration – particularly the 'considerations' I had been shown – it had been a fruitful and profitable stay; I had more than enough money to fly home and live easy for a few weeks. But that seemed a profligate waste of good beer money when there was a Norwegian merchantman lying in the river. So I signed on for the trip back to Europe. First stop, Spain.

Spain: fun, laughter, exciting and actually eatable food, guitars, clattering heels, raven-haired ladies with dark, flashing eyes. Alas, Sod's Law and Murphy's Law have much in common with Jacobs' Law, and Jacobs' Law states that if a ship can sail before a sailor on a marvellous run-ashore has finished having a good time, it will. When I got back to the docks for a shave, wash and brush up the berth was empty, the ship had sailed with all my clobber in it. Come to think of it, I have lost more clothes aboard ships disappearing over far horizons than Oxfam could collect in a prime shop in a month.

Nothing for it, buy a new suit, a natty overcoat against the rigours of an English summer and an airline ticket to London.

POSTSCRIPT TO CALCUTTA: when the occasion demanded, one of my duties at the Singh establishment was to stand around looking as big and hefty as possible. It happened when irate suppliers clamoured too pressingly for a few more rupees for their wares or aggrieved neighbouring tradesmen demanded compensation for goods stolen or ruined when our monkeys escaped. Mr. Singh would tell them: 'Any one of you greedy miscreants who sets a filthy foot in my emporium will have to deal with my manager, Mr. George, who is instructed to pugalise him'.

Sadly, looking big, Chelsea boots with Cuban heels and all, was not too difficult in that undernourished community and a couple of heads cracked together usually sorted out any trouble; nobody ever held it against me, they all smiled great sheepish grins when we met later.

The point of the story is that force was not a usual approach in the business: it ran much more on guile, subterfuge, cunning and the adroit placing of backhanders plus an appreciation that, outside the magic circle of animal dealers and buyers, few people knew anything –

51

a fact which bedevilled all efforts of concerned authorities to impose reasonable controls.

When the Indian Government tried conscientiously and desperately to clamp down to save their rapidly diminishing wildlife, big operators moved the centres of business to Thailand, Cambodia, Laos and Borneo, with strings all over Southeast Asia and the smugglers came into their own again. What Westerners often overlook or forget is that smuggling is a way of life in the East, they love it, running contraband – gold, liquor, precious stones, technology, drugs, car spare parts – adds an essential spice to life apart from the profit it brings.

The best intentioned measures for the protection of wildlife and its conservation are often counterproductive; so the *Red Data Book*, listing the rarest and most endangered species for the benefit and information of customs and control officials became the price guide to smugglers on the basis of the rarer, the costlier and the more profitable.

Two factors are pretty well insurmountable: ignorance – even in sophisticated, educated Western countries there are not all that many customs officers sufficiently well-trained to spot the difference between a rare, listed monkey and a common or garden species and fewer still who, say in the middle of the night at an obscure port of entry, are prepared to open a crate at the real risk of being bitten or savaged to examine the specimen in detail and check it against the book, and corruption – most Departments of the Interior are staffed by local, underpaid country boys ever open for a backhander for a quick official stamp on a phoney document, usually enough to get a rare animal out of the country. An enterprising German dealer was exposed by a television wildlife investigation for making and printing boxes of his own export licences, sending them to his corrupt contacts in Paraguay and bringing back whatever he wanted – all unknown to Paraguayan authorities.

Of course, the real disgrace of the business is that there is *always* a buyer available with a pocket full of money.

Chapter 5

Gerald Durrell's animals and other wild people

*With the whiff of India out of my nostrils, the clicking of cas-
tanets only faintly in my ears and what I could remember of
what I think must have been a marvellous time in España, the
bankroll was beginning to look as if it was afflicted with anorexia
nervosa. Three courses were open to me: starvation in the affluent
society, borrow from mum or get a good, steady, rewarding job
– so to the small ads in the animal man's job bible,* Cage and
Aviary Birds. *Gerald Durrell's Jersey Zoo wanted a keeper,
there's class, there's prestige. I telephoned and got the job immediately. But it wasn't as simple as all that . . .*

So there was this advertisement in *Cage and Aviary Birds*
for staff required by Gerald Durrell's zoo on the island of
Jersey. It must have been my luckiest of days or Gerald
Durrell was in the middle of a mental aberration, dreaming of faraway places for his next book, or possibly one or
more of his keepers had been slightly chewed up by their
charges. Because I telephoned from London and they said:
'Can you catch the night plane and start tomorrow
morning?'

Which is very unusual for Jersey Zoo, who are noted
for being extra choosey in selecting their staff since it is a
prestige, Rolls-Royce-of-zoos sort of place, very professional, very expert and a recognised frontrunner in animal
breeding and conservation techniques. They say, and I
found no reason to doubt it, that you can learn more
about wild animals in a month at Durrell's than you can
in a year on a university zoology course.

So that was how I arrived, fresh and keen, on Britain's

little paradise island in the sun, snuggly situated under the French coast, no income tax, duty free booze and cigarettes, gorgeous birds of the human species in uninhibited mood because they were on holiday . . . it might have been better if they had put me in a cage and let the animals loose, there was so much temptation.

Jersey has achieved a great number of firsts in breeding species but the most important thing you can learn there, if you want to keep your animals alive, is how to feed them; Jeremy Mallinson, the curator, working closely with Durrell, has become one of the world's experts in animal diet. Though, with a generosity which is unique in the zoo world, they go out of their way to acknowledge the contribution made by other zoos. Zoologists tend to be prima donnas who jealously guard their secrets and revel in the glory of discoveries and academic triumphs, not too willing to share credit with their fellows. More about that later.

Durrell is a remarkable man if only for his dedication; he works to make a fortune from his writing only to spend the lot, and often very much more indeed, on his animals: if sailing is, as they insist, standing fully clothed in a cold shower tearing up £10 notes, then zoo-owning is standing near naked up to the eyeballs in animal shit shovelling £20 notes down never satisfied throats (including the veterinary surgeon's).

It is one of the incomprehensible facts of the zoo world and a complete contradiction of common sense that while dealers thrive and fortunes change hands for rare animals at a rate of inflation unmatched in any other field, zoos run at frightening losses and have to be, largely, supported on local rates or by government grants if they are available.

Durrell's Jersey Wildlife Preservation Trust, which he set up to ease the financial problems of his zoo and, particularly, to support its ambitions, is one approach to the problem of paying for attempts to restore the damage we have so wantonly inflicted upon other species sharing the world – it isn't just *our* world.

But the scale of destruction is so vast that, no matter how admirable in its way, Durrell's is a puny effort, and the awful prospect is that having done the damage while we were rich, now that we are all poorer we can no longer afford to repair it.

Seven quid was the fare to Jersey, seven quid for the return fare, if memory serves correctly; and seven quid a week, the wages for working from dawn until dusk or the following dawn if required, nobody expects anything more or less from a zoo. The dealers, of course, were doing well out of it; a Birmingham dealer had sold N'Pongo, the gorilla, to Durrell for £1,500 – money which Durrell did not have available at the time, so he bought it on H.P. – but if you wanted a gorilla, that was the money you had to pay or do without; four years' wages to the poor sod who had to look after the animal, day in, day out, for the rest of its living days. Things have not changed since those times, everybody is now paid in Monopoly money but the ratios remain the same.

Durrell's zoo was new but rapidly establishing traditions: like nobody ever getting a Christmas dinner. Since the zoo had begun, every Christmas day when the staff sat down to a traditional Christmas dinner, the instant the carving knife touched the glowing, golden turkey breast and mouths began to water, the alarm went up: one or more of the animals had escaped – chimps, orang-utans . . . it didn't matter, they were out and had to be recaptured. So the turkey went back in the oven, vegetables were covered to keep warm and frizzle up on the hot plate and off went the merry lads to chase the escapees round the deserted zoo.

That was probably the cause of the trouble: Christmas day was the only day the zoo was closed and the animals wondered what on earth was going on, nobody to stare at, nobody to grimace at, no staff, nobody at all about, strange and disturbing – and very boring. So some of the more enterprising fiddled and played with their cages, found weak spots and were up, up and away in minutes. Then, for the staff, came the hours of chasing, coaxing and conning them back into safety.

A classic piece of coaxing happened at Jersey to a classic escaper, Pedro the bear. Escaping runs in bears' blood, they will break out of anything because they are enormously strong, they can climb, run, leap, and when a bear gets up a bit of pace it can clear prodigious distances, which as I remarked earlier, makes them very expensive to house. On top of all that, they are resourceful.

Pedro took every opportunity to scarper. Somebody left his cage door unsecured for a second – literally a split-second – and he was off, shambling along like a circus clown but covering the ground at speed, across the zoo car park, over the road and into a field with a gang of us in hot pursuit. Something in the field attracted his attention and we caught him up – but we had nothing to catch him with so we sent Frank Wymark back to get a rope.

Frank had been discharged from the navy for being too weedy. They had taken him on in the hope that he would fill out on a diet of navy cocoa and plum duff but he didn't and they grew embarrassed at having a bell-bottomed walking skeleton around the place with the danger that the Russians might photograph him and use him for propaganda purposes to show the state of things in HM's Senior Service.

He arrived with the rope and we made a lasso which we got round Pedro's neck with surprisingly little trouble while he was ruminating about some particularly fascinating scent he'd found in the field. We were persuading him back towards the zoo with gentle tugs, five to ten yards at a time, until Pedro realised what was going on and took off in the opposite direction dragging us all behind him until he finally shot up a pole. I thought it was a telegraph pole but Frank pointed out that it carried mains power.

Panic visions of barbecued bear dangling from the sparking wires, worse – *much worse* – the island in darkness, all those busy sucking, squelching Alva Laval milking machines in a thousand milking parlours suddenly stopped, prize jersey cows bursting at the udders, parties of angry farmers storming the zoo. . . .

So I screamed: 'Come down, you stupid bloody bear'. But Pedro wouldn't. He was three-quarters the way up the pole, with the gang clinging to the rope below and working out a system whereby one of us could shin up to the first of the metal steps sticking out from the side of the pole – the electricity company puts them just high enough up the pole to be out of reach of adventurous members of the public. Then we would momentarily slacken off while he whipped a hitch round the rung which would prevent Pedro getting higher and give us all a breather.

Then Pedro got bored and let go. He crashed on top of us but mostly on weedy Frank. It seemed to knock a bit of the stuffing out of both of them and they stood looking at each other rather balefully. What Frank lacked in brawn, he made up for in native cunning: fishing deep into his anorak pocket he pulled out a packet of Smarties – children's sugar-coated chocolate drops – and adroitly he flicked one under Pedro's nose. The bear snuffed and snorted until he found it in the grass. Then at a collected amble Frank went toward the zoo, pausing every ten yards or so to rattle the pack and drop another sweetie under Pedro's nose, and the great beast grunted in pleasure, falling upon the tiny bombshells of pleasure in ecstasy. Across the road, through the car park up to the cage door they went, Frank rattling and dropping, Pedro sniffing and gulping until, a few yards from the cage, Frank dropped a clutch of half-a-dozen.

While Pedro was occupied sniffing them out and rolling the pesky little things along the ground in his haste to snaffle them up, Frank, on hands and knees, was in the cage laying a trail of red, yellow, green and brown little tempters, carefully spaced into the front left corner, up to the back left corner, across to the back right corner – like fairy stepping stones. Then half way down the right hand side of the cage he stopped and waited. Pedro, all senses intent upon the brightly coloured little gems, trundled in following the trail . . . Frank backed out; we slammed the door, shot the bolts, snapped the padlock and guffawed.

But Frank, never of the happiest countenance, just stood looking sick and forlorn. I thought: 'It's a reaction, it must be a strain having a great, shambling bear breathing down your neck all that time'. Frank held out the Smartie packet, turned it upside down, shook it, then crushed it in his fist and wailed: 'He's eaten all my Smarties and they were meant to last me 'til Saturday – and I haven't any money left 'til pay day'.

Never let it be said that zoo men are ungenerous and unfeeling. We clubbed together, all five of us, and bought him another packet – half-a-pound, twice as big as his first one.

Fame produces some curious reactions in people. Durrell was already famous when I joined the zoo because of his books about animal collecting trips to exotic places and through dramatic, mysterious jungles. His books had made a deep impression on one young hopeful who applied for a job; the boy had worked with animals in laboratories and his letter of application suggested that he would be quite useful. However the day the lad arrived to start work, the zoo stopped in its tracks: he thought that Jersey Zoo was an extension of Durrell's expeditions. Which, in its way, it is – but not an extension in the way our young hopeful imagined. At the back of his mind he thought if the zoo needed an extra couple of specimens, Durrell would arrive on the scene one morning and say: 'Just popping over to West Africa to collect a couple of odds and ends we're short of, all the lads who want to go, hop in the back of the truck. . . .' Yes, this was the big stuff, he believed.

So the young hopeful arrived fully kitted out for the task: a safari suit, bush hat, knee boots, leather bands round his arms, a huge machete big enough to hack down half an Amazonian jungle, jungle knives and ropes. The staff, in their tattered jeans, stained and ill-fitting T-shirts and plimsolls with the toes torn out, looked at the apparition in amazement, too shocked even to laugh. He was immediately Christened Mungo Parkes because that was the only explorer we could think of at the moment.

Not that he alone excelled in sartorial elegance. Ken Smith, the manager, was a pretty snappy dresser – for a time. In a flush of affluence he had bought a magnificent suit, a masterpiece of the tailor's art which he would insist on ruining by wearing a thick, ugly belt – not a belt really, more a leather cummerbund.

Ken was a good animal man whom we all respected though we did not much appreciate his new-found finery which caused him to pussyfoot on heel and tiptoe through the animal dung with his trouser turn-ups hitched delicately above his ankles for fear of staining. But he cut a marvellous figure chatting up the dolly-bird visitors.

It so happened that an opossum died and those lads in

favour of a bit of devilment, which was everybody, took it down to a tall tree and arranged it in a lifelike pose among the uppermost branches.

Then, a little later, somebody told Ken that the opossum had gone missing and Ken, being a keen and conscientious keeper and manager, organised a search. By carefully engineering the situation, he was gently led in the direction of the tree where eagle-eyed Ken spotted the missing animal.

'Net the tree,' he ordered and dutifully we spread in a circle the catching nets. But nobody was willing to climb the tree. 'You are the expert, you ought to show us how,' suggested some cunning character appealing to his vanity – well, any man with a suit like that must be vain.

So up the tree went Ken. And it was a particularly twiggy, prickly, well-foliaged tree which required a lot of squirming under branches and sliding round the trunk. Soon dark sap stains began to appear on Ken's suit and there were ominous sounds of tearing.

'Oh, tough luck, Ken,' said a sympathetic voice from below.

'Shall I go and get your jeans?' another asked helpfully.

'Too bloody late now,' Ken's voice grunted from aloft.

Then came a strained, tortured gasp: 'The . . . flaming . . . thing . . . won't . . . budge. . . .'

Next came the forerunner of what has become one of the most famous lines spoken in the Monty Python television series, but instead of a parrot it was an opossum. 'This opossum's dead . . . grunt . . . grunt . . . but I can't move the thing. . . .' He couldn't move it because it was nailed to the tree by two six-inch nails.

The rest of the incident is shrouded in mystery and ignorance; none of us ever knew what happened because by the time Ken had climbed down there wasn't a soul in sight.

Jersey being a great holiday centre has its own sideshows and attractions during the season. One of these was the fabulous Nick Nyoka, the animal man, an impressive, magnificent figure of a man, resplendent in leopard skin headband, snakeskin tie, white trousers and jungle boots. Nick the fearless, owner of the biggest lion known in the world, Simba. That fact was authenticated and appeared in the *Guinness Book of Records*, but whether his two snakes also qualified for the claim was never established, though big they were, 24-foot reticulated pythons. The only thing that let the show down was that Nick's real name was Adrian Darling and there is no way you can say it to make it sound tough and fearless.

Crisis came in the middle of one of our night duties at the zoo. The police arrived at panic stations: Nick kept his animals in farm buildings he rented and they had caught fire. They could not find Nick who had last been seen heading for the fleshpots in his finery so, par for the course, call in the zoo people, they are the experts.

The buildings were well alight by the time we arrived and firemen at the top of extending ladders were not only fighting the blaze but also doing a spot of crowd control by squirting the press of rubber-neckers who had turned up even at that time in the small hours of the morning.

Shotgun and pitchfork in hand, the two of us from the zoo were pushed to the front of the crowd by escorting policemen. We broke through and were promptly lifted four foot in the air by a high-pressure jet of water, shot by an overkeen fireman. Dripping like tree branches in a fog with water trickling in rivulets down every nook and cranny of our bodies, but with two feet firmly on the ground again, we surveyed the prospects and worked out a plan of action – helped by an uninvited scratch committee who weren't going to help but had plenty of encouragement. It went like this, and all in the space of a couple of minutes:

First zoo man: 'We've got to get into the building first and that looks as if it's burning quite well on one side.'

Second zoo man: 'Then we've got to open the lion cage, if it isn't locked.'

Policeman: 'What are you waiting for? The place will go up in a minute.'

First zoo man: 'Then we've got to get the lion across this open field to Nick's caravan. He's got a travelling cage built in the back of the van, so somebody had better open both the doors.'

Second zoo man: 'We've nothing to hold the lion with even if he wants to be held, which is going to be a problem. And he might take fright at all these people.'

Policeman: 'For Christ's sake, you'd better get moving. . . .'

Old grandma in the crowd: 'Eee, that poor lion in there, it'll be going mad what with the smoke and those flames. Why don't you go in and get it. I'd go myself but I've got this bad back. . . .'

First zoo man: 'Thanks, Ma, that's very encouraging. . . .'

Policeman: 'You two are the bloody lion keepers, the experts, for Christ's sake do something, you're supposed to know all about lions.'

Second zoo man: 'Do you expect us to walk in there and say, "Look here, Simba, we're lion keepers, so don't bugger about. . . ." '

First zoo man: 'You clear a path through this crowd and

Chimps and Christmas crackers cannot mix.

get them *well* back, he might come out like a thunderbolt and savage half-a-dozen of the silly bastards. How? That's your problem, but get 'em back, right back.'

Second zoo man: 'Keep that gun cocked and aimed *all the time*. I'll try to prod it along with the pitch fork.'

Policeman: 'I hope you've got a licence for that gun. . . .'

Grandma: 'Are you at the zoo then? Well, fancy that. . . 'ere, Eric, they're at the zoo, these lads 'ere, they're going to get the lion out.'

First zoo man: 'Get that caravan door open, get that cage door open and clear a bloody path.'

Grandma's Eric told his neighbours that the zoo man were here: 'Going to get yon lion out.' The crowd surged towards us.

The elevated firemen blasted us with jets as we moved in and made a lot of steam to add to the smoke but they kept the flames back.

Simba was a big brute. He made my lions at the zoo look like pygmies, and he was getting a bit agitated by the commotion. The cage was not locked. I tripped the catch bolts and the door swung open. Simba loped out. He looked around confused. I pointed the pitchfork at the door, and he moved out still confused and swung his head inquiringly. I pointed the pitchfork toward the caravan, and he slunk in that direction, me leaping along beside him and my mate galloping along with the gun at his shoulder. I caught a fleeting glance of a mass of startled white faces which turned to black heads and retreating backsides as they scattered.

Simba slowed down to a muscle-stretching walk and started looking round like a gun dog for instructions. I pointed the pitchfork at the caravan door. He seemed to brace up as he recognised the familiar place, scurried towards it, through the door, into the cage and, almost with a gasp of relief, flopped into a corner with his tongue out like a panting dog.

Trembling we stood in a group outside. The policeman was sweating; I was too wet to sweat. We bummed a fag from the policeman, ours had disintegrated into a brown mush in our waterlogged pockets. We leaned together to share a light when FLASH! CRASH! WHOOMPH! The bloody gun tucked under my mate's arm went off. The shot dug a hole in the ground a foot from our legs, though thankfully not a pellet touched us.

The policeman said: 'Holy Jesus, you ought to have the sense to keep the safety catch on that thing.'

Simba was rattled by the explosion. He let out a mighty, snarling roar and rattled his temporary cage. And the policeman added: 'You've upset the flaming lion now.'

The snakes perished.

But Simba thrived. Most of you will have seen him and marvelled at his power and magnificence: he starred with Liz Taylor and Richard Burton in the film *Cleopatra*.

Chapter 6

The Buck begins here

Ambition, driving, burning ambition made me seek a change from the joys and pleasures of lovely Jersey. I was living at the heady rate of £12 a week but my income was only £7, so financial disaster was imminent. Cage and Aviary Birds *showed that wages of up to £11 were being offered on the mainland; such riches could not be ignored. But first, like I always did when I got that sinking feeling of insidious bankruptcy, I went back to sea for a few quick, short trips to restore solvency. Back ashore I answered an ad for Howletts, which was then John Aspinall's private zoo in Kent. Aspinall was the acknowledged Gambling King of London: the rich and mighty queued up to lose their fortunes to him at his Clermont Club, in Berkeley Square, London. He was, in his private life, fanatical about wild animals. Rich as Croesus, I thought. Money by the bucketful, thought I . . . could be good, very good. It wasn't as simple as all that . . .*

Kent is a county in which nature has skilfully contrived that it cannot be entirely ruined by the agricultural industry in the way that Essex and Lincolnshire have been devastated. By cutting into the landscape cunning little ravines, producing sudden steep hills dropping to unsuspected valleys, scouring deep courses for shallow streams to meander along and topping off the natural scene with tight-knit copses of gnarled trees, nature has ensured that the farmer stays within the confines of the terrain.

Country lanes and byways are etched deep between protecting banks so that hedgerows topping them remain for growing not grubbing-up, and hawthorn, beech, elder and blackberry shield the secrets of the fields beyond.

Of course, wherever possible, the great industrialised belts of grain are stretched to capacity to allow the combines free run but these are interspersed with orchards, strawberry fields, market gardens and small-holdings to keep the aspect to a scale suitable for the designation the Garden of England. As a county Kent remains English whereas others have been transformed into Mid-West American mini-prairies.

Howletts sits in a triangular island of rural isolation bounded on two sides by the sea and to the West by that thunderous trunk route from the rest of England to the Channel ports, Watling Street, as straight as the Romans originally built it.

Royal Sandwich is just down the country lane, that most famous and testing of golf courses which for 31 years prior to 1981 had been isolated from the British Open Golf Championship circuit because the roads to it couldn't cope with the traffic the event now draws.

To the West of Watling Street the road map is tinted light green to denote 'a designated area of outstanding Natural Beauty'. The modern-day joy of working with animals is that often they are kept in beautiful places like the parklands of great country houses and stately homes. Howletts is such a place though by no means on the scale of Longleat or Woburn Abbey.

The aristocracy and landed gentry of England's wealthy centuries built privacy into their vast estates as a matter of course. They constructed towering walls running for miles round the perimeters of their lands, planted trees to hide the houses and themselves from the common gaze and inside that enclave of exclusiveness they remodelled the landscape to as near perfection as possible.

At Howletts the process was taken a stage further: the artificially created natural perfection which had, in fact, grown natural over a couple of centuries was simply encased as unobtrusively as possible to form a natural habitat for the animals. So the trees grow within the cages and compounds, the flora remains unchanged, the fencing is no more apparent than on any other country estate where they are concerned only to keep marauding fallow deer out of the corn and vegetable garden.

I arrived in this oasis of tranquility to find Derek Rushmere, who balanced the situation by having a tumult of fire in his belly, poor soul: stomach ulcers which manifested themselves in towering, thundering rages when they played him up. The hours he was working didn't help. Derek had arrived at Howletts with the first delivery of animals, a capuchin monkey and a tigress followed by two Himalayan bears. I had applied to be keeper number two.

The collection had grown tremendously since Derek had arrived and what appeared to the local residents as strange and weird species had arrived in abundance, to be peeped at through gaps in the fencing. But few of those strange creatures could have had a more bizarre and exotic history than Derek himself.

His curriculum vitae spoke for itself, gold-panning in Australia and chimpanzee catching in West Africa, to name but two unorthodox occupations he had engaged in, and there were many others.

Chimp catching in West Africa was big business at the time and worth a lot of money. Zoos are never too happy to talk about how their prize chimp specimens are acquired. Most, in fact, would deny all knowledge of it, but they do know. They are aware of every nuance and trick of the trade but they do not discuss it because it reflects no credit upon them, particularly if they have climbed aboard the conservation, save-our-wildlife bandwagon, like many have without any genuine interest in the subject at all.

Chimps are captured more often than not as new-born babies and their parents are murdered so that they can be caught. It is a highly organised operation which, at one stage, reached quite incredible proportions and used astonishing methods.

Nothing was left to chance by the dealers, absolutely nothing; the chimp colony is located, the number of pairs, the breeding potential, distance from the town and airport; orders are taken from potential buyers, deals are fixed before the catch is begun.

To survive and build up strength for a long, arduous

flight to the Western zoo world, the baby chimp needs a wet nurse, and a human wet nurse is used.

To make absolutely certain that a supply of wet nurses is at hand at the right time, a 'stud' is sent out to ensure that the wet nurses are in the right condition at the right time – can't be a bad job for an ambitious young fellow willing to travel. Profits from the venture are well worth the waiting time; in early infancy chimps are very vulnerable little things, mothers' milk is the only safe and sure diet.

The horror of the business is that a colony of breeding chimps will be wiped out to secure the babies so that they can be reared in a zoo and eventually breed to boost the ego of the curator.

The human wet nurse will succour the baby chimp until it is strong enough to withstand the rigours of the air journey and fit enough to be weaned; the name of the game is not conservation, it is CASH.

All in all, an interesting and informative business to have been in but you couldn't get a job, say, at the local supermarket, insurance office or on Ford's assembly line on the strength of it.

'Previous experience, please?'

'Goldpanner and chimpanzee catcher. . .'

'What? Will you write that down, please. . . . I see, panning for gold in Australian rivers and catching chimpanzees in West Africa . . . let me have a word with the supervisor . . . well, it seems that we have nothing *quite* suitable at the moment, but if something turns up, we'll contact you . . . expect a call about 1999.'

Come to think of it my career wouldn't read much better: candidate's c.v.: public school, failed; dodging about a bit for animal dealers; whisky runner, ship jumper . . . forget it.

My interview with Aspinall which was scheduled for 10 a.m. took place at four o'clock in the afternoon because he slept most of the day to recover from the exertions of the previous night, coining a few thousand pounds in his club. The unreality of the money, the preposterousness of it all is illustrated by the fact that after Aspinall sold the Clermont Club for the give-away price of £560,000 in 1972 (he was running hard-up at the time because of his spending on the zoo) to Victor Lownes, the European Playboy chief, Lownes made the purchase price back in just two nights' business. So The Buck's Sleep was probably earned and justified.

Derek met the train at Bekesbourne station and greeted me with enthusiasm. I liked it, he was a keen lad, he rushed me round the zoo, showed me everything, explained the routine better than I had ever had a routine explained before, insisted on going over again any points I wasn't quite clear on.

Then he said: 'It's all yours tomorrow, George. I haven't had a bloody day off in three years and nothing is going to stop me taking tomorrow off.'

'No problem,' I said, full of confidence, 'take a week off if you feel like it, you deserve it.' It was clear that Derek's day off was a matter of great concern to everybody, the domestic staff repeatedly told me in the first couple of hours: 'Derek hasn't had a day off for three years . . . three years, don't know how he's kept going.'

Such was the excitement aroused by the prospect of a day off for Derek that I was swept up into it and failed to realise how bad it sounded. 'Join happy Howletts and get a day off – once in a blue moon.'

Now there was a gorilla house and the only way to the kitchen was through it. The morning's first duty was to take the crate of milk to the cook in the kitchen; the gorillas did not know me nor I them, a nosier bunch of creatures you have never met. The pathway between the gorilla cages was very narrow, so narrow that they could reach across and touch each other. As I set off with a full crate of milk, first one hairy arm reached out and grabbed a bottle of milk, then another grabbed my hair, my arms, my legs, the crate itself. That kitchen door could have been on the moon for all the chance I had of reaching it intact. When eventually I did fall through, tattered and dishevelled, I told cook: 'Ring for another crate of milk then let me in through the front door when it arrives, otherwise it will be black coffee all day.'

Derek's long stint had taken its toll of him. He suffered his excruciatingly painful ulcers which made him the most difficult animal in the zoo to cope with: non-ulcers-playing-up days, serene, marvellous; ulcers-active-days, life in a punk rock group would have been quieter and more restful; those were the days of the flashing meat-cleaver, the flying metal dustbin hurled at your head, the hurtling pitchfork to be dodged. The anguish and pain of Derek's ulcers extended as far as he could fling the nearest heavy object – preferably at somebody within range. Everybody knew Derek's ulcers; a scurrying housemaid would hiss: 'Ulcers!' – lock the door, bar the windows, keep fifty good paces between him and you at all times and you might survive the day. Everybody suffered more from Derek's ulcers than he did. In making life miserable, it was the only case of communal ulceration I have come across, not a private little ulcer but one to be shared.

They were the reason for the beginning of my on-off, run hot, run cold relationship with Howletts. The first time I quit was to get a rest from them. Once you've left and gone back, the second parting comes easier, so do the third and fourth. Sometimes the grinding poverty of the job gets you down, it overrides the interest. It is a curious job which causes you to think, 'I must go somewhere else to make some money so that I can afford to keep this up'.

But the zoo was expanding relentlessly. New specimens poured in, they had to be accommodated and cared for; new staff arrived and a great team evolved, every one an idiosyncratic lunatic in his own right but together a team; that fabled 'crack' had developed and everybody worked for everybody else, otherwise the job would have stopped.

Not all recruits stayed. Some were just too weird to keep on, but employing weirdos is one thing, getting rid of them is quite another matter. A truly enormous man was employed, a man so big that people would turn to stare at his size, and with strength to match his bulk. Work stopped one morning when we watched him pick-ing up hundredweight sacks of cement with one hand and tossing them into a trailer like throwing three kilo bags of flour across the kitchen. But he was no gentle giant. He had what we thought at first were fits of mood-iness and sudden fits of temper which flashed up like summer storms. At these times he was uncontrollable. The storms grew more frequent and he started to break things, and his temper became so uncertain that we were all becoming terrified. He produced a very curious feeling in all of us, quite inexplicably, at one certain moment, you would feel that you had to get away from him, at other times he was perfectly all right.

Since it was beginning to wear everybody down, it was decided that he would have to go. Aspinall was very wary since the man had shown clear signs that he resented authority, any kind or level of authority. In his rages he tended to seek the support of those he considered his friends and fellow sufferers. Aspinall said: 'You'd better get rid of him, George. But don't rub him up the wrong way.'

You will have gathered that a meat cleaver is to a zoo man what a kukri is to a Gurkha soldier – indispensable; it is there, of course, because you are chopping up meat all day and become adept with it. I took one with me, up the back of my donkey jacket, a couple of mates stood by, out of direct sight, with crowbars and axes, just in case.

I didn't tell the big man that he was sacked, I looked perplexed and worried and asked him: 'Can you think of anything else to do?' Then I added: 'Oh dear, there's no more work for you, you've done your three months' casual work and the Old Man's run out of jobs for you.' Each word echoed in my ears and I waited, tingling, for the outburst and the anger. Instead he smiled and said: 'That's all right, George, mate.' He collected his money and bags and left singing.

Trouble came with the morning. The big fellow, before leaving, had placed a plank across the bear pit. He had been seen to do it but the observer thought he was working there and took no notice. Whether it was spite or foolishness is impossible to tell, he was prone to actions like this which made sense to him but nobody else. It was one of the things about him which had worried all of us, sudden compulsive actions unrelated to anything which were clearly vitally important to him. But the things he did were potentially dangerous to himself and others.

The results this time added up to a bloody nuisance ending in farce, but they could have been disastrous. The bears were out.

They were not difficult to find, they were up the trees

in the highest branches; fruit, vegetables and all temptations failed to get them down.

Getting an eight hundredweight bear down a sixty-foot tree is no easy task, nor is getting up a sixty-foot tree to catch an eight hundredweight bear a simple matter. Long ladders were needed so we called the fire brigade – after all they are noted for rescuing cats from similar predicaments and getting their pictures in the papers for it.

Our intrepid fire fighters lacked for no advice or encouragement: 'Mind their claws, they're as big as an average cat is long.' 'Watch their teeth, they can take your hand off with a bite.' 'Don't get into a position where they can take a swing at you, they'll knock you twenty feet.'

As soon as the turntable ladders were in position, the bears moved. After circling the trees half a dozen times, each move a major operation of shunting, reversing, raising and lowering the turntable, the firemen's patience was running out.

'Connect the hoses to the mains hydrant,' the fire chief ordered. He hit them with a high-pressure jet and bounced them like table tennis balls on a water-jet in a fairground shooting gallery. They tumbled down the trees from branch to branch in a cascade of sparkling water. We were soaked through to the skin. It was the firemen's turn to grin and give advice. 'You ought to dress properly for a job like this,' they said as they shook the droplets from their oilskins. The bears were glad to scamper back across the plank into their pit, helped by a friendly squirt or two to speed up their progress.

As they say, all was made clear later when an official, whose status and function we never fully established beyond the fact that he had a file of official documents, a clipboard and a ballpoint pen, called to ask about the big fellow. After a chat and learning that the big fellow had left, our friend, who was from the probation, after-care or health services, explained: 'The poor chap's done a couple of spells in Rampton and Broadmoor. We like to keep a friendly, helpful eye on them when they come out, just to see that they are getting on all right and coping, you understand.' We understood. If they had told us earlier we would have understood his behaviour better – but, then, it is doubtful whether he would have got the job at all.

Chapter 7

Nature will out – too often in public

I dallied awhile in Kent enjoying the delights of leafy Bekesbourne and the relaxing peace of rural life. The trouble is that animals have minds of their own and sometimes take it into their heads to do their own thing. I have a mind of my own and sometimes do my own thing; often other people with minds of their own do their own thing. They all combine to complicate matters. I try to keep things orderly and straightforward. But it isn't as simple as all that . . .

Escapes excite the media and frighten the public. They excite and frighten keepers too and they happen all the time in every zoo. If they didn't it would be because the animals were moribund, so the better the zoo, the more likely are escapes.

But zoo keeping is such a closed society and consequently so introspective that the alarm caused to the public when wild animals run free in their midst is resented and misunderstood by the zoo fraternity, as much as the public resents what it sees as a threat to its safety. Wolves which escaped from Howletts caused a furore and the matter was even raised in the House of Commons, yet zoo keepers knew that the wolves would not immediately think of gobbling up the nearest passing villager, they would be much more concerned with seeking a tasty morsel for lunch among the fauna of the district. Farmers could possibly have the right to be alarmed on behalf of their stock, but public hysteria is almost entirely unjustified. When, to put the business into perspective, did you last hear of a member of the public mauled or devoured

73

by an escaped wild creature? Not in Britain, not in Europe and not in America.

Yet the public does have a right to feel aggrieved because of the shockingly inadequate safety standards of three-quarters of the zoos in Britain. A spokeswoman for the R.S.P.C.A. told the House of Commons that, of the 150 zoos in Britain examined by the society, less than 25 per cent came anywhere near meeting minimum standards of health, hygiene and safety. Another speaker in the debate revealed that 2,000 wild animals had escaped from Britain's slum zoos and had never been recaptured.

There are indeed dangers: when the Indian honey badgers escaped from Howletts, they got out of a compound which, by all the rules, to the safety conscious eye and common sense should have been escape proof.

A lovely, safe compound except that the basic fact of nature was overlooked – trees grow and their branches extend; so the tree in the compound which was one of its attractive features grew bigger and its branches overlapped the fence; the badgers climbed up, slid along a branch and dropped to freedom.

A honey badger (behind that deceptively charming name lurks a killer) is one of nature's most dangerous creations: Not only is it not afraid of any living creature but it also has a wickedly aggressive streak in its make-up. Brock the badger is a comforting, homely designation suggesting a shuffling, grumpy old fellow with a walrus moustache and a heart of gold, but even our own native species is not all that chummy a chap if caught in a tight corner, not that he could hold a candle to his Indian cousin.

This was action stations for the whole zoo staff: Richard and I spent the night in woods where they had been reported – not a whisper of them. And no luck at a dozen other venues where sightings had allegedly been made. Ponder the problem: a cunning, strong, resourceful creature inclined to hole up during daylight hours and go about his nefarious business in the dark, a quickish mover if needs be, a traveller. *Where* do you begin to look? And the public has to be warned: 'For goodness sake, don't go near it.' So if it is sighted, it could be miles away by the time the re-capture team arrives.

Then the lady called from a village near Dover, 15 miles away. 'Your missing badger has been in my chicken shed twice. I think it will come back.'

Cool, collected, and a keen observer of bird and wildlife from her kitchen window, she delighted in everything she saw. What a marvellous witness! She described the beast exactly to the last stripe. We arrived and she showed us her son's wildlife chart: 'This is the thing, I watched it carefully, there can be no mistake, those are the tracks it made and that is the way it came.'

We sat out the first night watching the clouds scudding across the moon to darken the view while cold crept up from the toes to the neck, and limbs tingled from immobility; grey light seeped from the eastern sky, curious policemen eyed the two odd men motionless in the car, early risers like milkmen cast quizzical glances. Nothing.

Five hours into the second night's vigil there was a movement to the left, where it should not have been. The chicken house was surrounded by lawn which was bright in the thin moonlight; it was the badger and he went straight to the flap and hole in the side of the hut. We waited for the uproar, but not a murmur, not one screech, cluck or tweet, not even a rustle of feathers. 'He's gone past,' said Richard, 'but he can't have done, we saw him go in. Perhaps he's gone out the other side.'

He had left a trail in the dew on the grass. It ended at the hatch and it did not start again at the other hatch. Yet no noise. A fox in that chicken coop and the neighbourhood would have been awakened.

'He can't be inside. . . .'

We slapped the sides and poked a broom handle inside. He was there – his awful growl and roar confirmed it. And that is when the cold sweat breaks out no matter how experienced an animal man you are; we both knew the damage he could do if we made a mistake.

A vigilant guardian of the law was waiting by the car when we went to collect the nets and catching gear, having first blocked the chicken coop hatches.

'A badger,' he said with ill concealed contempt, 'put the bugger in a bag and chuck it in the boot. C'm on, I'll help you.'

'But this one is a killer.'

75

'Bollocks, a killer badger, pull the other one.'

His walkie talkie crackled and he listened for a few seconds, then with a grin he spoke into the mike: 'I've got two lads here from the zoo with a killer bloody badger.' He stressed the last phrase. Then his smile faded and his eyes opened wide. 'Bloody 'ell,' he said. And then he told us in a voice into which a tone of brusqueness had intruded and as if imparting vital information: 'It's on the list, this one, the dangerous list. It can be bloody nasty, there's a reward for it. Well, you lads seem to know all about it, I'll leave you to it . . . unless you want some help.'

There did not seem too much conviction in the offer and, no matter how willing, an inexperienced pair of hands can be more of a disadvantage than a help in such circumstances.

The nets were rigged and secured at Richard's end of the hut. The moon set. 'Why does it always happen in the pitch dark when you can't see what you're doing,' Richard bemoaned.

All deadly, disturbingly quiet inside the shed. The danger was that he would come crashing out of my door as soon as it opened. With trepidation I pushed in the broom and began walloping it about with a great clatter. I thought I felt it make contact but couldn't be sure, so I kept on working the broom and making the racket until my breath ran out.

It always happens in a flurry and a mad rush. Suddenly he was in the nets growling and roaring in a pig-eyed fury, beside himself with rage and frustration at being ensnared and entangled. Like playing a salmon, all you can do is wait until he tires and his breath runs out, then drop him in the box.

Flushed with success, we telephoned the boss asleep in his London flat, he growled worse than the badger and slammed down the phone. It was just after four o'clock in the morning. Down the road we met the guardian of the law. He stepped out from the deep shadow of a tree. 'Everything all right, lads?' he asked warily.

'He's in the bag,' we told him.

As we left the scene we heard his walkie talkie crackle into life. He was telling HQ: 'We've got that dangerous badger thing in the bag, Sir. No, no trouble really, bit tricky at times but it's all right now.'

Foolish it may be, but it is surprising how – when you are cold, exhausted, full of frustrated sleep, hungry, dirty and it is the blackest part of the night before dawn – little things like a phone being slammed down and a chance remark can be excessively irritating. Particularly when you have to be at work again when daylight comes.

The trouble with animals and keeping them is that you cannot switch them off until you are ready to deal with them. They go on inexorably living, eating, going about their business. Put an animal into captivity and immediately you become its slave and handmaiden.

Possibly the reason people are so smug when they have occasion to say 'virtue rewarded' is that virtue so often goes unrewarded. Justice had a habit of coming rough in our tight-knit world. Rough enough to induce a philosophical acceptance of what ever life throws up, or doesn't throw up, or throws up as a near miss – like the time Sheikh Zayed of Abu Dhabi came on a visit of inspection. He was being wooed for some of his oil riches to help keep the place running. This was at the height of the Arab invasion of Britain when they arrived by the hundreds, dripping gold in rivulets into the pockets of casino owners, hoteliers, call girls and con men.

At the time it was vital to Aspinall because he was feeling the pinch: he could not get planning permission to open regularly to the public, costs were mounting and every penny had to come from his private pocket. The Sheikh apparently offered financial support.

Sultans and sheikhs were fabled for chucking money about and doling out expensive gifts, usually in solid gold. The zoo staff all donned their best blue jeans and turned out looking as pretty and wholesome as they could with big smiles for the sheikh and his retinue, but the gold watches were a long time in coming out. The greed sparkled in our eyes but when the goodies did eventually materialise, they were produced in the wrong place at the wrong time.

Horror, shock, scandal and fury swept the camp when the sheikh began to hand out gold watches, old-fashioned hunters worth about £300 each, to a group of part-time casual labourers working in the gardens. They collected all the Arab treasure – not one member of the full-time regular staff got anything, we were sick. Yes, we are a greedy lot. At such times it is hard to turn the other cheek and smile. There are compensations, job satisfaction, beautiful surroundings, there can be few more pleasant places than Howletts in high summer . . . but you cannot spend the compensations.

Yet Howletts' conditions are good. By zoo standards, the money is first-rate and accommodation is fabulous. The truth is that it is just an appallingly paid job and as long as animals eat as much as they do and need to be expensively housed, it will remain a life on the subsistence level for those who look after them.

Life was good when The Buck was flush and flashing wads of 'extras' round the boys and when, if some item of equipment was urgently needed, you could go to the office and draw the ready cash. It changed fundamentally when the zoo opened to the public and an organisation was imposed with chits, requisitions and forms in triplicate the order of the day. It is amazing how well a shambles can work if left to itself and then when it is organised, how quickly a 'them and us' attitude develops between staff and management. When 'management', as such, comes in, some soul goes out of an organisation.

The Sheikh of Abu Dhabi pulled out of the Howletts deal. It upset Aspinall and he was a bit churlish about it, but maybe the sheikh was right: The Buck has subsequently admitted that the whole project, Howletts and Port Lympne combined, was a gamble that did not pay off. His fanaticism made it all worthwhile in his eyes, but it obviously looked a bad investment to the astronomically wealthy but wary Zayed. However, Aspers is not short of friends and some of them stepped in to pull him out of the mire. The Goldsmith brothers, Sir James and Teddy with Lord Londonderry must top the list. Sir James has poured in money; Teddy, the ecologist, has poured in support; Selim Zilkha, the Mothercare tycoon, is a supporter along with Jim Slater – all big money men, all putting hard cash into an enterprise with scant hope of profitable return.

Yet, in the media, Aspinall is bad news, Jim Slater is

not good news and Sir James, to many sections of the press, is a positive anathema. If the press can print the bad news about Aspinall, it will and does; the good news is left unwritten. Aspinall is unloved by press and public whereas other animal men like Gerald Durrell, David Attenborough and Johnny Morris are doted on, respected and admired with never a nasty word written about them. This attitude rebounds on the zoo.

Black Sunday was the day when the beautiful model girl, Merilyn Lamb, visited Howletts with James Osborne, The Buck's half brother. As is usual, the after lunch treat was a tour of the zoo with much closer contact with the animals than is possible in a public zoo. What happened was the subject of a lengthy court case, the outcome of which was that Merilyn was awarded £10,600 damages against James and he was ordered to pay her costs of £25,000, which, in early 1970s values, was a lot of money.

The story in the press was that she tickled a tiger on the nose, the tiger grabbed her and inflicted severe damage on her arm. In defence of the tiger, it did not maul her as was suggested. It seized her hand and pulled her arm through the weldmesh fence. The wire did the damage, but that wasn't much consolation for a young girl with a mutilated arm.

It happened at the time of day when The Buck usually went out to play with the tigers and put on an act for his guests. However, on this occasion he was abroad and so had nothing to do with the incident. But the fact that it happened at Aspinall's Howletts was enough to ensure that big, black headlines told the world the story in all the newspapers the following morning.

It was a tragedy for the girl. An arm mangled and shredded through a wire grille must have been hideously shocking and painful. But the thought of putting a limb within reaching distance of a strange tiger sends shudders down the spine of any experienced tiger man.

It is easy to sense danger, and easy to forecast that disaster will come from certain attitudes and actions. However, it is not wise to talk about it too much because talking about it minimises the risk if disaster does not strike quickly. There is a set pattern to breeding dangerous complacency: you sense the danger and are extra wary, nothing happens so you relax, still nothing happens, and you become so relaxed that there is a risk of becoming insensitive to possible danger; nothing happens and you begin to think that you were wrong in the first place and then you become utterly confused and that is when it is most dangerous; the *facts* have not changed, only interpretation and attitudes to them have altered. It took years for it to happen at Howletts, but when all our misgivings were finally realised, it was horrific and dreadful, and close friends, Brian Stocks and Bob Wilson, two big cat keepers, were killed.

London was swinging and getting more and more permissive, East Kent and the diocese of Canterbury wasn't; so when Swinging London invaded Bekesbourne it scandalised the neighbourhood.

The annual staff party was an all-night barbecue with booze, beautiful women, food to build up the strength when energy flagged from the pace of the roistering and more booze: The Buck was never a man to stint his guests and he must be classed as one of the world's all-time experts at throwing a party.

In Chelsea or Kensington . . . so what? In Bekesbourne . . . horrors. Lips pursed censoriously, eyelids were dropped in reproval, faces set in indignation and the words disgusting, degrading, immoral, outrageous gained great currency in the village.

'The party!' snapped one affronted lady resident with the rasp of barbed wire scratching ice in her voice, 'no I did not hear about the party. But I did hear about the orgy. I wonder they weren't all arrested.'

Like the day after when two children asked why the elephants were carrying hay on their heads. I thought it was very sharp of them so I explained in detail that it was an exceptionally hot day and the elephants were out in the open with no shade so we put the hats on to stop them getting sunstroke. Indian elephants are prone to sunstroke because of that huge expanse of heads. They are jungle animals and not used to the hot sun beating down on their necks, so sensibly, they seek the shade in the heat of the day, in the same way that gorillas take a siesta between noon and three o'clock in the heat. Happy, the kids went back to their parents. Their father's face set in anger and I heard him say: 'But they come from India and Africa and it's hot out there. I know because I was there in the war.' He came to me and said: 'Look, smart-arse, if my kids ask a sensible question, give them a sensible answer. I paid a few quid to bring them round here, for education, not cock-and-bull stories.'

If there is something not quite right with the image of Howletts because a controversial lifestyle rubs off in the wrong way on all the right reasons for running a zoo, it should not diminish the value of the gems to be found in the spread of the great Howletts' chestnut, the Gingko tree, turkey oak and the mass of sweet chestnut, lime, cedar and beech. Probably there is far too much for the public to absorb.

The public often wants only the spectacular: great apes, big cats, elephants, amusing monkeys – the traditional excitements and amusements of a zoo, the things they know and can understand. But Howletts is crammed with much more than that. With all the passion of a dedicated collector, Aspinall has assembled a unique exhibition of the animal world's rarities. But who, except those who know, would be impressed by the rare and beautiful four-horned antelope, or even the roan antelope which is becoming increasingly rare in modern Africa. The snow and clouded leopards are there to see, exquisite to the accustomed eye but, sadly, often unappreciated – as are the tapirs, yet they too are an increasingly rare species. There are very few things at Howletts which could be called common. It is a zoologists' collection which, by its uniqueness, highlights the problems of modern zoos: go commercial and use the animals as exhibits and side shows, or go conservation and blow the profits.

Never a dull moment: an articulated lorry arrived on a Saturday morning to deliver an elephant – and no lifting gear to hoist it off. Desperate solution: manpower, go to the local pub and transport thirty stalwarts back to the elephant house for lifting duties.

Shoulders to the crate, the men heaved and the strain brought about a great belching as the beer swilled about inside them. A pause to clear excess wind and gather strength; another heave gained lift off, followed by a stagger backwards as the elephant moved to the back of the crate. Then forward in a rush as it changed its stance. The left side plunged as jumbo swayed; then the right side as it adjusted balance. The lifters shuffled backwards, stopped, then heels were dug in, and forced forwards again; they gained a foot, lost two, and were back where they began. The crate went up, down, and sideways, undulating like a rudderless boat in a heavy swell. The crazy dance routine went on until in a mad backwards rush, rapidly approaching a gallop, the whole lot, lifters, driver, onlookers, womenfolk advisers, were all dumped in a heap behind the trailer.

Silence from inside the crate, silence from the tangled mass of humanity outside until one helper, purple in the face from effort, wiping sweat from head, face and neck and wringing out the soaked handkerchief, exclaimed: 'By heck! I don't expect I'll be asked to do that again for another fifty years . . . some silly bugger coming into the pub Sat'dy lunchtime and asking, "Give us a hand to get this elephant on the lorry". '

Dignity doesn't necessarily go hand in hand with animal handling. They have a habit of gaining the upper hand physically and reducing the keeper trying to enforce his will to a comic figure who can only let the farce run its course: Richard Johnstone Scott had the seemingly simple task of moving the wild boar from an old pen to a new one, but wild boar are tricky, slippery, agile and amazingly powerful. At Chilham Castle they tried to contain them with strong chain link fencing, the boars charged through it head on. Contrary beasts, they do not like going where you want them to.

Any organisation and methods man could be reduced to a state of gibbering idiocy by a week's work in a zoo. The mundane chore of re-penning the boar – half-an-hour's work at the most, we had estimated – had stretched to three hours of Keystone Cops chases, captures, escapes from the nets, tumbles, up-endings, ripped jeans and bruised limbs plus infuriating frustration. The wild boar were just being bloody-minded and not open to persuasion, temptation or guile. One man dived at a passing beast, grabbed it by the hind legs and rolled it over. He held on to the legs, scrambled to his feet and wheelbarrowed the astonished creature into the waiting trailer.

'That's the answer,' we all said, 'grab the back legs.' Richard dived, grappled, and scrambled to his feet with a firm grip on the upper limbs and feet tucked tightly under elbows: success. Until the boar decided to go the other way; faster and faster they charged round the compound, the boar crashing through all obstacles and Richard dragging behind yelling: 'What the Hell do I do with this one?' Pooling the combined weight of our experience and wisdom we could not advise him. 'Hang on a bit while we work it out, we'll send you a postcard,' said one exhausted chaser, sitting on a log and pulling hard on a cigarette.

Be prepared to be embarrassed by your animals – even be prepared to be embarrassed by your friends: both are usually equally unpredictable. In both cases nature will out. The difference is that in the case of your friends you can often talk it back in or, *in extremis*, wallop it back in; but with animals, not well-versed in the proprieties, nature outs and stays out until it is ready of its own volition to go back in – and it has a habit of outing at the most inconvenient moment possible.

The most adorable little animal pal can be embarrassing. We kept a personal donkey, a delightful, lovely little creature with a marvellous temperament. She was called Twiggy. She earned her fodder by pulling us around in a donkey cart. There is really no greater contentment in life than riding in a donkey cart, clip-clopping down a leafy country lane, dappled in summer sunshine, with the din of birdsong fresh and clean in your ears, sharper than any stereo, with a background of the penetrating hum of insects in the hedgerow and the noise of distant farm work drifting across the open fields. You listen to the abrasive rustle of growing corn as it moves in the breeze, good, rich earthy smells come undiluted to the nostrils and wildflowers scent the air – bliss. All these sensations and pleasures are impossible to experience in a car. We trotted to the shops and the pub on Sundays with time to look over the hedges and into the trees with no fear of Twiggy swerving off the road, so we missed nothing of interest going on.

The time came for Twiggy to be mated. It was arranged that we would take her to a neighbouring hamlet,

Brabourne Lees to meet the Jack donkey and she was duly loaded into a horse box for the tryst. Dodger Hogbin, a 19 stone friend, came along to lend some weight to the occasion – and a fat lot of use he turned out to be.

At eight-thirty in the morning we unloaded Twiggy into our friend's paddock and the lady went to collect her Jack donkey and perform the introductions. Either Twiggy was not quite ready or she didn't like the idea or the look of the Jack, or maybe she just wanted to be chased, but, quite out of character, she bolted.

Over the wall she went like a steeplechaser and off down the narrow country lane. The mistake which became rapidly very apparent was that, though at any other time of the day that lane was virtually deserted, between eight-thirty and nine o'clock in the morning, it was crammed with wives driving commuter husbands to the station and mums driving children to school. Twiggy caused confusion.

By now, Jack donkey had got the scent of Twiggy, and realising what was afoot, his ardour was fully aroused in every way. He bucked, kicked, brayed and shook off his owner who was holding his bridle and, with big Dodger Hogbin, hanging on to his tail bobbing along behind like an old boot tied on a wedding car, charged the fence dumping Dodger in a tangle of shattered timber and wire. Down the road he galloped, weaving and dodging between the cars which Twiggy had brought to a standstill; she too had been stopped by oncoming traffic and was prancing about in bewilderment with her ways forward or back blocked by traffic jams.

It was there that Jack donkey caught her. Once a Jack donkey has the tingle of lust in his veins and the object of his affection in sight, there is nothing in the world going to stop him – nothing. So he mounted little Twiggy instantly and had his wicked way with her in full view of a circle of fuming, embarrassed onlookers with husbands and wives chatting nonchalantly about this and that and flustered mothers playing I-spy with fascinated kiddywinks who didn't want to spy anything except what was going on in front of their very eyes.

Chapter 8

Lowdown on high life in swinging Thanet

*Earthy though we may be, we have our dreams of higher things.
I used to think how nice it would be to be a country singing star
like, say, Johnny Cash and, since I do have a bit of a voice and
I love showing off, after work at Howletts, I used to sing in local
clubs in Kent. There are girls and beer in clubs and that has
often proved a lethal mixture for me because after the girls and
beer come the bouncers. But I behaved myself because I liked the
extra money 'stardom' was bringing in and I reasoned that I had
a nice little number going which allowed me to have fun with a
sufficiency of free booze. But it wasn't as simple as that . . .*

They loved me in Ramsgate. I was king. East Kent's answer to Johnny Cash and billed as the 'Country and Western' singing sensation. It must have been *fairly* good
because they kept asking me back to the Refectory Club
and I had my own fan following; good enough anyway to
take up singing semi-professionally.

It was quite literally a case of singing for my supper.
The money was urgently needed. On wages of £16 a week
you can't see much high-life: a weekly visit to the chip
shop severely strains the exchequer. So I sang like a
thrush. I think that fear of the awful consequences of
failure, like no beer, skittles or girls, put my voice up at
least an octave on top high notes and pumped an added
throb of passion into the slush songs.

The routine was to tuck up my elephants for the night,
steam across to Ramsgate in one of the zoo's vans and
wow 'em with my renditions of *North to Alaska* and *Ring
of Fire*.

But Ramsgate knew Howletts keepers better as hellraisers than songsters. Zoo men stick together like soldiers in the same platoon. They work together, drink together and fight together – if there's nobody else around, they fight each other. They have a word for it, they call it 'crack' – the camaraderie of the job which comes from working very closely together in odd and dangerous circumstances, being forced to rely utterly and completely on each other and knowing that, every time you open a cage door, if something goes wrong the others will come in and get you out . . . it happens all the time, sometimes it makes headlines, most times it just becomes part of the folklore and chat, good for a giggle in the pub.

Everybody talks shop all the time and gains a lot from it: you learn how to recognise the particular twitch of a tiger's ear, or the peculiar flick of a wild elephant's trunk which signal trouble, things you cannot really learn from personal experience because you might be dead by then. You learn to sense when a seemingly docile, beautiful but menacing black panther is manoeuvring to get behind you for the kill. You learn to recognise the almost imperceptible change in the cat's gait, the set of its feelers when the killer instinct is running through its veins; you know immediately because you have been told and talked about it.

Through the chat you know that most dead panther keepers are found without a scratch or mark on their bodies. You know that some have died in the fleeting instant of time it takes companions to turn, empty a shovel into a wheelbarrow, turn back and find their colleagues dead on the floor. A panther, with deadly intent and in deathly silence, will catapult itself fifty feet from a standing start, break its quarry's neck instantaneously by impact and, without stopping, be squatting forty feet up an opposite branch, yellow eyes burning through the foliage, all in the space of that split second.

The talk keeps you sharp, it tops up the adrenalin which flows everytime you walk into a cage. That is the sort of shared experience which keeps zoo men together as a close and closed community. Let's face it, there are not many people daft and reckless enough to walk into tiger cages or play 'touch' with frustrated panthers, so there are not many other people who you can swap yarns with except zoo men.

But most hard-working, hard-playing, tight-knit communities tend to behave in the same way: oil wildcatters, construction gangs, seamen all go mad when 'loosed', even staid businessmen on a convention kick over the traces; booze flows in and conventions flood out.

Kurt Paulich, the big-cat keeper at Howletts, regularly eased his tensions in the nearby East Kent seaside resorts where pubs, clubs and companionable young ladies abound. There came the inevitable night when he couldn't go for a drink because he was barred from every drinking haunt in Ramsgate. His social credit was a bit overdrawn. Yet somehow he had managed to get paralytic. It must have been a good day for the off licences.

My date was waiting for me in Nero's Club, so I went alone to plead Kurt's case, ask for forgiveness and vouch for his good behaviour.

A couple of hundred people were queueing but, since I was a local 'star', the bouncers gave me a big hello and let me in.

But Kurt? They drew in their breath and said. ' 'e's been very naugh'y the last couple of times, torn chandeliers out of the ceiling, jumped from the balcony, laid out a couple of blokes.'

'He's all right tonight, he's harmless. I'll look after him,' I promise. So they agreed that when they'd let in a few more from the queue and the boss had gone round the back, they would quietly slip him through.

As we chatted, there was a crash and pandemonium broke out. The blue Transit van was in the middle of the dance floor, the dance floor swing doors on its bonnet, Kurt tumbled out and headed for the bar. He had driven through the window.

'So I got in, did I?' he said, oblivious of what he'd done.

I jammed him back in the passenger seat, scrambled into the cab and reversed out through the shambles. Outside I stood on the pavement to take stock when, suddenly: 'Whoomph!' Somebody was loosing off with a twelve bore shotgun. I leapt on Kurt and rolled the pair of us under the van.

I thought: 'Hell, the Ramsgate Godfather is after Kurt and he might get me as well.'

The shooting went on for a few more rounds and, again, I thought: 'It can't go on for ever and the police are definitely bound to arrive any minute . . . and all I was doing was trying to get him a drink. It's better to face the drunken driving job than the other, so lie still.'

But the police didn't come. The street cleared, no law, no angry club men, no queueing disco fans, no passersby. Just the odd tinkle as a sliver of broken glass detached itself and fell to the pavement. Quietly I got the pair of us back into the cab, worked out the quickest way out and expected all bedlam to break out when I switched on.

But . . . nothing. So we went home with a bent and damaged vehicle, sore heads and butterflies in the pit of the stomach, anticipating the custard hitting the fan the following day.

Strangely it didn't. Except that John Aspinall fumed: 'You boys will have to stop taking the transport and writing it off, ripping it off all over the place. £6,000 Land Rovers left outside pubs because you've forgotten them and taken a taxi home, vans and pick-ups costing a fortune in repairs. You two are banned from taking zoo transport anywhere. The keys must be handed in to Beryl at the mansion every night.'

No wonder, when he had to introduce us to visitors or his private guests, he would always say: 'Now . . . I suppose you'll have to meet my pirate crew.' And there was usually a pained expression on his face.

On one occasion when he had important callers we gathered round, unwashed, unshaven, trousers held up by string, Nick Marks squatting on the grass barefoot. Out of the side of his mouth Aspinall hissed: 'Ask Nick not to pick his toenails with a Bowie knife in front of the guests'.

It wasn't long before Mad Kurt – did I tell you that he was always called Mad Kurt? – was feeling depressed and moaning: 'I do fancy a bit of that Ramsgate tonight, but no transport.' Then he sank into a deep Austrian gloom of deprivation. In that mood he was like a bear. I have said how you can tell the moods of tigers by their ear-twitching and elephants by their trunk flicks. Every animal gives some sort of warning, eyes, nostrils, feet, tail, some distinctive behaviour not in their usual posture. What makes bears the most dangerous and unpredictable of all is that they are completely expressionless, not a flicker of an eye, not a ripple of a muscle; deadpan killers when the mood takes them, poker-faced players who could just be coming over for a romp or to rip out your guts, whichever way the mood takes them.

It was best to humour Kurt. So I told him: 'The only thing they haven't taken the key from is the tractor.' An enormous Fordson 2500. His face lit up. We hitched up the muck trailer, swept it out, trundled the three-piece suite from my front room aboard and set off for the village of Ash to pick up Rosie and Val, who used to be our dancing partners. On with the duffle coats and off we GO. Nobody ever stops and breathalyses a tractor: they think that it's an old farm lad doing a bit of night harvesting. We travelled like that for months, though the contraption did look a bit odd parked among the Lotus Elites, Jags and MGs at the club.

It was after a night of such debauchery with Kurt that I decided to go back to sea. Captain Harri Voss and his good ship *Steinberg* were in town and desperate to find a cook before sailing. In fact, he couldn't sail without one and somebody suggested me.

Chapter 9

'Shanghaied' by Captain Harri's buccaneers

My singing elephant keeper act won me local fame and not a little popularity but, with a little help from my friends, it also sent me off a-wandering again; when the wine is in, in my case, the wanderlust will out. They introduced me to a ship's captain desperate for a crew, so I went to sea once more. But it wasn't as simple as all that . . .

You know the *Steinberg*, of course you do. The archetypal timber-trade coaster which slides up muddy estuaries to tie up in unlikely semi-inland docks at the far reach of a tide. She's the type of ship which looks friendly and family and you wonder what part she can possibly play in the great maritime trade of the world alongside the super-tankers and fat-bellied container ships.

A very important part: She is bigger than she appears and carries a motorway full of articulated lorry cargoes. She and her sisters operate from ports convenient to the industries that use them; she has an acute sense of proportion when it comes to charging her customers and she gets from place to place usually on time and without fuss. Since she avoids the enormous container ports, her cargoes do not get lost as often as those aboard the monster ships.

Steinberg is a nice ship: she is the epitome of small is beautiful. Apart from that her crew are, well . . . not as *formal* as masters, officers and seamen in the big, prestige fleets.

Captain Harri Voss was in a dilemma in Ramsgate, he had lost his cook. Or vice versa the cook had lost his ship.

Nobody seemed quite clear. All that could be firmly established was that there was no cook aboard and Captain Harri urgently wanted to sail on the next tide.

At this stage we were introduced and Austrian Kurt, being fluent in Captain Harri's language, persuaded him that I was one of God's more wonderful creations, particularly with a pan in my hand. Captain Harri pleaded with me to join him. I told him I couldn't possibly go without taking my pet monkey, Minnie, a Java Macaque. 'Of course you take her, George,' said Captain Harri, 'take your mistress, take your grandmother, take who you want, but will you do the cooking?'

The *Steinberg* was sailing the following morning on the night tide at 01.00 hours, so I arranged my farewell concert at the Refectory. Word got around that I was leaving, like it does in a small town, producing the biggest house and take of my career. If it had been like that every night, I might have stayed.

Come midnight and they all spontaneously decided to give me a send off. Four hundred strong we marched through the streets to the harbour and the commotion brought out the police and harbourmaster to join in the fun.

We sang 'Now is the Hour', 'We'll Meet Again' and, because it was a German ship, 'Deutschland, Deutschland Über Alles'. I staggered along, blind drunk, with a case of Heineken in one hand, kitbag in the other, guitar slung on my back and Minnie on my shoulder. Tears streamed down my cheeks at the gangplank, Captain Harri blubbed at the top of the gangplank. The harbourmaster said: 'What in heaven's name is going on?' The pilot said: 'Oh, my God.' And *M.V. Steinberg* put to sea, Captain Harri, seven crew and Minnie. First stop Hamburg, then to Finland, where mostly everything is grey, sombre and dull – and what isn't is forbidden.

Captain Harri was over the moon about Minnie, she had her own cabin. Since I was the cook he gave me money to buy the food, £150 for the crew, £20 for Minnie. 'Nudding but the best for mein leiber monkey, Ja?' Best grapes, bananas, nuts, the pick of the exotic tropical fruits of the market and Minnie blossomed.

The *Steinberg* crew kept at bay the terrors of the deep

by partially anaesthetising themselves with a constant supply of alcohol; to soften the shock of my cooking I put a crate of strong lager on the mess table every morning before breakfast and kept it topped up all day.

We were a smuggling ship; at least, as far as the crew was concerned, that was the primary function of the voyage, to take supplies of vodka to the besieged, down-trodden population of teetotal Finland. A wholly commendable and humanitarian enterprise in their view and all the better if a little profit rubbed off along the route. The vodka was bought at three deutschmarks a bottle in Hamburg and sold for 80, 100 Finnmarks or more: it was a powerful distillation, the stuff they run the Hamburg buses on.

And still Minnie continued to entrance Captain Harri. On a morning when the Northern sea and sky were merged in a grey wash like a monochrome illustration in the old *London Illustrated News* and divots of white spume detached themselves from the sea to splatter like spit against the bridge windows, Captain Harri, well slaked with vodka against the cold and impending inclement weather, was up top cradling Minnie in his arms.

The glass was falling quickly as the sea was rising and the *Steinberg* was beginning to plunge and roll with wind and swell, when the helmsman demanded a course to steer. '**** the course,' screamed Captain Harri, 'run mit der sea, mein klein leiber monkey is feeling seasick.'

Eventually, Haukipŏudas, our port of call, was somewhere out there in the murk, enticing as cold bacon in congealed fat and looking like it. The pilot came aboard sparkling with the zest of an anaemic Count Dracula and declared the first helmsman drunk; he also declared the second, third and fourth helmsmen drunk; he even declared Charlie the Turk, a devout Muslim and dry as the Rub 'al Khali, to be too drunk to steer. Poor old Charlie whose sole ambition in life was to buy a taxi and who was prepared to suffer Hell to fulfil it; all Turks want to buy a taxi, owning a taxi in Turkey puts you in the same bracket as a vice-president of General Motors in the United States.

'Send for the cook,' commanded Captain Harri, 'he's the only one on the ship who can steer, including me.'

92

But the look of me didn't appeal to the pilot and we finally resorted to the 14-year-old deck boy who shivered so much from nerves that the pilot declared him drunkest of the lot. He took the wheel himself.

Nothing much ever happens in Finland but nothing itself is huge excitement in Haukipŏudas. The engineer swore that the whores, if you could find one, paid *you*, just to prove they were still alive.

So the arrival of the *Steinberg* was a sensation. The local newspaper headlined it with the pilot's report that the crew were drunk. 'The only sober one aboard was the monkey,' he claimed. He demanded a total ban on the ship from sailing in Finnish waters and a 20,000 Finnmark fine.

With bubbling Finnish humour the local sub-editors dubbed our little sobersides 'Captain Minnie' and the fuss and attention were too much for her, she disappeared. We questioned all the women loading timber, we offered £20, £30, £40 – make it £50 – instructed the desolated Captain Harri, as a reward for her return. Eventually the 'find Minnie fund' topped 700 Finnmarks, about £200. She was spotted on the roof of the biggest hotel in town.

Wolfgang Bronowski, the first mate, a hard man of the highest order who had once wrestled bears for a living in Bavaria, went to rescue her. He was found sitting in front of the hotel, strumming a guitar and serenading Minnie with the only English song he knew, 'I Only have Eyes for You'. He played the song incessantly on the ship and thought that she would recognise the tune and come leaping to him. But the Finnish police arrived first, arrested him on the suspicion of being drunk in a dry country, slapped him in handcuffs and brought him back to the ship.

'Mein Gott!' bellowed Captain Harri, 'mein ship in chains because of the damned pilot and I am telling them, "Nein, Nein, this is impossible to happen in the Merchant Marine of the Federal German Republic, we haf no drink for the crew, they are good, sober men who go to church." Then my First Mate is arrested as a drunkard in the main square. They are made of ice and fir cones, these dumb Finns, they haf no souls.'

So instalment two of the saga of the hunt for 'Captain

Minnie' was duly reported with a picture of Wolfgang under escort in chains on the front page.

Captain Harri glared at it and split another case of vodka, the better stuff we kept for the ship – not the Hamburg bus fuel – to drink to the subjugation, decline and final demise of all frigid Finns, and may all their digits drop off with frostbite.

It was at this moment that the man arrived alongside with Minnie in the back of his car, and a sorry little macaque she looked, huddled up and shivering. Captain Harri wept copiously as he pressed his nose to the car windows and made clucking noises at her through the glass.

But the man would not take money, we upped the 700 Finnmarks to 1,000, but NO. 'Vodka . . . t'ree bottles', that was all he wanted and nothing else. Alas, we had sold every drop of illicit hooch we'd brought in and we had just polished off the remainder of the legitimate supply we were allowed to keep out of the bonded store.

'Vodka . . . t'ree bottles,' the man repeated, his set chin and fixed stare reflecting a resolution and steadfastness of purpose that the whiff of money would never budge.

Captain Harri paused in deep reflection. 'Vait,' he told the Finn and we trooped back aboard. 'The axe,' he ordered. Three dextrous, mighty swings and the locks on the bonded stores were severed.

Without a smile the Finn took his t'ree bottles. He held each in turn like a priest holds an infant at a christening, regarding it with reverence, before carefully placing it on the car seat. Minnie clung to Captain Harri, her arms twined tightly round his neck.

Dawn crept into our fuddled brains the way cold seeps into a room when the fire has died. The euphoria of the night before lifted like sea mist under a warming sun to reveal the stark reality of the landscape – the customs house on the wharf, the police station along the road, all those pistol-packin' poker-faced Finnish officials each looking as if he had been specially schooled by his personal overlord in the KGB.

Head in hands, Captain Harri gasped: 'Mein Gott, there will be repercussions,' he searched for English words to describe the enormity of it all, 'prodigious repercussions, mein klein leiber monkey,' and he sobbed.

'Mein Gott, my ship in chains, my mate to be tried . . . now the bonded store, and the bonded store is VORST.' His voice rose to a crescendo: 'You vill nefer get out of a Finnish prison alife if they find you haf broken into the bonded store, they couldn't care more if you shot the President'.

He gave a little sob and Wofgang joined him. 'My ship, my two million deutschmark ship, all I've got, all gone for a little monkey.' He picked up Minnie, stroked her head and fed her a grape, 'Mein klein leiber monkey'.

In the Seaman's Mission in town were a few nice old boys who looked as if, in their time, they had seen other parts of the world as if through a glass darkly and would appreciate the *natural* injustice of Captain Harri's situation. It was a simple matter to relieve the bonded store, with its door still swinging loose, of a few more fluid ounces of its precious stock and Gerhard the Beast, the ship's AB, and I went to visit the old Finnish salts.

Of course they appreciated the Captain's position, it was an outrage, he was being victimised because of his deep humanitarian principles. After the fourth bottle they were inflamed at the transparent harassment and injustice to all the gallant crew of the *Steinberg*; Ollie Rollensen, or Ollafsen, or some-sen-or-other had cable cutters in his construction workshop and if another case was left under tarpaulin behind the bollard, they were sure he would be delighted to assist.

'At dusk,' we told Captain Harri, 'we're shoving off.'

'My ship is chained,' he sobbed, 'the chains are locked. . . .'

A truck trundled along the wharf, two mysterious parcels were examined and quickly stowed aboard, the men climbed back and the truck began to reverse. 'I vill murder them,' Gerhard the Beast shrieked, 'I vill tear them apart vis my bare hants, the bastards.' And coming from him that was no idle threat.

Then the truck stopped, two shadow figures slipped under the canvas cover and walked alongside as it began to crawl slowly back. Clink, clunk; twang; clunk, click; zwang . . . the riptide swung out the bows pointing them down river . . . Zerrdung! The final cable taking all the strain flashed through the air and whacked *Steinberg's* stern, and we were in midstream.

'Mein Gott, mein Gott,' said Captain Harri, 'I vill nefer be able to return to Finland.'

'Make up your mind,' said Wolfgang, 'do you want to stay in Finland for ever, or do you want nefer to come back?'

The Minnie saga did not end there, she became the femme fatale again in Hamburg.

If Wolfgang was a hard man, Gerhard the Beast was weathered granite to the mate's sandstone; undoubtedly the strongest man I have ever set eyes on in my career, he made professional circus strong men I have worked with seem like jelly babies.

He wore a badge proclaiming: 'I'm hairy all over'. And he was, thick, black knotted coconut-matting covered him from tip of head to toe – and on his toes. He was the ugliest man in the world, but nobody dared ever tell him so. I have a recurring nightmare of being so drunk one night with Gerhard that I say to him: 'God, you're ugly, you're hideous.' Then I see pieces of my dismembered body floating through the air. . .

His strength was phenomenal. Docking one day in bad weather, the motor-tyre fenders had gone adrift and it looked as if the bow would be badly dented by crashing into the side of the jetty. Gerhard jumped over the side, put his back against the boat, his legs on the staging and he pushed us off. A display like that just causes a ruminative silence while everybody makes a mental note: 'Don't argue with Gerhard, be polite and nice to him at all times'.

In Stralsund, East Germany, Communist guards stopped him and refused to let him ashore unless he cut his hair. 'Nobody goes ashore in East Germany with de-cadent long hair, get it cut,' the Guard Commander declaimed with typical Peoples Socialist Democratic Army arrogance. Eyes flashing, Gerhard responded: 'Nobody tells me when or how to get my hair cut or when I can go ashore'. In the resulting ruckus sub-machine guns were flying through the air with and without bodies attached and, amazingly twenty guards were injured but Gerhard was unscathed.

'You must keep this beast in chains while you are in port,' the local Commandant fumed at Captain Harri.

'We will, my friend, willingly,' replied Captain Harri, 'if you will put him in the chains for us first.'

The Captain doted on Gerhard. 'Worth two donkey engines and cheaper to run.'

Gerhard, like the rest of the crew, was very much taken with Minnie, he loved her as much as Captain Harri did. He took her ashore one night in Hamburg to show her the bright lights. Next morning, when I went to feed her, I found The Beast in a state of great emotional distress; a frightening sight, sobs wracked his great frame, tears streamed through the hairy jungle on his face.

Beauty and 'The Beast'.

97

'I 'ave done a terrible t'ing, I 'ave lost Minnie. I took her to the Reiperbahn and I vent vis a girl, I had no money left to pay this girl, so I left Minnie as a bond, I forget the girl and I forget where she live. Minnie vill hate me, the Captain vill hate me, nobody vill speak to me. . . .'

He locked himself in his cabin shaking his bunk in his remorse. The crew gathered outside in silent wonderment at the spectacle. Gently, I persuaded him to open the door and talk to me. He owed the girl 40 marks, he had met her in the Silver Sack, he gave me 40 marks plus 20 for taxis and I set off in search.

The owner of the Silver Sack was another gigantic German. 'I know the svine,' he said, 'the ape with hair all over him, the one who picks up policemen and bounces them, the one who throws pimps over my bar and breaks the glasses, ja?'

'That is he,' I agreed in my politest manner.

'Nice fellow, good man,' the barman confided, 'with a monkey on his shoulder, lovely little monkey, nice little thing.' He said it with an air of puzzled incredulity suggesting 'what's a nice monkey like that doing in a place like this with a bloke like Gerhard?' He added: 'The girl he went vis will be in shortly, wait for her'.

Clearly a man with all his priorities right, I was happy to wait and drink his beers.

The girl came straight to the point. 'Your friend owes me 40 marks.' She was obviously a better class of whore with a heart, one who was prepared to give credit in a usually strictly hard-cash trade. I concluded that she would have treated Minnie well and looked after her kindly. We did the business, took a taxi and collected Minnie safe and sound and very chatty – probably a little more wordly wise, but a girl has to learn sometime.

Gerhard was ecstatic. 'Tonight we celebrate, we dine in the most expensive restaurant in Hamburg, all of us, everybody. Minnie will have choice of the best.' They have plenty of money, these German seamen, and they don't mind spending it.

He did it again. After a magnificent meal and a Noah's flood of German beer, wine, brandy . . . he went to the lavatory carrying Minnie on his shoulder and got Shanghaied by another whore, leaving us at the table. It took two days to find her that time.

Minnie was ecstatically happy on that ship, she was queen and she seemed to know it. She got on with and trusted every crew member though she reserved her prime attention for Captain Harri, who was clearly her favourite. I had to leave to go home, Minnie stayed, still clinging to Captain Harri.

Chapter 10

The firewater man

The North American Indian is a member of an oppressed race which has been badly done by ever since the white man stole its lands at gunpoint and softened its resistance with firewater.

They are the underdogs of North American society and having always been an underdog myself I am on their side.

Nowadays, almost too late, they have their influential champions, foremost of whom is actor Marlon Brando who has poured most of his huge fortune into their defence.

They have a case before the courts in America which may reap them millions of dollars if they are successful in their claims.

When they win, I hope they will remember me because I did my level best to bring a little joy and happiness into their depressed lives.

But it wasn't as simple as all that . . .

Canada, when I used to go there during my time at sea, was no place for a hot-blooded, lusty young Turk with a hefty thirst. Where we used to dock, in the dreary backwoods, was exactly that – the backwoods, all trees and piety.

It was so dreary that it looked all the same. For years I thought it was Newcastle, Nova Scotia, but since that is not in the atlas, it must have been Newcastle, New Brunswick, which is just across the water from Nova Scotia and even duller.

The dullest time to dock in Newcastle, New Brunswick or Nova Scotia – and I fall asleep trying to check which just at the memory of it since Newcastle is that sort of place – is just before midnight when sleepsville is tucked up in its cots.

But there is usually somewhere to find a drink and a bit of life, so I slunk out of the dock gates and headed for the town centre.

'George,' somebody called my name. I couldn't believe it. There was nobody else about and my name was called again. The voice of the caller seemed to come from a saloon car parked in the High street. I ambled over and there, sitting in the driver's seat, was a bloke I used to know in Notting Hill Gate, London, six years previously. From Notting Hill Gate to New Brunswick is quite a step, a step in the wrong direction and wholly unexpected. Enough, in fact, to make a man temporarily speechless, but the thought crossed my mind, 'He's got a big car, obviously he knows the place, he must know where to get a drink . . . and whatever else follows.'

By the time I had reasoned this and climbed into the car, I had remembered his name. 'Hello, John,' I said, in the tones of Dr. Livingstone, I presume, 'what the hell are you doing in a Godforsaken hole like this?' It was all very original stuff.

'Me? I'm a seaman on the ship that has just docked. Yes, a deckhand', I told him when he asked.

'But I thought your Mum wanted you to be a lawyer, or a doctor, or a top civil servant. I remember she was dead keen about it, university and all that crap.'

So I gave him ears-bashing about preferring to be educated in the University of Life, and so what? And where the hell could we get a drink and chat up some beautiful women in this desperate place?

'No problem about that,' he assured me with a confidence which could not be argued with. 'You'll have to keep your head down a bit. But first of all I've got a bit of business to do, it won't take more than a couple of minutes. In fact, here's my man now. See you in a jiffy,' he added.

With that, he slipped out of the car to talk to a funny, huddled figure by the car boot. A bit of business? In a car, in the main street, such as it was, and at half-past midnight? Ah, well, he seemed to know what he was doing.

He certainly knew the place where there was plenty of

101

booze and some very pretty, dark haired-ladies who were a bundle of fun and remarkable for the amount they could tipple back and the enthusiasm with which they did it.

The ship was in to load newsprint and timber, about all that could ever be loaded out of here. But having met John, it looked as if Newcastle could be a little more interesting than it at first had promised.

If I was a chump, then he had to be a king chump. He told me how he had come to be in New Brunswick. He had left London to come out here on a 'highly-paid selling job' – £400 a week was not uncommon, the recruiting supervisor had told him, and that was when £15 a week was a fortune.

He had been recruited as an encyclopaedia salesman and agreed to come to Nova Scotia and New Brunswick on a 'high pressure sales drive to make a killing'.

In Fredericton, the university town, encyclopaedia salesmen had been thicker on the ground than the snows of winter, and New Brunswick is a cold, cold province. In the backwoods settlements they only read the Bible or had not got past the-cat-sat-on-the-mat stage of reading.

He didn't sell many encyclopaedias and hadn't the fare home.

'But,' he said, drawing deeply on a fat cigar, 'I found a little number, a good little number. And, Georgie boy, you might be able to do me a bit of good. There could be a few pennies in it for you, quite a few pennies.'

Naturally, I said I was interested – because I was interested being in my usual penurious state, about which I make no bones.

'Well,' said John, 'there are lots of Indians around here, Red Indians. And they live on reservations . . . like the one we're on at the moment.'

'Are we?' I was obliged to ask.

'We are, I'm very friendly with the local Red Indians,' said John, 'you see, they have problems, and I help them solve these problems and they are very grateful for the help.'

'What problems have they got?' I questioned.

'Well, the main one is that they're not legally allowed to buy liquor on the reservation, which I think is an in-

102

fringement of their human rights, so I help them,' John explained.

'I tumbled on this when I was flogging the encyclopaedias. I thought at first that they were very interested in encyclopaedias because they were all very interested when I first produced the big, thick demonstration book. But as soon as I opened it they lost interest and vamoosed, it was disheartening.

'So I asked one of the chiefs why they suddenly lost interest like that. He told me that when I first got the book out they thought it was a hollowed out book and I would have a couple of bottles of hooch inside, like the bloke who sold the Bibles had . . . that tipped me the wink.'

He was the local bootlegger and doing a roaring trade – making a fortune.

'What about the law, don't they interfere?' I asked, 'surely it must be a bit risky.'

'The law and I have an understanding – follow me?' he replied adding: 'They like the strong stuff, something with a bite, rough as you like. What have you got on board?'

We were nearly gunnels under with the stuff, it was a marvellous opportunity, in my eyes. I explained that, being a Norwegian ship, we had cases and cases of 100 proof Aquavit. Duty free to us but a very expensive drink in North America. He was delighted.

The Red Indians will do almost anything for a drink, though they are not very good drinkers, they don't hold it well which means that a lot of barmen will not serve them. Also they are barred from a lot of bars because they are second-class citizens in the barman's eyes.

It is curious that they work either at heavy labouring, logging, stevedoring on the docksides or at that incredibly skilled and dangerous job of high-climbing steel erectors, spidermen. The men who walk nonchalantly along thin girders hundreds of feet above the ground building skyscrapers.

They are the finest steel erectors in North America and much in demand, though I have never walked underneath an American skyscraper in construction since I got to know Red Indians. I give it a wide berth and walk on the other side of the street.

They are always drunk. They are pissed out of their

minds up there talking to the birds. A Red Indian will sell you anything to get a drink, the coat off his back, his shirt, his shoes. It really is a tragedy, they have been put down so much that drink is all most of them have left.

It is so bad with them that employers in Canada prefer to pay them on a daily basis so that they will turn up for work the next day, those who are paid weekly go on the town with a pocket full of money and are lost for days. They drink until the money runs out and then spend a couple of days sleeping it off.

But I wasn't to know anything of this when I was in Newcastle at that time.

The following day we slipped three crates of Aquavit ashore without any trouble. It went down well on the reservation, extremely well, the braves loved it and their squaws loved it even more. I became the most popular man aboard, learning of the source of such ample supplies, the Red Indian girls swarmed to the ship, there wasn't a cabin in the crew's quarters without its own little totem pole party going on. Newcastle had taken on a whole new, better aspect and the captain was pleasantly astonished that nobody complained and threatened to walk off when some hitch caused a delay in loading.

'No, love it here, captain, don't mind if we stay a month,' said the jovial crew, instead of bellyaching and complaining and demanding hard-lying money.

One of the money-making functions the reserve Indians undertook was to perform a mock war dance for the benefit of visiting tourists and a payment of fifteen dollars, they were reduced to that. Then they nipped back to the shack for a quick snort of whatever was available.

We had made a delivery of Aquavit at lunchtime and the braves had imbibed a few tots before the first afternoon war dance. They immediately blew the first fifteen dollar reward on more supplies and were beginning to get steamed up.

Come the third and final war dance of the afternoon they were on top form and belligerent with it.

The war dance began to the usual ohs and ahs of the crowd. Then it began to get wilder and the leaps got higher. Soon it turned frenzied and fearful whoops rent the air while tomahawks flashed dangerously near to whiteman and whitewoman scalps. The crowd had fallen strangely quiet. A few drifted away and began to hurry as soon as they were clear of the crush, more followed and began to rush, then the whole lot scarpered as fast as they could for their cars.

The local police chief in attendance, leaning against a tree and drinking coke from a can, waved his arms as the Indians broke into a whooping pursuit of the fleeing crowd and cried: 'Hey, fellas, cool it, cool it. What the suffering saints has gotten into you. C'mon now, fellas, slow it down.'

But the fellas were not in the mood to cool it. They grabbed whatever Aquivit they could from the shack, piled into and on to their jallopies, jumped on horses or just ran whooping and shrieking into the town centre, where, for the rest of the night, they ran amok ignoring the pleas of the police chief through his loud hailer to 'Cool it, fellas, forchris'sake cool it'.

I had collected as many fifteen dollars as I could in the circumstances from the shack and made a discreet withdrawal. But the harassed police, at a complete loss to know what was happening, picked up John to find out.

Terrified by the whoops and shrieks all around and the sight of normally quiet cronies performing rodeo feats in the main street and driving the frightened, law abiding citizens of the town off the streets, John had lost his bottle.

'We know you supply the Indians,' the police told him, 'and we turn a blind eye to that. But, God'nheaven, what have you given them this time? You sure must have given 'em pure firewater, it sure has driven 'em plum crazy.'

John, in his state of shock, blubbered that he had got the hooch from me.

I was pretending to be asleep in my cabin when the police deputation arrived but I saw it was no use pleading innocence because one of the policemen was a man who I had met on my first evening ashore at the party with John.

The air was blue. The Riot Act was read. I got an almighty bollocking. The chief policeman demanded my passport which he said he would keep until he had decided what action to take.

It was useless to protest or argue. There were drunken squaws all over the ship who kept knocking on the cabin door and asking: 'You gott'another little drink, George?'

They left and I sat in deep despondency on my bunk thinking, 'Another nick, how long this time?'

There was a knock on the door, a policeman popped his head round, threw my passport on to the bunk, and said: 'Hi, George, say have you got a crate of that hooch for us at the same price? The boys sure would appreciate it.'

Chapter 11

Aspers, gamblers' gold and simple country folk

I went to Howletts, I left, I came back again . . . drawn like a villain revisiting the scene of his crime. There has to be a lot about John Aspinall and Howletts in this narrative because he has made himself and his zoo-home very important in the animal world and he has become a controversial conservationalist world figure. He has the knack of attracting attention though those who are attracted have the knack of becoming infuriated, exasperated, dismayed or just plain bored by him. He is a rich man with great talents and a big ego. But it isn't as simple as all that . . .

Stringent, egalitarian times have brought one great pleasure, almost taken for granted as a right by younger generations, to the general public which, for centuries, was the preserve of but a few. The great masterpieces of landscaping and gardening in fine country houses are now available for all to enjoy as owners open their gates, at a price, to defray expenses.

It takes a crisp spring day, an early morning in May, an August afternoon heavy with the heat and hum of summer or an autumnal evening when the world is red and aglow in late sunshine to appreciate Howletts at its best; though there is also magic when a marsh fret hangs in wisps low in the trees in a murky November mist. And then you wonder at the amazing foresight of our forebears who planned it all centuries ago with never a hope or thought of seeing the fruits of their labour in their own lifetime, nor even in their children's lifetimes. It would take full four generations before their creation could be seen in the glory of its maturity. They truly planned for posterity and no matter how you view their role in history, it was a selfless act. Taking God's wilderness they worked and transformed it into a garden of pleasure for each and every season and through the centuries it has continued to reproduce its magic throughout the succeeding seasons.

The records say that one of Henry VIII's admirals, Sir Henry Palmer, owned the manor, so the foundations of its beauty must go down to him, certainly some of the trees date back to his time. The present mansion is nearly 200-years-old having been built in 1787 by Sir John Leach for Isaac Baugh, a merchant who had made a vast fortune in the East India trade. It has an unenviable history as a gambler's prize: Sir Thomas Deering, whose claim to fame or notoriety was as a big gambler, bought it. That was after Baugh's death but it didn't stay in the Deering family for long: he lost the whole estate in one evening's gaming at White's Club, in London. At which point a money lender, Abraham Gipps took over and left his heir well placed enough to set up that respectable pillar of the establishment, Martin's Bank, now absorbed into the Big Five clearing banks.

Then, in 1956, another gambler took possession through a big betting win, John Aspinall. He relishes the story of how, after caning the bookmakers for a fortune with a win on a horse called Prelone in the Cesarewitch, at Newmarket, he bought the dilapidated estate and restored it to its former glory. He spent vast sums of money and did the job brilliantly. The park today, our place of work, is a vivid, glowing testimonial to his painstaking work; it goes to prove that all that is needed to put these great estates back in order is unlimited cash.

Howletts smiles on speculators and gamblers: Aspinall discovered two rare maps when he moved in, sold them at auction and recovered the purchase price of the estate. He boldly, proudly asserts that the whole enormous enterprise is financed and built on 'Gamblers' Gold'. Conservative-minded neighbours do not, alas, necessarily smile on gamblers or their gold; some even consider gambling sinful.

Gamblers believe that they, their cronies and their

world is riveting in its fascination and that the world is clamouring to join in. They can never understand that people outside the business may regard them as mindless wastrels, buffoons or even a malevolent, social influence; they cannot comprehend that in the minds of many, gambling carries great social stigma because they regard it as reprehensible and evil. Down in darkest Kent they do, and in the precincts of Canterbury Cathedral too, and the great church at the heart of Christianity in England carries a deal of weight thereabouts. Neither country-minded commoner nor churchman dignitary cared for the way Aspinall made his fortune. Spend what he would, spend as he may to the benefit of local trade they still considered it tainted money. He fumed at local opposition to him and his plans for the zoo. '. . . *village council . . . rural district council and the county authorities combined against me,*' he wrote in petulance about his failed efforts to extend his operation to nearby Chilham Castle. About his success later in gaining planning permission to open a zoo at Port Lymphe, a few miles down the road from Howletts, he said: '*By now the relevant authorities had decided that I was no safari-park entrepreneur or circus impresario.*'

With the gambler's introspection he had misread public opinion at Chilham. He had planned to open a spectacular animal park in the grounds of the castle, owned by his friend, the Viscount Masserene and Ferrard. But, because of his actions, the public suspected that he was a safari-park entrepreneur and circus impresario – and they suspected his allies even more.

The Buck's proven performance in animal keeping and conservation meant that his personal passion for the welfare of the threatened wild could not be doubted. But villagers were not so sure about Lord Masserene's commitment to the cause of nature; they thought that his enthusiasm might be more for the prospect of an injection of the currency of the realm into his coffers. Chilham was not a lavishly run estate, locals knew that funds were needed to shore up his Lordship's crumbling ballroom (badly afflicted with dry rot) and keep the flag flying above the battlements of his Norman keep. They believed that the noble 13th Viscount's ancient line was feeling the pinch and that his appetite had been whetted by the success and new leases of life safari parks had given to such great institutions as Longleat and Woburn Abbey.

Within the zoo we are as introspective and probably as arrogant as the casino crowd at the other end of the life-support line. We have our own personal fascinations and a feeling that the world ought to know, acknowledge and admire what we are trying to do; we can't imagine people not being intrigued by wild animals and not wishing to help to conserve them. We feel this in the same way that airline operators, motor racing enthusiasts, car rally organisers, pop festival promoters and others whose interests impose some degree of nuisance or inconvenience on the otherwise disinterested public protest that they cannot understand public opposition to their plans which will, in their own heartfelt conviction, bring benefit and pleasure to the public at large.

Noise, smells and crowds tend to arouse passionate public reaction from those who have to suffer them.

Inside the perimeter fences, in our own private world, we keep clear of controversy and public antagonism until the crucial moment something goes wrong, like an escape, which is liable to impinge on the public awareness. Then suddenly we become acutely conscious of the problems of – in its true sense – public relations.

The Buck saw public relations in a different light, he understood it as public opinion manipulation and for him it came drastically unstuck over the Chilham Castle adventure. He was going to take over the 300 acre estate of his pal and neighbour, Lord 'Jock' Masserene, which surrounds the beautiful and magnificently sited Chilham Castle, and open a safari park. In spite of Aspinall's protestations about safari-park entrepreneurs, it was difficult to see in his plans how it would have been any different from Longleat, Woburn or even Windsor safari parks except in its rather pretentious designation as a sanctuary or conservation park.

What was meant to be the clincher in the deal turned out to be folly. Aspinall threw a huge party to which all the villagers were invited. It was meant to show off the applicants for planning permission as nice, highly civilised and considerate guys. And, above all, it was meant to impress. It did impress, but in quite the wrong way. A great marquee was hired and erected at Howletts. Fortnum and Masons put on a lavish, exotic spread. The Buck's London cronies turned up and he displayed his extrovert nature at its most outgoing: moules mariniere, lobster thermidor and fillet steak sandwiches by the dozen, strident voices of the Clermont Club set, and champagne. It was the Mayfair set at play with the backwoodsmen watching. Gossip columns reported the flamboyance and expense; councillors, officials, local societies representatives and local residents noted the ostentation and it confirmed their worst fears. The minds of the Man of Mayfair and the Men of Kent were not as one.

Aspinall himself best explains the resentments he unwittingly creates: quotes selected at random from almost any page in the book he wrote about Howletts – and himself – tell a lot about him. He called his book *Best of Friends* and proceeded to make enemies by it. Some passages were, to say the least, provocative:

If I had gone into politics my gift for persuasion, my oratorical powers, my capacity to incite admiration would have found an outlet that could have furnished me with influence and power far greater than the modicum that I now have at my disposal.

Gambler that I have always been, brave man that I am, I tremble with fear before the oncoming storm.

The book is splattered with similar observations and the staff at Howletts who have to suffer reaction to them believe that he doesn't realise the effect they have upon strangers. Like the prospective buyer at the zoo who browsed through the book and commented: 'This guv'nor of yours has got a fantastic tit for himself, you ought to put him in a special cage, he's the most wonderful animal in the zoo.' Having said that, he did not buy.

Still, The Buck knew how to keep animals. Whatever faults he might have shown in the projection of his personality and the presentation of his case, he made up for in imagination and creative ability in housing and understanding them. The cages were beautifully considered, built to use every natural asset of the park: living trees became part of the structures, plantations were unobtrusively fenced in and secured to form compounds, every

111

dell and depression found its place as an animal's home. If you can subscribe to the theory that if it looks right, it usually is right, then Aspinall's planning is a success. And if you can subscribe to Gerald Durrell's theory that to get an animal to breed in captivity it must be happy, then the animals obviously liked it too for they began to breed with great consistency.

Much of the adverse criticism that came Aspinall's way was only partly his fault. He liked to play with his animals particularly his gorillas and tigers and the fact became well known. London gossip columnists who had made an industry out of Aspinall stories and the hijinks at his club, encouraged him to romp and swim with the wild ones, television men joined in and then they all turned round – having got their stories – and virtually said: 'Look at Aspinall showing off again, playing the big-head.' And the accidents at Howletts became front page news whereas at other zoos they would have warranted a couple of paragraphs.

He was, indeed still is, a brave man, he goes fearlessly into the tiger compounds and gorilla cages whenever he can in a way which few of his keepers would ever do. But whereas the keepers live with the animals day by day, he sees them only once a week; on a time basis alone keepers know the animals two-and-a-half times as well as he does, they also feed them and attend to their comfort. The Buck writes and talks about the probability of him being killed by a wild animal, he accepts it: keepers do not like the idea one little bit, our idea is to keep the animals happy and stay alive. The best way to do that is not to put temptation in their way.

Some days live in the memory more than others. The Buck's 'gorilla rambles' and 'tiger rambles' became a feature of his visits. He took the animals for a stroll round the park with them tagging along like pet dogs.

This day it was the turn of the tiger but Aspinall ordered: 'Bring Mr. Thurston along too.' Mr. Thurston was one of the Indian honey badgers and most people could think of more sensible things to do rather than take one of those critters out walkies on his own, let alone with a frisky tiger.

Off we set and the animals seemed to be enjoying the

novelty of it all, keeping themselves to themselves and deeply interested in the new smells under their nostrils. We never knew what upset Mr. Thurston or why he should so suddenly turn on the tiger. A honey badger doesn't need a reason, they are just evil tempered when the mood takes them and aggressive with it, four-legged muggers who would chew up their own grandmothers if they made a snuff out of place. Mr. Thurston flew at the tiger. Now a tiger is a nimble creature with power, agility and speed in those rippling, undulating muscles, but not quick enough for a honey badger, and singularly incapacitated by a badger's method of attack. Mr. Thurston went straight for the tiger's balls, his jaws snapped tight on those dangling testicles and he held on. The shrieks were terrifying and claws like a chainsaw on the loose flailed in every direction. All that could be done was to dodge, duck and pull until we could drag them apart. Mr. Thurston's attack showed the value of surprise: the tiger was shocked and his dignity far too disturbed to launch a counterattack. He needed time to collect himself in the privacy of his quarters, so there was no trouble in getting him back into his cage.

Which raises the point that tigers, no matter what their reputation, are not always the winners. They quite often fall victim to their own quarry in the wild; a slip in concentration during attack and they can be fatally wrong-footed.

The hedonist in Mr. Thurston's nature can be his downfall. He loves to curl into a ball and be rolled along; it is one of his greatest pleasures. He curled into a defensive ball when pulled off the tiger and I rolled him. Once rolled he stays rolled, he cannot resist it and that is how he went back to his compound.

It takes odd people to take a tiger and a honey badger for an afternoon walk together. However, though zoos have some odd people on the staff, many odder people live outside and they are often attracted to visit. Certainly few more eccentric have ever called than the early morning arrival on the doorstep of John Aspinall's mother, Lady Osborne. Lady Osborne had a cottage on the estate and I used to collect a crate of milk from there in the morning. I found the man on the doorstep and asked what he was doing.

'Just resting, mate,' he said, 'just resting.'

Poor old tramp, he looked shattered and at the end of his tether so I said: 'All right, old son,' and went about my business.

Ten minutes later Mrs. Fielder, who did the cleaning, arrived in an agitated state. ' 'ere,' she exclaimed, 'there's a gangster sitting on my doorstep, I don't think that's right, I don't like finding gangsters on my doorstep.'

'That old boy – he's a tramp', I assured her.

'He's a *gangster*,' she insisted indignantly, 'I've seen him on the tele and he's all over the papers. He's that big bank robber, Foxy something.'

The newspapers were full of the daring escape of Foxy Fowler, a notorious gangland figure of the time. His photograph was printed and shown on television and the police issued a stern warning: 'The public are warned do not approach this man, he is dangerous. Contact your local police station if you see him.'

'It's him, it's him,' Mrs. Fielder insisted.

So, nonchalantly, I ambled back to the cottage trying to look as if I was going there anyway in the normal course of duty.

' 'allo, mate, you 'ere again,' he said.

In a chatty mood I smiled and said: 'Who are you? What are you doing round here? We don't get many strangers about at this time.'

'Just passing through,' he replied 'I missed the train, thought I'd wander about the village a bit until the next one comes. It looked so nice here, I thought I'd sit in the sunshine for a few minutes, hope you don't mind, there's nobody about.'

If he was public enemy number one, as the police insisted, he was the most disarming public enemy I had ever met. The newspapers and television had obviously played on Mrs. Fielder's imagination. So I said: 'That's all right, mate, make yourself comfortable, there's a train in an hour'.

I left him to it and wandered back to the mansion. Mrs. Fielder thrust the newspaper under my nose, jabbed the photograph and, getting angry, shouted: 'It's him, have a good look. Anyone could tell it's him.' It certainly looked like him; the resemblance was too marked to ignore. I had scrutinised him while we were talking and now it seemed all too obvious that this was a photograph of the man sunning himself on Lady O's doorstep. The warning under the picture suddenly looked ten times the size it had a few minutes ago: 'This man is dangerous, do not approach him'.

The less you want the facts to be true, the more niggling doubts creep into the mind. Bekesbourne is a small village which makes a difference: in a town foolishness can soon be forgotten, not so in a rural community. If I rang the law and the local police turned out to discover an old tramp, I would never live it down, it would plague my life. If I did nothing Mrs. Fielder would plague my life, I could see the accusing look dawning in her eye: 'A big, strapping lout like you, gorilla keeper, tiger man . . . and you can't sort out a little old gangster on the doorstep.'

Again I wandered to the cottage, with luck he might have moved on, but, just in case he hadn't, I rehearsed what I would say. His legs were sticking out beyond the doorstep into the path, my heart sank. He said: 'You again, they do keep you runnin' about'.

All my rehearsal went for nothing, I tripped over my own tongue and blurted out: 'I accuse you of being Foxy Fowler. . . .' The effect was electrifying: the relaxed old tramp's body was suddenly shot through with power, movement and action while I was still working out what I should have said and why I hadn't. He moved tremendously athletically and I was off balance when he hit me. Instinctively I grabbed and we swayed and rocked about as we wrestled for a while, then suddenly I was on my backside in the pathway and feeling decidedly foolish, trying to work out what was happening, I simply had not believed that public enemy number one could possibly be sitting on our cottage doorstep. It still might not be him, the old tramp might have just been terrified by the accusation. But the speed with which he was now disappearing down the path was a bit quickish for a worn-out old tramp, he took the five barred gate with a vault and was away down the road.

All I could think was the idiot thought: why do things

like this happen when you least expect them, it was too early in the morning to think clearly. So I was on my feet and after him until the thought flashed into my mind, what would I do with him if I caught him? I stopped. By now I was having a full-scale debate with myself – to go, or not to go, to chase or not to chase. Hell, I'll never catch him now, he's got far too big a start, so I turned and lolloped back to the mansion to telephone. My own indecision worried me. I should have done something different, I could have been Super-George and caught him single-handed instead of sitting on my bottom in the drive. The police were on the ball: 'Where? What? Which way? On foot? Stay where you are.' Not a single note of disbelief.

The country is a far more constricting place than the city for a man on the run, because wide open spaces are his prison: he is far too obvious. Bekesbourne Lane takes a long time, walking, to lead nowhere. There are the fields but a lot of people work in them and spot a stranger immediately.

In the country lanes, police cars swarmed. It was a surprise to know that there were so many about which could be called so quickly. Commuters walking to the station were hot and embarrassed by the intense scrutiny of police officers in passing cars. They found him on Bekesbourne station a few minutes before the commuter train arrived. He had realised that he would soon be picked up in the lanes but if he got on the train and headed for town or city he might slip through the net. Foxy gave up quietly.

Newspapers told the story in big, black headlines and classic manhunt phrases; it sounded very different from Mrs. Fielder agitatedly saying: ' 'ere, there's a gangster on my doorstep'.

Another 'hard man' came unstuck at Howletts. Zoos have a habit of cutting people down to size, a sort of natural justice prevails. This man was Mickey B, a real toughie, the most feared man in Kent, club bouncer, regulator, collector and hit man for various gangs in London and Kent. He was the man who did the dirty work and violence for his employers and revelled in it; he was known for such antics as biting off men's ears.

116

Kurt Paulich had been committing outrageous indiscretions again. This time he had formed a warm relationship with the wife of a local godfather, or as he put it: 'I have been knockink auf zis vife of zis gangster, he ees terrible man, she ees nice voman'. Such a situation leads to complications and ugly complications in the form of Mickey B, the godfather's hit man, arrived at the zoo one Sunday afternoon.

Having seen the local godfather, you couldn't blame the woman: Kurt was infinitely better looking and twice as much fun as the boring old, brutish thug she was married to. But having seen Mickey B, you sincerely wished that Kurt hadn't been quite so solicitous of her problems.

Kurt was in the tiger cage cleaning out before Aspinall arrived to do his Sunday stunt of playing with the tigers, and a crowd had assembled waiting for the show. The appalling Mickey said: 'You Kurt? I want a little chat with you, my guv'nor's sent me to teach you a little respect.'

Kurt replied: 'I'm a bit busy at the moment. . . .'

'Not too busy to see me, I wanna whisper in your ear,' said Mickey, clearly enjoying the tension he was creating, 'c'mon you bloody Kraut, you can't dodge out of this one. You and me is gonna 'ave a little chat.'

'O.K.,' said the apparently very subdued Kurt, 'you'd better come in.' He opened the gate and the swaggering and menacing Mickey slipped through; immediately Kurt slammed the door with its self-locking catch, skipped across the cage to the second gate, opened it and let the tigers in.

He turned to the fearsome Mickey and, with his awful, earthy Austrian humour, said: 'I zhink you'd better take your trousers off, because you are going to wetz yourself in a minute . . . the minute I tell zeese friends of mine to jump. Ja?'

Mickey B stood transfixed and riveted against the wire, he couldn't move.

Kurt said: 'My bootlace is undone, tie it up for me . . . and while you're down there, kiss it.' He was wearing Wellies at the time but fearsome Mickey complied. The crowd thought it was part of the act, like they always do when funny things happen in a zoo.

117

Kurt said: 'If I let you out of here, and I haven't decided whether I will let you out, I want you to go back to your boss and tell him that I vill come and visit him viz one of my furry frients, the big one over there, if he causes me any more trouble.'

The tigers prowled, turning in the corners as if on a pivot, and pacing the length of the cage in the determined, impatient manner they have; Mickey B's florid complexion had drained to a waxen pallor, he was utterly immobilised, so still that the tigers probably hadn't noticed him as an interesting object. Kurt prepared to open the gate, but Mickey B didn't notice him, his eyes, with the pupils centred, were fixed only on the tigers. As Kurt eased him towards the gate, he moved like an automaton, stiffly, jerkily, two inches at a time with not the slightest bend in his body. Outside the cage it took several minutes for the terror to thaw out of him, you could see it dripping from him and he looked very ill. The experience left the 'hard man' soft and weak, he left and was never heard of again in our circle.

Chapter 12

What got up Mrs. Mills's nose

Gordon Mills had Tom Jones and Englebert Humperdinck among others in his pop music stable and their combined talents made them all very rich – millions rich. Gordon was a 'good punter' at Aspinall's Clermont Club, in Berkeley Square, London, and as such was feted at Howletts quite frequently. Visiting the zoo, he got the animal craze and decided to set up a zoo for himself. He asked me to go along to organise and run it for him. Apart from being a good punter he was also a lucky one; he could afford to lose a few thousands a night at the tables but as often as not he won. In the firm belief that luck rubs off, I joined him – apart from that again, he was also a very nice person. But it wasn't as simple as that . . .

Let the good times roll. Working for millionaires can be very pleasant. They tend to live in nice houses well-situated in green and pleasant countryside and free from irksome neighbours. They keep their houses well-heated or cooled to suit the seasons; they are often enthusiastic swimmers who keep a heated pool handy. They do not stint on the grub and consider that five or six cars are a minimum requirement for comfort. Good looking women seem to be attracted by millionaires and positively blossom under their patronage, fitting very well into the scenery particularly round the heated pool. People are nice to millionaires and some of that rubs off on members of their entourage. And, taking that latter point into consideration, it is as well to remember Daymon Runyon's – Mr. Guys and Dolls – axiom that, if you stay close enough to money some of it will rub off on you also.

Well, worth a try at least, and better than a squalid flea-pit in Calcutta.

Mr. Gordon Mills was a millionaire who lived in such a style. He was also a nice guy and keen to own a zoo. He is the man who discovered and promoted such household name stars as Tom Jones, Englebert Humperdinck, Gilbert O'Sullivan and Leapy Lee. Two superstars of the calibre and staying power of Tom and Englebert are an asset and a gold mine in any pop stable and they kept getting bigger, and bigger, and bigger . . . so the millions rolled in and kept on rolling in. Money available in such huge quantities changes the actual conception of money for the people who make it, and also changes the way they use it.

Compare Gerald Durrell with Gordon Mills in the question of keeping animals: Gerald Durrell, because of the money his very popular books earned for him, could be considered moderately wealthy, yet the Jersey zoo teetered all the time on the edge of a financial precipice with the threat of a banker's avalanche rolling down the mountain to engulf it. So it had, of necessity, to be run as a penny-pinching operation because available cash had to be spread so thinly that, no matter how much Durrell poured in, it was never quite enough to sustain the place in a condition where the gorillas were kept well fed and happy while at the same time the bank manager was kept smiling.

The animals were always kept well feasted and eventually Durrell formed a Trust which brought a glimmer of a smile to the bank manager's face, as Durrell records in his books.

For Durrell a zoo was an obsession, a career and a dedication; for Mills it was fun, a new interest and he being in the financial super-league could say: 'I want a private zoo with nothing but the best,' and it was there.

In the incredible 'Golden Disc' pop boom of the 1960s, to adapt a famous phrase, never was so much earned for so few from so many – the pop stars could almost have paid for Sir Winston Churchill's war out of their revenues. The Mills's bank account was more liquid than Niagara Falls.

From a bus driver's weekly wage for flogging up and

down dreary, slag-heap scarred Welsh mining valleys to an income which could equal the Gross National Product of a small developing nation is a huge step which Gordon Mills managed to take in his stride. And, unlike a lot of others, so did the members of his stable. They lived high, sometimes wild but they kept their feet on the ground and were still able to mix and communicate with a mud-bespattered knockabout like me who had farmyard grime under his fingernails.

Gordon had bought himself a modest millionaire's 'shack', standing in six acres, in the plush stockbroker belt of countryside around Weybridge, in Surrey. It was an L-shaped, fully-thatched minor mansion with all the trimmings – swimming pool and such like, down to an all-night security patrol with dogs. I had the base of the letter L as my quarters and animal nursery.

They were all neighbours and saw a lot of each other. Tom Jones revelled in his success. He enjoyed every minute of it and every succeeding stage on the upwards ladder. He'd loved moving his family from South Wales to a modern 'Span' estate placed behind a high prefabricated concrete 'privacy wall' in Shepperton – where his wife, Linda, could indulge a private childhood passion for garden ornaments so that Tom would pause at the gate through the wall and laughingly tell his guests: 'Be careful, don't fall over the bloody gnomes, pixies and frogs. We've got more gnomes, pixies, frogs and toadstools in this yard than in a fairy grotto.' Now they all had mansions though they never forgot their roots. Gordon's new estate was called 'Little Rhondda'.

Often we all went down to the pub, the Flint Gate, for a few pints together, except that, more often than not, they were pints of champagne. I liked it because, unlike some other stuff I have mentioned drinking in my time, it didn't actually send you blind. And Englebert would exercise his well known 'little peculiarities' – like a strong reluctance to buy a round and Tom would pin him in a corner, threaten him with a knuckle sandwich and say, politely as possible: 'Look, you tight-fisted bastard, get a bloody round in'.

My introduction to the Flint Gate was revealing in a curious way. The advent of such a novelty as a brand new private zoo in a classy residential district like Weybridge causes local comment and the advent of zoo keepers causes more. It is not a trade the general public often comes across. So when they ask what your job is, it isn't like saying: 'I'm a butcher, baker or sagger maker's bottom knocker,' something they know about, so when you tell them: 'I'm a tiger keeper,' you see them think: 'He's a liar, nut-case, joker or sly bastard – probably all three,' but they still ask questions.

I first called in the pub straight from work one day and the flustered landlord apologetically muttered: 'I'm sorry, you can't come in dressed like that'. I didn't blame him: me in muck-caked wellies and scruffy clothes, smelling like a sewage farm – I had hoped to find a public bar available.

Then a rich Welsh voice hollered: 'It's all right, let him in, he's one of ours'. Since he was the caucus of the pub, everybody smiled and let me through to the bar. Tom said: 'Right, now get the round in'. My heart dropped to my muddy boots: there was a crowd of them drinking stuff I'd only read about in James Bond books. Even in those inexpensive days the round came to £18. My wages were £25 a week. Thank God it happened to be pay day.

It left me short for a week but my 'buying in' round stood me in good stead for the rest of the time I stayed in Weybridge. I liked being asked to buy a drink but I was staggered at the cost. But what I later realised was that Tom's ploy worked: I was immediately included among the accepted pub regulars on equal terms. For the rest of my time there I almost had to fight to buy a round.

The adrenalin was pulsing through their veins at such outrageous success that they lived on a semi-permanent high in the high spots of the world, thriving on the synthetic, electronic excitement they created with their talents. And they played the games the world's high-livers indulge in. Gordon became well known in John Aspinall's Clermont Club, at the time the most exclusive gaming club in the world and a Mecca for high-stakes players; nightingales either sang an octave higher and doubly sweet for Aspinall's clients in Berkeley Square or croaked like corn crakes with sore throats depending on how the cards ran.

Mostly they sang merry tunes for Gordon. He was a lucky gambler and quite skilled at it. But inevitably came the night when the cards ran badly and all his 21s turned up 22s so when settling up time came he was told apologetically: 'We're sorry, but it's £30,000'.

The curious and envious looked on with unconcealed interest, a lot of guests at the Clermont were there as voyeurs whose greatest pleasure came from watching the big-punting aristocrats, city gents, captains of industry, property developers, merchant bankers, film stars and celebrities take an almighty tumble. One of them, determined to rub salt in the wound, said: 'Hell, £30,000, that'll set you back a bit'. Gordon, with quite a few drinks under his belt, smiled, wrote the cheque and replied: 'I couldn't give a monkey's f . . .'. Then the hangers-on went about muttering: 'Bighead, riding for a fall, he'll be back driving buses in a couple of years . . .' and other such backstabbing remarks, like they do.

Although he could treat the loss of such a huge sum in an arrogant, cavalier way, he could also bristle at waste and flashy extravagance – the Welsh upbringing came to the surface and broke through on such occasions, like the time at John Aspinall's mansion, Howletts.

The big punters in the club were often invited to spend a weekend at Howletts where Aspinall full-bloodedly lived the life of a Regency buck – he preened himself when newspapers called him 'The Buck'. The keynote for guests was lavish entertainment, abundance of booze and food, games with the zoo animals. Sunday lunch meant a table groaning under the weight of a traditional Sunday lunch complete with baron of beef. After lunch, one weekend, when the butler was clearing away the substantial remains on the beef trolley, Aspinall, always the great extrovert, thundered: 'Chuck it in the pig bin . . .'

With shock and horror Gordon interrupted: 'Don't do that! It's sinful, don't waste good food like that, man, it's a crime.' Then noticing the amused silence that had fallen round the table where most of the occupants had never seen the inside of a butcher's shop, a kitchen oven or a bus driver's wife's weekend shopping basket, he added: 'Even I couldn't afford to do that'.

Aspinall's animals fascinated Gordon. It was a whole

123

new world to him and a whole new experience. It happens to a number of people when they come into close contact with wild animals and feel the stirring interest in the hidden half of the world. Suddenly the interest becomes a compulsion, you feel that you must get to know about these creatures.

Aspinall sold two tiger cubs and sent me to Gordon. So I began an idyllic period living in the short side of the L in the L-shaped house, with the sole duties of playing with two kittenish tiger cubs all day and drinking beer or champagne in the pub at night. All baby creatures are fun but tiger cubs are terrific fun – amusing, intelligent and absorbing; part of the interest is that you know that at some stage they are going to outgrow you and assert themselves, so you watch them grow with respect. Even so, when you raise them by hand, feed them from a baby's bottle, clean them, comb them, wipe them, put them to bed and generally run their infant lives so that they come to look on you as a substitute mum, you feel, for a time, that basically they are just like kittens or puppies which will develop into the faithful old hound sleeping by your feet in front of the fire or the old cat purring on your knee. But it isn't so, we all think we know the difference between wild and tame, or more so, between wild and domesticated, but nobody really knows just where the dividing line comes in an animal's make-up.

Old timer big-cat keepers tell you that at best it is an uneasy relationship between cat and man and one which can never be taken for granted, no matter how long it has been established and working successfully. Big cats, though you might think you know their every whisker and nuance, are unpredictable – as we were to find out in a hideously frightening way. But meanwhile they were in the flat. The flat that was to house gorillas, orang-utans, leopards and – most unforgettably – a pair of the world's biggest birds of prey.

That story began the day when Gordon was offered a pair of Andean condors, something which couldn't be turned down, but there was no accommodation for them.

The grandeur of a condor is unmatched in the bird world: the South American vulture (*Vultur Gryphus*) is the largest existing bird of flight. It has a body length of four feet and a wing spread nine or ten feet from wingtip to wingtip. They flap their wings to take off but thereafter they sail in the air, and Charles Darwin, that most acute of observers, during his expedition to the High Andes from *H.M.S. Beagle*, watched one for half-an-hour without detecting a single motion of its wings. The explorer Humboldt observed one over Chimborazo at a height of 23,000 feet. They nest in the Andes, 10,000 to 16,000 feet high, on inaccessible ledges and I can add my personal observations of the species which will not be found in any textbook: they choose such places of spartan solitude not because of their naturally shy and retiring natures but because they have such disgusting habits that no self-respecting gaucho, iguana or mountain llama would have them within 100 miles as neighbours.

Condors feed mostly on carrion but frequently carry away a goat, sheep or deer; ornithologists describe them as voracious feeders which is an understatement because they are insatiable gluttons who literally will gorge themselves until they collapse in an overfed stupor to sleep it off. And they are the heaviest sleepers known in the wildlife world, nothing will waken them until they have slept off their gross overindulgence. Which is how they come to be captured: the native hunter waits until they have finished another Lucullan orgy and fallen asleep, then he climbs up to their roost, slips a noose round their necks and pops them in the bag – easy.

The actual capture, that is, is too easy, but traversing several hundred miles of jungle and climbing 16,000 feet up the snowy Andes is a little more difficult and time consuming.

A condor's head and neck has no feathers. The male is crowned with a comb or caruncle and his neck is wattled. In both sexes the feathers start with a white frill round the base of the neck surmounting the rest of their jet-black, shining plumage, though there are white splotched feathers under the wings.

The second Jacobs observation on condors is that they are baldies because of their revolting eating habits: nature has protected them against their own obnoxious follies. To eat, they rip open their prey and plunge their heads into the carcass tearing, ripping, shaking and gulping down without ever removing their heads until it is completely devoured. They eat from the inside outwards. Blood, guts, entrails, bile and fur fly like spray from an Atlantic roller hitting rocks; then they withdraw to sit with the mess of blood, guts and entrails dripping from their bald heads on to their plumage and running in rivulets through their feathers. Whereupon they fall asleep and let it all ferment. If they had feathered heads they would be so caked in dried animals' insides that they would be top-heavy and unable to see.

A newly decorated flat in the lowlands of Surrey, England, painted in white emulsion and brilliant white gloss is not a suitable replacement for the high, wide open spaces of the Andes and problems soon arose.

We fed them with hares, rabbits, squirrels – anything we could lay our hands on. Soon there was not a spot of white visible in the room: walls, ceiling, doors and windows ran red, brown and green with splattered blood and entrails and you slipped in the gory slime on the floor. Then came the smell: stultifying, mind-blowing, a sensory nuclear bomb of a stink. The sort of smell that follows and haunts you and when it catches up with you, knocks you down. Sleeping next door to it became difficult to impossible. I tried gauze face-masks and went to bed looking like Dr. Kildare – useless; cotton wool soaked in eau de cologne was not much better; the only answer was a midnight-early morning jog round the estate to breath in some untainted air and hope it would last for a couple of hours back in the stink chamber.

The hose couldn't be used to sluice down the room: there was nowhere for the water to run away and there was the risk that the fabric of the flat would be completely destroyed. And slowly the smell spread like a menacing, deadly fungus in a sci-fi film embracing everything in the immediate area. Domestic staff from the house were to be seen lifting manhole covers and prodding down drains but within days the source of contamination was too powerful *outside* to be disguised.

Jo Mills, the patient, uncomplaining mistress of the house, commanded: 'Those bloody condors go, immediately, or I do'. Never was a bird-house finished more quickly, down wind from the house, with walls and surfaces that could be power-hosed clean. De-contamination squads moved into the flat. We all began to breath again without wincing.

Condors in captivity worry me. Most creatures acclimatise to the restrictions of captivity but the sheer scale of a condor's natural freedom is incompatible with being caged. A bird which in its element soars to heights of 23,000 feet with a thousand square miles of hunting territory beneath its wings seems wrong in confinement.

Gordon Mills had a remarkable aptitude for picking embarrassing animals for his zoo, not deliberately – but that's the way the cattle-cake crumbles. Monsieur Louis was a case in point. There was always something odd about M. Louis, even in the way he was collected from his previous owners at dead of night. He was a very good looking orang-utan, a species which were, even then, becoming scarce on the market and were protected by export restrictions imposed by the government of Borneo.

'Take the truck and pick up an orang-utan,' I was told, 'get there about midnight and it will be ready.' It sounded a bit 'iffy' but in the animal game you do not ask questions – and when you are personally involved in pulling a stroke, you don't answer them either; ignorance solves all.

So the furtive deal was done at dead of night in the grounds of some obscure safari park and I returned home with a box full of monkey tricks . . . the strangest tricks I have ever come across in any primate I have looked after.

I opened the crate and M. Louis hopped out not at all suspicious of his new surroundings, not at all nervous, in fact, friendly. So friendly that in minutes he was climbing all over me and I thought to myself what an affectionate chappie he was and shook him off. Then he became over-affectionate and wouldn't stop molesting me. If it had been a woman doing what he did, I might have had her charged with indecent assault. Eventually I got him bedded down and comfortable for the night and went to bed. Come morning, affectionate approaches began again with renewed intensity. I had to fight him off. I locked him in the flat when I went to work and I told Gordon:

'We'd better get a mate for M. Louis a bit quickish, he's a randy little devil'.

For the next few days his erotic advances continued unabated and I put it down to the shock of being moved and all the new people around him. But you could not let him near a woman. He had to be kept on a tight chain, otherwise it would have been instant molestation on the spot: he lifted ladies' skirts, or if they were wearing jeans, his active little pink paws flew immediately to sensitive and embarrassing areas while all the time he chattered excitedly to himself. Men were not much safer and a number of them were forced to retreat with that curious semi-crouched stance of a shy man caught coming naked out of the shower and covering himself fig leaf style. He would be all right once he's settled in, we wisely confided to each other.

On my day off, Gordon took him for his afternoon walk. I did not arrive home until midnight to find a collapsed and exhausted Gordon in his sitting room bravely trying with the aid of drapes and cushions to ward off the affectionate advances of a delirious M. Louis. 'It is impossible to stop him,' Gordon gasped, 'he's a sex-maniac monkey, you can't hold him off.'

A sexually depraved anthropoid, particularly one which seems to take a shine to both sexes of the human race, is a rarity and I began to suspect that this might be the reason why we had got him, if not cheap, inexpensively. So in the morning I telephoned the safari park and spoke to a pal of mine on the staff. There was an ominous silence at the other end of the phone.

'Come on, what is it with him,' I demanded to know.

'He's had a funny old life,' my pal told me, 'we got him from France, we picked him up cheap. We had to get him out of the country a bit sharpish and a bit quickish otherwise he would have been destroyed.'

'Yes, all very touching, but what's his problem?' I pressed.

'Well, he was in a blue-movie studio which was busted by the gendarmerie. He'd starred in nearly 90 films . . . believe me, he's done *everything* – and I mean *the lot*, AC, DC, it makes no difference to him. Though fellatio is a bit of a speciality with him. He just needs breaking of the habit.'

We got M. Louis into a cage very quickly after hearing that and left him to live with his memories for a few weeks before letting him out into polite society again.

The zoo came on fast with great care lavished on design and detail. There was the advantage that Aspinall's designs for cages were available and any snags he had discovered could be ironed out. Aspinall's designs were good both from the point of view of the animals and keepers and also spectacularly pleasing in aspect so that *The Observer*, not a newspaper given to pointless flattery, could write: 'Howletts is to other zoos what the Dorchester is to a doss house'. And the engineering company that built them, South Coast Welding, were called in to do the construction job for Gordon. All the buildings were made just that little bit bigger, just a fraction roomier, tiling and finishing was stepped up a couple of qualities based on what Aspinall had discovered from hard experience.

Experience is a funny old thing, you never now how you acquire it. For instance, one story has stuck in my mind: at Chicago Zoo a gorilla kept breaking the bars of his cage. The corner posts were bolted on the inside of the cage with nuts tightened on to one-inch diameter bolts which the gorilla kept shaking loose. An engineer was called to tighten them with a torque wrench to 27lbs-a-square-inch, three nuts per bolt, spring washers as well. Full of curiosity, the ape watched from his night quarters while the man worked. 'Right,' said the engineer as he left the cage, 'that'll put a stop to his little tricks.' Out bounded the gorilla thinking it all a marvellous joke. He squatted in the corner, put out a tentative hand to the fixture and with his fingers unscrewed the lot one by one flinging them at the observers. Experience now says: nuts, bolts – no good for gorillas.

A few months saw gorilla, tiger and jaguar houses at Weybridge completed though we still worried about the condors. 'We'll never possibly build anything nearly big enough for them,' Gordon fretted. So it was decided to sell them. It took weeks of clinical examination of the world's zoos' and aviaries' statistics to find a place which could house them. Gordon said: 'The sky isn't really big enough for birds like that'.

You obtain animal stock in a variety of different and curious ways. How we got the gibbon was as odd as any. Down the road from Little Rhondda was a pub called Thatchers run by Dave and June Robinson. As an attraction they had a little animal garden in the back garden, tiny but with some rather nice stuff in it, particularly the gibbon which Gordon wanted to buy and Dave couldn't be persuaded to sell. Dave was a drinking mate of mine but no matter how hard I tried, he would not sell.

June, his wife, was Tom Jones's number one fan. She had all his records and never missed a television appearance. 'You get me a personal introduction to Tom and I'll give you the gibbon,' she offered one evening. I nipped round to see Tom and asked: 'As a favour to Gordon let me introduce this lady to you when you're next in the pub'. The unspoken rule in the Flint Gate was that he was never pestered. Nobody had arranged or asked for it to be so, it had just happened. Good neighbours realised the pressure that is often applied to superstars and allowed him privacy and neighbourliness.

We arranged to meet at Sunday lunchtime and I took June along though she protested all the way: 'He'll never be there'. He was and she became hysterical. 'Don't give her a vodka, give her a Valium,' said a friend laughing at her state of nerves. It took the first half of the Sunday lunchtime session for her to pluck up courage to come over and be introduced and the rest for her to simmer down.

Put that down as another zoological first in the Jacobs record: the first time a gibbon was swapped for Tom Jones.

Being rich is fun, being around the very rich is also fun, but it can be harrowing and when you share the good times, you also suffer the anguish with the people who have become your friends as well as employers. The Mills are family people. In my time with them they had four daughters, now I think, they have six so they have always lived in a home, never just a house.

It was alarming to find Jo Mills in tears in the kitchen one morning with Gordon pacing the floor in great agitation; first thoughts must be that there has been a domestic tiff and the best thing to do is to beat an embarrassed retreat. But Gordon snapped: 'No, come in, George, sit down'.

They were silent for a time and I was confused until Gordon said: 'We have just received a kidnap threat about one of the kids. We don't know which one but the police say that we have got to take it seriously, bloody seriously. Jo is dreading letting them out of her sight. 'The demand is that we leave £25,000 in the postbox outside the gate, don't tell the police, don't set any traps . . . the usual stuff. But we've told the police and it's up to them now. There will be a lot of them about today, very quietly, inconspicuously, but around.'

And he added: 'George, I'd be grateful if you didn't go out tonight, would that be all right by you?'

Perhaps that will tell you why I so liked the Mills family.

The police advised putting the money as instructed, real money, not a fake package in case something should go wrong and the intending kidnapper slipped the net to discover he'd been hoaxed which might inflame him to some more disastrous action against the children.

I made my evening rounds to make sure that everything was secure. Knowing every tree and bush in the place it wasn't too difficult for me to make out shadowy figures here and there. There seemed to be dozens of them but they were deathly, unnervingly quiet, today's policemen are not all flatfoots by any means. I went back to my flat to wait and listen. In situations like that you listen so intently that your eardrums begin to sing.

I remembered that I should have been having a pint with my best mate Telfer Thomas, another lunatic friend of mine – I attract them. Telfer drove a taxi for a living and had some mad habits: such as he would call to see me on Sunday morning and say: 'I fancy a pint in the West Country today, boyyo'. And we would drive to Devon for a Sunday drink, sleep off the effects during the afternoon and drive back in time for one in the Flint Gate before closing time. Mad.

A car drove up and there was a knock on my front door, I opened up to find Telfer standing there. 'Sorry I couldn't make it, Telfer,' I said, 'there's a hassle on to-night, I can't really tell you about it'.

'Don't worry, I thought you might be having some animal troubles, so I brought a couple of bottles up with me,' he said, slumping on the settee, 'oh, by the way, I found this in the post box . . .' He tossed the envelope with the £25,000 in it on to the table.

I had forgotten; considerate Telfer always brought the mail up if there was any in the postbox to save me the walk to the gate. He sat goggle-eyed and amazed when I grabbed the envelope, shot through the door like a bear with a bee up its bottom and across the yard to the office where I knew the police chief and Gordon were waiting in darkness so as not to alert the unwanted, expected caller.

Back in the flat Telfer protested: 'Half the bloody Surrey constabulary suddenly burst in through the door, what the Hell goes on?'

Nothing, happily, happened over the kidnap threat; maybe the threatener kidnapper was scared off; if it was a hoax, it was the product of a warped, putrid mind. I would prefer living with a nest of king cobras than with somebody like that.

Men are usually kind to animals or, at least, most of them try to be. Animals, on the other hand, can be piti-lessly cruel to each other for no apparent reason, and they can suffer cruelty inflicted upon them also for no apparent reason. We inherited a leopard which led to two of the most bizarre incidents I have witnessed in the animal world.

He had lived on a houseboat at Walton-on-Thames with a man called Tony Travers who kept him as a pet and took him shopping and down the pub for a drink, thus putting the fear of God into a fair proportion of the genteel citizenry of mellow Walton who are more given to keeping King Charles spaniels and golden labradors as household pets.

A local publican friend confided in me that the time Tony and his leopard were most welcome was at five minutes to closing time because their presence appreciably shortened the period of drinking-up time after last orders. This enabled him, in the afternoon, to get round to the

132

bookies in time to listen to the finish of the three o'clock at Sandown, or wherever, and actually hear his money going down the drain, and in the evening to catch the beginning of the late night movie on TV. Another profound social observation he made was that customers who made a fuss of the leopard and thus displayed their valour and unique personalities were not noticeably good beer drinkers and decidedly poor spirits tipplers who liked to draw attention to themselves in the hope of picking up a free noggin. He would, he explained with admirable clarity and brevity, prefer their space to their company and they were welcome to play with the leopard in the coffee bar down the street. In support of his views his spouse added that she would rather wear it than walk it about.

Wisely, Tony decided that his feline friend was becoming possibly a little too assertive and would be happier and safer behind adequate bars in a proper place, so we took him on. At the appropriate time we housed him in a spacious cage in the new jaguar house. Such a beautiful structure, the jaguar house, built in the middle of a wood, incorporating the trees into the design and completely natural in feel.

Before he was placed in the new cage, one small incident underlined Tony's wisdom in seeking a new home for him. Some of the security guards employed at enormous cost, did not play exactly fair with Mr. Mills. They would make a great show of going about their security duties while the family was up and about until the lights in the main house went out when they would scuttle away to their own little shake-downs for the rest of the night. One or two of them had the cheek to ask me: 'Give us a shake in the morning, George, I've got an early start'. They were working nine to five for one boss and 10 p.m. until 6 a.m. for the security company – at Gordon's expense. Until the cages were ready, the leopard was kept in my flat. One morning, purely by chance, I walked into the back room where he slept and found him crouched on the window sill by the open window in the pounce position, trembling with excitement and pulsating with anticipation, his front paws being extended, lifted and curled in the slowest of slow motion preparatory to leaping. He always wore his collar and chain, I caught the chain just as he moved. Below in the yard was one of our tired security patrollers stretching, yawning and blinking the sleep from his eyes while his equally tired alsatian stretched and gulped down the fresh morning air: totally unaware of what had been going on the guard was shaking out his sleeping bag to stow in his car boot. If the leopard had moved it would have wakened them quicker than a cold shower – or put them to sleep permanently.

The leopard's cage in the jaguar house had a sleeping bench bolted half way up the bars dividing it from a jaguar cage. The first morning after we had installed him we found him lying unconcernedly on the bench in a pool of blood; his tail had dangled through the bars into the cage next door and the jaguar had bitten it off near the root. The vet was called to perform an emergency operation. The leopard soon healed and seemed quite happy to be rudderless, which is strange because a leopard's tail is not only his glory but seems so essential a part of him.

After convalescence during which we moved the bench and lined the dividing bars with close mesh weldmesh we put him back in. We found him lying on the floor by the dividing bars; there was a two inch gap between bars and floor to allow water to run away, he'd pushed his leg through that tiny gap during the night and the jaguar had bitten it off well above the knee, he was squatting on his haunches when I first saw him and it wasn't until he stood that I realised what had happened. There is no explanation for such behaviour, we were baffled. We returned him to his original owner and years later he was still hopping merrily around tailless and three-legged. We were still baffled.

The place was expanding so rapidly that extra staff was needed and one of Jimmy Le Blonde's men was recruited. Le Blonde is a famous animal dealer with a reputation for being larger than life, so was his bloke. It would have been safer to lock him up at night and leave the tigers and gorillas roaming free. He couldn't possibly last long in respectable, high-class Weybridge – and he didn't. A simple error of judgment was his undoing during one of Gordon's lavish poolside parties where there was enough booze to fill the swimming pool and enough grub to eat to sink you like a stone if you fell in. All the knobs of the county were there having a whale of a time and our wild-man pal, in a mood of boisterous playfulness picked up a geyser and threw him into the pool. Unfortunately it was the Chief Constable of Surrey in his dress uniform.

It couldn't last for ever, though I wish it had. An unexpected turn of events brought it all to an end. John Aspinall had bought some African elephants and there was nobody at Howletts with experience of elephants, so Aspinall asked Gordon Mills if he could have me back. Much as you like what you are doing, something different is a challenge and stimulating. The idea of elephants thrilled me. I had come to realise that, of all creatures, these were *my* animals, without doubt my favourite beasts. I love elephants. I had always delighted in working with them, so the temptation was too great and I agreed to go.

My replacement was to be Nick Marx, also from Howletts. I had first met Nick working on a building site and desperate to find a job in a zoo. He had the usual history, a fascination with animals since his childhood and a determination to work closely with them. But there the usual history ended: Nick was the son of a fabulously wealthy family. His father was a well-known merchant banker and they had a mansion almost next door to Gordon Mills, in St. George's Hill, Weybridge. He had been sent to the right schools, given all the opportunities, had every door in the City open to him . . . and he walked out on it all to go labouring until he could find a job shovelling shit in a zoo. And zoo men regarded him with astonishment. He was a good worker who really got stuck in and never shirked. He arrived to spend a week with me to get the run of the place. Being old mates we thought that was long enough to sort it out.

One day Nick and I walked into the tiger compound so that he could be properly introduced since they were to be his responsibility. They were quietly padding round, unconcerned and docile. I was chatting to them, and Nick was smiling delightedly. The tigers were as good as gold, absolute little darlings. They were healthy, fit and happy in their splendid new quarters with lots of space, things to climb on, a deep pond because they like water, and

135

warm and comfortable night quarters. It had been a great thrill to me to watch them grow and settle in so well.

Now we had three, Ugli (pronounced Ooogli), Benji, quite a lad, and Shere Khan; you could stand with them and really feel that you were living Kipling's *Jungle Book*. Most of the literature I had read about tigers came into my head as I watched them; to see, day after day, their power and intrinsic nobility made you realise why Blake's overworked and hackneyed, 'What immortal hand or eye could frame thy fearful symmetry?' had become overworked and hackneyed: it summed up the tiger and it was true.

If there is any romance in zoo keeping then, I supposed, this was it: three fantastic creatures, beautifully housed, living naturally, contentedly and well, and looking superb. In a way it was the end product, the result zoo keepers dream of. There is a lot of muck, sweat, grinding, milling, carborundum stone and broken finger nails put into a Rolls Royce before it appears gleaming in perfection in the showroom, so it was with our tigers. These were my babies and my confidence had risen to unprecedented heights because of them. They were a justification of my way of life which seemed to prove that you can establish a working relationship with another species.

Suddenly, in a micro-second, the air was full of venom, hate, fury and thundering, flashing, snarling anger; the burning brightness of eyes bellows-blown to an intensity of resentment, the latent, pent-up power of high-tensile muscles and sinews unleashed in a paroxysm of rage. The day disappeared, no daylight, no sunshine, just a black tunnel of fear and incomprehension: these were my tigers but each one had donned a hangman's black mask of anonymity and the tunnel reverberated with terrifying roars and snarls. Claws like cavalrymen's sabres slashed the air, mouths curled back revealing formidable canine teeth and the air was rank with the acrid reek of feline outrage.

My ears felt deaf with the pounding of blood in them and every hair on my body tingled with dread. My brain was unhinged and spinning like a crazy roulette wheel which I couldn't stop, the ball would not drop into one slot and let me decide what to do. Then, over the din of action and blood in my ears, I heard the only truly spine-chilling sound I have ever experienced: the sound of Nick's bones crunching. Shere Khan had got him. She had dragged him into the pond and she was tearing at his arm with those great incisors crushing his bones as if they were pretzels. His blood spurted in fountains and the pond, lashed to a foam, was staining red. I glimpsed his arm now opened up like an anatomist's specimen on a dissecting table.

I had a pitchfork, I had a pitchfork in my hand, the pitchfork was still in my hand. When the realisation came I do not know, I cannot tell you, but the pitchfork was there. I had taken it with me because I was going to change the bedding – and it was still there, in my hand. It felt as if God had given me my own personal thunderbolt to protect me from all evil. I was not totally defenceless. It might have been only a penny in a beggar's hat but to me it seemed salvation. It stopped the roulette wheel in my head and I can remember the thoughts which came to me as if the secret of life had been revealed: get the other two into their den then attend to Nick and Shere Khan. The nature of the game had changed: I was thinking and I was armed. Hindsight may say that tigers are not multiple killers, few big cats are. Lions will take out one victim from a herd of antelope and the rest of the herd will continue grazing knowing that, for the time being, they are safe. Tigers think, they recognise danger, they know when *they* are being hunted. I prodded the wonderful pitchfork with frantic intensity, by reflex – it must have been a reflex action – and Ugli shot into the night quarters. I prodded and swung the pitchfork again and so-and-so shot in after him. They spun round ready to relaunch their attack but the grid clattered down over the opening with a shattering crash.

Now Nick. Nobody in such a situation can ever tell exactly what happened or how it was done because you truly do not know. The mind reconstructs the events. You sit outside yourself watching from a distance; you think you might already be dead and watching it all from a distance. You think it can't be *me* doing this. You cannot differentiate between thought and terror; the mind puts up an automatic mental blackout otherwise the probability

137

is that you would die in you tracks of sheer fright. I seem to remember prodding those vicious prongs at Shere Khan; I think I remember her snarls, her crouching, the tensing of her muscles ready for attack.

But meanwhile she had Nick in the pond with her teeth sunk deep into his arm. His bones were cracking and his flesh being ripped from his arm. I knew I was watching death within touching distance, within possible seconds, with life receding like a digital read-out on a television screen during an Olympic slalom ski event. It had to be stopped, but I couldn't think except in shop-talk. I've talked of shop-talk, that idiot indulgence of this and all trades, before. It flashed answers into my stunned senses: the tongue, grab the tongue and it forces them to let their prey drop, that's what they always told you and you sniffed and made no comment. It is quite a different matter to get at a tiger's tongue when she's thrashing and raging about in four foot of water.

Inexplicably the mind clears. You don't think. You don't reason but the truth flashes into your brain. 'She can't get me while she's got him, she won't let him drop now she's got a grip.' I plunged into the pond and my Chelsea boots filled with water so that they dragged like divers' weights. I could see red stains on my clothes but I couldn't clearly see her mouth through the foaming spume being lashed up. Now I was pressing between them and sheer physical effort surmounted all other reactions. My hand lunged down into the water and I felt the abrasive rasp of her tongue against it and grabbed. A tongue isn't slippery even when wet; I got a firm grip and tugged sideways and backwards. She choked, sucked in water, and her grip on Nick loosened. She struggled backwards slipping and floundering. My grip broke, and she shot to a corner of the cage to get her breath. I staggered out of the pond dragging Nick and seized the fork. Don't ask how, I cannot tell you.

In my subconscious is a mental picture of thrusting at her just at the instant she was at her point of balance and poised to spring so that she momentarily recoiled and had to regroup herself for another leap. If she had managed to launch herself, that would have been the end, curtains for both of us. I seem to recall dragging Nick by his uninjured arm and pushing him along with my boot, but it is all dreamlike. What I actually remember and what I reconstructed later there is no way of telling. But what is indelibly ingrained in my memory is the distance to that gate: it measured not in yards but in eternities until we were through it and I slammed fast the bolts. The mechanics of holding Nick in one hand, the pitchfork in the other hand, slipping the bolts, lifting the catch, swinging open the gate and dragging Nick through, I have never worked out. It is not until you arrive at an obstacle like a gate, even with an arm full of shopping, that you realise what a complex operation a simple task like that can be even without a frenzied tiger on the wrong side of it.

Another non-memory is awakening in a hazy dream, apparently in a familiar house with distraught and anxious people crowding round and asking: 'Are you all right, George? You've been out stone cold.' I do not remember passing out or even feeling like passing out: if you are ever caught in a similar situation take courage from the

Big birds with bad habits.

139

fact that you don't need courage, you just go NUMB, the automaton within you takes control and only lets you back into your own body when it is all over.

Nick was a horrific mess, a tangled hunk of humanity with an arm like offal hanging on a butcher's hook. In truth, only two things saved him: he was employed by one millionaire and the son of another. The finest surgeons in all necessary branches of medicine were rushed to attend to him. The most consummate skills available put him together again and tended him with dedication and loving care: in all probability they would not have been obtainable in such haste for an average man-in-the-street.

No, there is no proven explanation of why it happened. There is no obvious reason why a normal, calm, happy day should turn into a nightmare of ferocity. We have a theory and it seems to be the most likely reason for the attack: Nick had been working with the tigers at Howletts and he had been wearing the same overalls there, so the scent of Aspinall's cats may have clung to them and ours may have picked it up. But even so, why such a spontaneous murderous assault? Tiger does not necessarily immediately attack strange tiger. There is usually a 'sussing out' period which gives sufficient time for warning to be taken.

A gnarled old tiger man, with forty or more years' experience of big cats in circus ring and zoo, who disapproved of John Aspinall romping and fooling with his tigers, used to mutter: 'One day they'll have him, it may be tomorrow, it may be in ten years, but one day they'll have him. Cats are predictable for ten years and unpredictable for ten seconds and that's all it need take.'

And we used to tell him: 'Oh, shut up, you daft old sod, you're telling old wives' tales again'.

Nick came back to his job of looking after wild animals – gorillas, bears, elephants . . . tigers, anything. We became great mates and stayed that way, until he proved that he definitely was a lunatic.

He watched that television programme *The Good Life*, caught the self-sufficiency, simple-living bug from it, shot off to the West Country to buy a two-acre plot and a pig and cut himself adrift from the civilised world. Which

140

proves that a television set in your sitting room is a greater danger than a compound full of tigers.

Nick's father died and left a fortune of millions, making Nick himself a rich man but he still carried on the simple life. To add a few bobs to the self-sufficiency budget he put an advert in the local papers saying that if anybody wanted any heavy digging done, Nick was the man for the job. So if anybody near Liskeard, in Cornwall, would like the status symbol and one-upmanship of having a millionaire dig his garden or do his labouring, Nick's the boy. And if anybody thinks it is all a big act he is putting on, take it from me, I know it isn't.

Chapter 13

Fickle cows and a load of bull

Jumbo was the name of a huge elephant and passed into the language as the identification of the whole species: Disney slandered the breed by adapting it to Dumbo. There is nothing dumb about elephants except their keepers. Elephants have an attraction for human beings even greater than horses. You question that? Put a horse and an elephant together and see which pulls the greater crowd. We like them because they are fickle and temperamental as a woman and just as mysterious; you never quite know how their minds work. Only a dumb elephantophile would quit the pleasures of Gordon Mills's establishment to live in a caravan and look after elephants. Howletts was acquiring a new herd; I went to look after them. But it wasn't as simple as all that . . .

The poet whose habit was to turn out masterpieces wrote:

> Nature's great masterpiece, an Elephant,
> The only harmless great thing. . .
> Still sleeping stood; vexed not his fantasy
> Black dreams; like an unbent bow, carelessly,
> His sinewy proboscis did remissly lie.

But John Donne got it wrong: we have learned something since 1600 or thereabouts, not a great deal, but something about elephants and their habits.

Elephants kill more of their handlers than the rest of captive animals put together; in its natural habitat as a working beast in Asia a good Indian bull elephant will go through three or maybe four mahouts in his lifetime. Bulls

142

as working animals or in captivity are a rarity, but they are kept for specific tasks in Asiatic forests. The mahouts who handle them are on top money which includes danger money because nobody can ever tell what will happen from day to day, though it could easily be year to year. One day you are the best of pals, the next he may kill you for no reason – just like that.

An elephant will take an instant dislike to somebody or something for no discernible reason at all and nothing will pacify him until that object is killed or removed from his sight. It could be a man in the crowd at the zoo and it could be that he wears spectacles, or a hat, or the colour of his shirt or that he stands in a funny way – nobody knows – and the elephant will go for him. Not just men. My favourite, Toto, took such an instantaneous hatred to a poor woman who had paused momentarily behind the safety barrier to glance into the elephant yard. Toto seized a tree branch and lashed out across the barricade and safety barrier and all but killed her. There were two dozen other people watching at the time but he took no notice of them, only this woman who had been on the scene for less than half-a-minute enraged him.

It happens with other elephants too and with other animals. At feeding time I might have forty-old assorted deer in and around the yard to scavenge what they can. My elephants tolerate them with hardly a glance in their direction, but if a nilgai wanders in they go berserk and are out for the kill instantaneously.

Elephants are known to be vegetarians and that is how they seem to like their food. Yet there is one instance, the only one most elephant men can recount, when one elephant suffered an aberration and a change of diet. That was in the horrible incident in the Swiss zoo when a keeper went back to the elephant house after closing time to check on something. He went into his own charge's shed and the elephant killed him and ate him. All they found in the morning were tatters of his unifrom and a few bones. The awful irony of that story is that the zoo authorities had been wary of that particular elephant's behaviour for some time and had been urging that it should be destroyed since it could become a public danger. Only the keeper had protested and argued that there

143

was nothing wrong with the elephant that time wouldn't cure; he argued that there was no evil in the beastie, only playfulness.

Do not be misled by the elephant's benign appearance, be wary, be respectful and feel for the brute's moods. They are moody because they are intelligent though their intelligence is often underrated. In the teak forests elephants work to between thirty and forty commands of three or four words each and they react instantaneously, which gives them an active 'vocabulary' of 120 words, as many if not more than a great number of human beings.

A friend of mine who worked elephants in forestry around Asia told me of an experience which might indicate their understanding of a situation. He explained: 'We worked the elephants ten months and sent them away for a two months' holiday rest every year. They knew when holiday time was coming around and got quite excited about it; even the newcomers to the team who had not been away before caught the excitement. The mahouts insisted that the elephants knew the time of year though it did seem a bit farfetched to us in management that elephants could work by the calendar. By an oversight one was left behind when she should have gone with the groups going on holiday and she literally went on strike. She would not lift a trunk or roll a log. She would not do a thing. It was not as if they worked a team all the time. They were switched from job to job. It was only when her mahout told her 'holiday time' that she perked up and trotted off happy as a sandboy. She came back like a giant refreshed and got stuck in with a will.

Anybody who wishes to work with and know elephants must accept that they have minds of their own, minds they can change if it pleases them. The oldest adage in a zoo is that an elephant will always pick its keeper; if it doesn't like whoever is presented as a prospective keeper, that is the end of the matter. No amount of ingratiation, persuasion or bullying will change the animal's mind. There will never be a relationship and there will always be trouble with only one possible result: either the keeper or the elephant will end up dead.

The attraction of Howlets was that there were to be eleven elephants all arriving at the same time and all

144

living together as a group; there would be five Africans and six Asiatics, each group with two bulls – a rarity indeed.

You can count the number of bulls kept in captivity in Britain in single figures. Nobody wants them because they are trouble. They grow too big, eleven to twelve feet high from shoulder to ground, act too dangerously when the mood and nature takes them and become unmanageable. The cost of accommodation built strongly enough to restrain them when the bad mood is on them is prohibitive to most zoos. Some of the big bulls kept in American zoos require a ton of extra chain to keep them controlled when they are in *musth*, otherwise they would be a danger to all other elephants, animals, public and the fabric of the zoo itself.

The reluctance to keep bulls is one of the main reasons why only one elephant has ever been born in captivity in England, at Chester Zoo. That plus the fact that breeding elephants is a long-term project taking fifteen to twenty years. (They have a long lifespan of 60 to 70 years and breed from about fifteen.)

Musth is a phenomenon peculiar to bull elephants and one of the greatest mysteries of the animal world. A great number of learned zoologists and other scientists have studied it and failed to come up with a complete answer. It could be some sexual urge or it could be something else. It is as vague as that. A lot of clever people have spent a lot of time on it and they haven't come up with a hundred per cent solution. It begins when a bull is about twelve-years-old. All elephants have temporal glands at the side of their heads and grown bulls produce a black, oily secretion from theirs which is called the musth and when it happens they go absolutely dulally.

At first, it is a junior musth but it builds up and up so that by the time they reach twenty, it becomes an unspeakable rage. All they want to do is to destroy buildings and kill. It is a homicidal madness and nothing is safe from it. By its effects you might equate it to the severest migraine in a human being and then multiply it by ten.

But it is not like a period in a woman or a season in an animal. It might come on today and last a few years, it might come on today and be over in three days. It will

145

happen four times in a year and not again for two years. There is warning that it is about to happen when the gland begins to secrete. Then you take precautions by putting the biggest chains on all four legs; you might have to chain its trunk and head as well. You cut down food and water to the absolute minimum, just enough rough hay to keep the stomach working. If you feed a full diet to a bull whilst in musth, you would never control it; the musth creates an extraordinary supplement of strength – strength through rage, sexual impulse, frustration, pain, nobody knows – in an animal which, at the quietest, most docile of times, has formidable strength.

Why chain the trunk? That trunk could easily break a man's back with a flick; those flailing tusks on a tossing head could rip a man in half. An elephant's tail looks as effective and menacing as a string tail on a sugar mouse on the Christmas tree, but, at the best of times, they have an annoying habit of flicking you with it and that is akin to being bullwhipped. Handlers know too well the weals across body and face which can result from a moment's unwariness.

In musth, an elephant will not recognise his handler. He has no reaction or feeling other than the torment he is obviously going through and, in return, the handler can have but one thought: he's dangerous. There is one reassurance for the public visiting zoos: if they go to one which does keep a bull of ten years or over, then it is certain that the keeper is pretty competent and knows what he is doing so the rest of the elephants will be safe.

All the hundreds of elephants imported during the last hundred years for circuses and zoos, and those in the boom years since safari parks suddenly required herds of twenty or so, have been cows. Nobody wants to take on bulls. I have seen them given away. In fact, I have seen people paid to take them away.

What might sound like a brilliant showman's stunt can turn into a nightmare. Even minor troubles turn into problems as was the case with Big Charlie, which Billy Butlin bought as an attraction for his holiday camps. In 1957 he advertised in *The Times* newspaper that he would pay £1,000 to anybody who could transport Big Charlie 'the biggest elephant in captivity' from his holiday camp at

Ayr, Scotland, to the camp at Filey, Yorkshire. It is one big job to get six tons of mobile, stamping, swaying aggression secured in a trailer and driven a few hundred miles. But that was as nothing compared to the problem when Big Charlie's handler, an Indian called Sheikh Ibrahim, died and they tried to dispose of the elephant. Nobody would take him on and he had to be shot. Most people who know feel – rightly – that a bull's handler should have been with it since it was young because they do not take easily to strangers.

A few rich zoos in the world do breed elephants: Hannover, in Germany, is one, Philadelphia, in America, is another plus a couple in Russia. Hannover must have bred ten, but they have the greatest elephant keeper in the world, Wolfgang Rhamin. A very small, swarthy man, he is brilliant. He had the biggest bull in captivity, an African elephant called Tembo which stood eleven feet tall, the cow was Iringa. Wolfgang handled them like little children, he could do anything with them and they loved him.

Once an elephant is your mate, it stays your mate for life. That is when you have really got to know and understand the animal and when he or she has taken to you but it really only works infallibly if you have had the elephant since it was a baby. A curious fact is that most elephant keepers drink. They are like steel workers, they have got to put back what they sweat out, and the more they drink the better keepers they seem to be. I have fallen asleep, drunk, in the straw in the elephant shed and wakened to find them gently nudging me with their trunks to make sure that I'm all right. I have gone to sleep under my big bull Toto's belly, between his legs and in the morning I have found him lying beside me with me curled up alongside his belly. He is chained one front and one back leg for the night so he must have manoeuvred with remarkable delicacy to avoid stepping on me.

I play a game with them by falling on to the straw and feigning dead, lying limp and not breathing. The panic soon sets in, they begin to squeak and shuffle and become very agitated. Then they try tentative, gentle prods with their trunks and there is an audible gasp of relief when I do move.

Wolfgang Rhamin showed me the way to develop such a relationship with the species – as much by example as by instruction. I went to work with him to learn, and the arts and sciences of the business shone through every day of the experience. There is magic in the man and he transmits it to his animals and his pupils alike. There are a thousand points about which you could say, 'I learned that from Wolfgang,' but there is not a single factor about which you could say, 'Wolfgang taught me that'. That, of course, is the true art of the great teacher, he is able to make you learn for yourself without knowing it. And if he thought that you were dedicated and genuine about elephants he would transmit his . . . not just plain knowledge but, in the truest sense, expertise, to you no matter what the language difficulties.

Hannover was the first and only place where I had worked with a full-grown bull in his prime and it was a double education firstly in zoology and secondly in human nature in the raw. A bull elephant is a randy creature and his sexual apparatus is awesome when he gets excited. The zoo was frequented by elegant German women, made rich and over-indulged by the economic miracle then coming to its peak; a Continental zoo is much more of a social place than its British counterpart, people use it as a social habit and meeting place and not just an educational outing. But the reactions of some of the women was astonishing, they would work themselves into a frenzy at the sight of Tembo rampant. We even had cases of them beginning to strip off in front of the enclosure – such is the power of auto-suggestion.

Really the elephants commonly known as Indian elephants should more properly be called Asiatic because they come from not only India but also Thailand, Burma, Sri Lanka – they are very wide ranging. African elephants come from Africa which makes it simpler to categorise them. One fallacy always raised is that African elephants are wilder and untameable compared with Asiatics. It is not true though it is only partly wrong. The critical factor is that Asia has a culture with centuries of tradition in domesticating and working elephants, they worked them in peaceful construction tasks and used them as battle tanks in war for the Romans and Hannibal. The great princes of the subcontinent had stables of hundreds each with its own mahout, three hundred with three hundred mahouts was not uncommon for a rajah and their duties ranged from splendid ceremonial to beasts of burden on his estates.

But the bush negroes of Africa did not have the savvy to catch and use elephants. They shot them to eat and sell the ivory which was the extent of their capabilities. But in the 1930s the Belgians set up training schools in the Belgian Congo and produced great teams of working elephants. Nowadays they are coming predominately into use in circuses and zoos because Asiatics are becoming scarce and expensive, if you can buy them at all. You can buy an African elephant now for what it would have cost to buy an Asiatic a few years ago. But, if you think that a bargain, before you rush to the local dealer to order one consider the cost of its upkeep: take a 1980 baseline for food, hay, cattle cake, cereals and vital fruit – £15 a day; with essential heat, and they must be kept warm, allot £120 weekly and add or subtract the food price inflation rate applying at the time you buy; that will give you a pretty accurate costing – a bit more than Fido costs.

Those were the problems Paul Ottley and I faced when we took on the Howletts' newly arrived herd, all babies, all fresh and frisky, all needing to be broken and sorted out. In the first chapter I described unloading and breaking Shebe, the latest baby addition to the herd, multiply that by eleven and you will recognise the daunting nature of problem one.

Gorillas and big cats I had begun to find a bit boring and, in honesty, I wasn't all that stuck on elephants. I did not know what I wanted to do. I had looked after innumerable elephants, a couple of old cows in one zoo, an odd one in a circus or sideshow and though I liked them, they didn't excite me until I went to Hannover. The truth, of course, is that 90 per cent of the world's working population finds its job by accident, most people just drift into it. That was how it happened at Howletts; I had experience with elephants and elephant keepers are very thin on the ground, so John Aspinall wanted me back from Gordon Mills. The idea of a lot of elephants together interested me; a brand new experience, do what you want with them as best you can and do something innovative and new.

But Paul, dear old Paul – poor old Paul – if it was new to me it was a revelation to him: a shock, a bewilderment, a soul-shattering experience. He had never worked in a zoo before, he was an insurance salesman. The idea had come to him while watching kiddies' programmes on television. How marvellous, he thought, playing with all those cuddly little creatures and getting on first name terms with those tigers and things, better than trying to flog life insurance to disinterested, jaundiced executives.

He turned out a very fine elephant man, one of the very best. But, my God, he suffered in the process: his back was nigh broken, his arms all but fell off, he was grimed, grazed, bruised, frozen, frightened, boiled and exhausted to the point of dropping. All the things that could never happen to a man in an office, but he grinned and became a fine elephant man. When they asked him why he gave up a good, progressive job in insurance to spend his life shovelling elephant muck, he told them: 'Well, it's different. And it's very expensive muck.'

Everybody who goes into the animal business seriously has to give up a lot in time and comfort just for the honour of an animal's trust and friendship. Aspinall has often told me: 'George, if it wasn't for the zoo, I would be one of the richest men in Britain'. I believe that to be true. In the days when Howletts was entirely private, allowed to admit the paying public on only 28 days a year, it was costing him £160,000 a year; at the time of writing costs have risen to £2,000 a day and though open to the public all the time, he still has to pump in £250,000 a year of his own money to support the enterprise.

You need the combined skills of a city slicker, three-card trickster and Zurich Gnome to stay alive in the animal business. They say that it takes a ro . . ., sorry, adroit man to know an adroit man and when I have been applying my gnomery to improve my parlous financial position, Aspinall has often remarked: 'George, your mind is a labyrinth of perks'.

In twenty years, Howletts has become far more than a conventional zoo for both keepers and animals: more of a zoological enterprise and experiment, not a place for the commercial exploitation of animals but one of breeding and conservation – and hang the cost. Which, despite his failings in the eyes of the pure and godly, sets Aspinall apart from other men. He has done something truly *creative*.

And that in the most fundamental meaning of the word. Breeding was not in our minds at the time our eleven little rompers arrived, survival – for them and us – was the more pressing priority. So we had them chained – at last – which meant that we could put them away for the night with reasonable confidence and get a night's sleep ourselves. Such little luxuries as sleep become so vitally important as to top the list of priorities when the demands of the job are so pressing that you are not getting enough. We could also think about what was going to happen and what we were going to do with the truculent troupe.

In the wild, bulls are solitary creatures which live alone and only visit in the mating season; the dominant cow runs the herd. Here they were all together and we had to keep a watchful eye to see that they did not damage each other while the correct pecking-order was established. There was a lot of hargy-bargy, roaring, buffeting and bullying until Assam, the one who had come from Hannover Zoo and not been born in the wild, established himself as dominant bull while Rani became dominant cow.

Things were beginning to sort themselves out, except for the diet. They had been fed on rice and we found we were spending the whole day cooking boilerfuls of the stuff, shovelling it into the cooking boilers like the fireman of the old steam Royal Scot shovelling in coal. It became imperative to wean them on to good hay, cattle cake for protein and fresh fruit; the local fruit wholesaler wondered what had hit him when his order book went up by 400 lbs a day, cases and crates of anything, we instructed him.

There were three of us actually handling the elephants; Falli, the mahout who had brought the six over from India was still in attendance. But he found the green pastures of England very queer.

To him it was a puzzling, mysterious and forbidding country indeed and it worried him: a worried Indian is one of the most worried things you can find, he makes the deepest anxiety complex in the Western mind look like a slight touch of euphoria such is his anguish. My theory is that fakirs and the like can walk on red hot stones and sit on beds of nails because they have worried themselves so sick that they don't notice: the knack is not a question of mind over matter but the daddy of all anxiety complexes taking over.

Falli slumped from a blue mood into a glazed-eye deep depression because of the phrase 'it is forbidden'. 'Forbeed,' he would say, 'why ees forbeed, sahib? Why ees wrong, sahib? Why ees bad, sahib? Ees good, sahib, ees good for elephants, ees not bad.' The trouble was that he wanted to plant an acre or so of marijuana and the local law did not think it a good idea. In fact, they were quite cross when they found Falli's little hash plot sprouting robustly. But Falli knew, as every good Indian mahout knows, that if you sock a good chew of marijuana to a fractious elephant it calms it down and the world becomes beautiful again to the beast. And if you take an elephant on a long journey, as a reward for good behaviour you bung it a good chew of opium, which is the least you can do to compensate for the inconvenience it has suffered. Apart from that there wasn't any available for him to smoke or chew and he found Players Number Six cigarettes a very poor substitute. It made him very sad – morose, you could say and it added to the chill of what he considered a cold, inhospitable climate. Falli went home. Which was a great pity because he loved those little elephants and he had brought them a long way round the world.

Meanwhile we were busy establishing relationships with our new charges: ideally you want them like a herd of cows so that they gather round and are well behaved at feeding time, and at night they each walk to their allotted space like a cow goes into its stall at milking time. Then you want them to stand still while you put on the night chains. But elephants are more self-willed than cows and not nearly so timorous, so there must be discipline which means an occasional gentle reminder with an elephant goad around their tender spots behind the ears, under the forelegs – like the armpit – and top of the back.

People often try to bribe them into doing what is required by offering fruit and titbits but once that is done, it is impossible to change the habit. They have to be taught to do what you tell them when you tell them. If you say 'in', then in they must go; if you say 'down' then down they must get, otherwise life becomes a practical impossibility. The ultimate is to have them as much under control and cooperating as Wolfgang Rhamin had his. They tell the story in Hannover of when Wolfgang was in hospital, he had to be brought on a stretcher to the elephant house every morning to let them out and give them instructions for the day. That way they are happy and they show it.

Control is one thing, cleanliness is something else: they have to be washed, hosed, scrubbed down with a long-handled scrubbing brush and oiled; oiling they love, it makes their skin feel good and keeps it in fine fettle. They are quite delicate creatures really and, even with the utmost care, they develop terrible abscesses. The slightest wound turns into an abscess and treating them is a monumental task. It is not a one-man job, it needs a surgical army. So when the preventive medicine of expensive Aramis and mustard seed oil fails, the expensive vet is called in.

One of the cows, Belah, developed an abscess under her chin. It was open but it just did not seem to be draining quickly enough. The problem with an elephant is knowing just when to act. Delicate as they are, they still manage to get over most slight ailments without too much fuss, but there is no gradation of illness with them. You cannot describe them as comfortable, poorly, serious and so on to the last rites as you would with humans and many other species. When an elephant becomes ill it becomes very, very ill, alarmingly ill. It goes from well to critical in a flash and the great danger is that if it is too ill to stand it tends to kill itself by lying down when the pressure caused by the sheer weight of the body becomes too much. At that stage the only way is to winch them to their feet; if for some reason you can't winch them, old elephant hands try the dodge of rubbing tobacco into their eyes which gets them into such a rage that they struggle to their feet.

Our cow was darted with anaesthetic to put her down

then the gang, headed by the vet, moved in. The only way to get into the abscess was by using a Black and Decker power drill. The skin is tough, and the growth had calcified and was hard as rock, so the calcification between fibre and bone had to be chipped away by hammer and chisel. And it had to be done fast, because of the reasons I have explained. Rough work, tough on the vet's hands and aching arms but absolutely essential if the animal is to survive. Pus soon drained away but it looks as if there will always be the remnants of a lump there; she doesn't seem to worry.

One interesting factor did arise. Nearly every member of the zoo came to watch, they gave up their days off to be there and learn from the experience, which, in a way, sums up the fascination of animals; the more you know, or think you know, the more you want to learn.

All the time the inexplicable happens and insoluble problems are posed; the baffling nature of some problems is part of the challenge of the job. We will never know why Assam, after years of apparently happy coexistence with Rani, suddenly took an intense dislike to her. The very sight of her drove him into a rage, her close proximity goaded him to violent assault and he tried to kill her. Now we have to keep them separated and out of each other's way. There is no reason we can imagine for it. He wasn't in musth at the time: he was being gentle and good natured with everything and everybody, but the sight of Rani turned him into a raging monster.

His tusks are now lethal. He could kill her at a blow – given the chance. Only bulls have big tusks, cows often do not grow any at all and if they do they are short, stubby little things. More cases than I care to recall are recounted of handlers speared by tusks; in one gruesome case the tusk went right through the handler's body and embedded itself in the wall behind, the animal had to break off its own tusk to free itself from the dead man.

Elephants are dangerous to handlers because they are close contact animals: with big cats, big apes, bears and nearly all the other so called killers, the animal can be segregated by using sliding doors to put it in one section of its accommodation while you clean the other or feed it. If you want to go in with the animal, that's OK, but if you don't fancy its mood then you can stay out and leave the cuddles and playtime until another day. Not so with elephants. The handler has to get in with the creatures, unchain them, turn them out, clean and oil them. If one has turned nasty, it is no use saying: 'I don't fancy that one today, I'll leave it'. The only way is to bravely go back in, get on top of the animal and get on top of the job no matter how much your legs are shaking.

These are agile creatures with a surprising mobility which enables them to spin around, dance on a drumhead as they do when balancing on barrels in circus rings, put on an astonishing turn of foot to easily outrun a man and cruise along at 30 m.p.h. with no strain and, above all, they are astonishingly well balanced as, again, the circus ring demonstrates.

Handlers watch a new recruit keeper's approach to the animals and know within minutes how experienced he is. Simple things are the pointers: a good man will never walk between an elephant and a wall or between two elephants, he will instinctively take the animals' wide side, nor will he put himself in a position where he can be 'trunked' or worse still knelt on. He will watch the wicked tail and keep well out of range of kicks from those tree-trunk back legs. He will show, if he is well steeped in elephant lore, a respect for the animal until the introduction has grown into something stronger than an acquaintanceship; an elephant cannot be rushed and it has got to give its consent before familiarity can be assumed.

But when that friendship is established they will lift their legs to have their feet pedicured. Their feet get into an awful state; if an elephant is walking timber-toed it is because of calluses and hard skin and the toenails need trimming. Fresh from a chiropodist's session an elephant will almost dance away.

Then they will want to play. I stuff my pockets with goodies, make a show of taking something out and popping it in my mouth, then wait for the trunks to slip into my pocket and steal whatever is there. They are as thrilled as children putting one over on a favourite uncle, particularly if you put on a show of mock anger.

Those trunks are so sensitive that their delicacy is un-

155

believable. Accidentally drop a raisin in the straw and they will pick it up. The tip of that trunk is as sensitive and responsive as our fingers, in fact, more so. A raisin in the straw is one example. It is tough enough for a man using his eyes at close range with his fingers grubbing about to locate and pick up such a small object, but an elephant's trunk can sort out a raisin among a group of similarly sized pebbles on a saucer. Compare the size of a raisin with that of an elephant and it hardly seems worth the effort of picking it up and popping it into the mouth, its senses of smell and taste must also be acutely sensitive.

Elephants in a group are fascinating, wholly different from those kept singly or in pairs. So different that the plight of the solitary ones becomes all the more pronounced in the sense that what was not noticeable before becomes all too obvious as the daily life of an elephant family is revealed. They form an integrated community and act like any other living community. They play together, interest each other, fall out and squabble, make up, boss others and are bossed themselves. Even the bitter feud between Assam and Rani is part of the game, the salt on the celery; in short, they are ALIVE, they look alive, act alive and express their characters. Compare that with the state of a poor old cow standing in the corner of her cage in a zoo, bored to oblivion, stupefied by loneliness, her feet on hard concrete and her outlook constrained by iron bars; compared with elephants in a family she is a creature condemned to the equivalent of thirty years' solitary for an inmate of a top security jail.

There is a pond in the compound at Howletts and a 'splash', a simple little device where they can roll in water and mud and wallow. They love it. You can see and feel the pleasure they gain rolling and spluttering around. Not many zoos can put in a wallow; they haven't the space. Far too many zoos would not bother because of the expense, all they want is a couple of jumbos for the kids to stare at. As times get more and more expensive, serious zoology is becoming ever less compatible with commercial exploitation. So the harsh and inescapable fact of life is that many are kept in atrocious conditions and so it will remain.

Elephant talk is very curious, not at all in keeping with

their bulk except when they roar. Most of the time they utter little squeaks as if a colony of bats was lodged up their trunks. When I have been away for some length of time the squeaks and mumbles of welcome on my return sound like a belfry at twilight; trumpeting and roaring comes in anger and pleasure and only an ear well attuned to it can tell the difference.

If they are trumpeting, watch the trunks; if they are curled up like a coiled hosepipe under the chin – move. That is the attitude when they are going to charge; it is done to protect the trunk, the most sensitive and vulnerable part of their bodies. And when they do charge, nothing will stop them.

Running about with trunks flailing is just high spirits, as it was on the Saturday they broke out at Howletts. Originally the compound was made by pile-driving telegraph poles five foot into the ground with five foot remaining on top to form a fence. But they chewed the projecting part of the poles – that wasn't in the diet book. Then, in frisky mood, they snapped off the weakened poles, tossed them around like matchsticks and went for a romp in the park – to the consternation of everybody watching who all suddenly realised that eleven elephants galumphing along quick as two-year-olds on a race track constitute a menace to public order.

The Anchor at Littlebourne was the local, a good pub with a decent drop of bitter beer, a good 'slate' and I rather fancied the landlord's daughter. In all, a fair combination for a good booze-up and every Saturday was my booze-up day (my real booze-up day, I mean. Every day is a good beering day but Saturday is a bit special.) I was busy making fast with the pints and the landlord's daughter, the beer was in good nick and the landlord's daughter better. And then this chap came in and said: 'George, your elephants are out.'

You get to know zoo men and the strokes they pull so, like you do when you know that you are being conned, I said: 'Oh yes . . .' and ordered another pint.

Then a little army came crashing in all yelling at once: 'George, your elephants are out.'

Each adding his titbit:

'They're wrecking the place . . . .'

'Half the fencing is down . . . .'

'They're ripping up trees . . . .'

'They keep charging down the paddock . . . .'

'Last time I saw them they were heading towards Bekesbourne Lane . . . .'

The remote possibility of my elephants trundling down the public highway and meeting the vicar, or any of his parishioners, coming in the opposite direction in his Mini was slightly alarming. I put my pint behind the bar in the charge of the landlord because I am not daft and I have seen pints disappear like that before, jumped in the Land Rover and went back.

They were not kidding. They were all there having the time of their lives: Assam and Toto ripping branches off trees; Rani, Motki, Bella and Buria knocking over ornamental shrubs; Pugli and Bwana shaking other ornamental shrubs out of their tubs. The others were examining the deer fencing and chasing sundry keepers who were waving arms at them and shouting 'Whoa!', 'Back boy!', 'Shoo!' and anything else that came to mind. Words my lot were not familiar with and consequently useless. After a moment's disbelief, I spoke to them in anger. But I am sure in my own mind that I did not behave in exactly the way that Kurt said I did.

Kurt regaled the pub with vivid descriptions of the action. He said: 'George fell out of the Land Rover screaming, "What the *Zap!* do you think you're doing? You stupid *Wham! Zing! Zapping!* idiots – back, get back in the bloody shed. Who said you could come out? You'll come out when you're bloody told." There are ladies here, I can't say those shockink verds he used – they dropped all the branches and the shrubs and all their trunks went down, and they all looked shifty like little boys caught robbing an orchard, then they all turned round and started to shuffle back toward the shed, then they started to trot, then run and they were in such a hurry to get back in the shed they got jammed in the door. And George was puffing up behind them yelling, "I'll belt the bloody daylights out of you all." And everytime he yelled they went a bit quicker. . . .'

That's his story. I thought I managed in a very orderly manner by quiet persuasion and gentle coaxing.

Incidentally, I later married the landlord's daughter – and what is managing a herd of elephants after that?

Stories about escapes infuriate zoo owners and curators who would like to pretend that they don't happen when they happen all the time. If the press gets to know about them it is always bad publicity.

Like the night we thought the boiler had blown up – if there had been a boiler thereabouts to explode. The small, still hours of the morning were made horrendous by deafening crashes, echoing booms, the splintering of timber and the shattering of glass in the enclosed courtyard; windows shook, doors rattled and the whole place shook and reverberated as flying debris hit solid object and ricocheted into other flying debris. Lights came on and cautious heads peered from opened windows. The elephants had broken out again and gone walkabout round the park until they found the courtyard and the dustbins. Big industrial-sized bins as well as domestic ones. They began to toss them around and, loving the din they made, tossed them further and higher.

It sounded like Armageddon.

Midnight frolics elephant style.

159

Chapter 14

Life on the other side of the cage door

Let us interrupt the flow of narrative in the interest of truth and that all shall be revealed. I was going to call this chapter 'Time Out', in the modern idiom, but realised that 'Time In' might be more accurate, so let's just call it a diversion. Once or twice the smooth progression of my career has been disrupted by malevolent outside interests – usually dressed in a smart uniform with shiny buttons and badges on it, a whistle in its pocket, nightstick and shooter on its belt. Naturally I never went seeking trouble and always tried to avoid it. But it wasn't as simple as all that . . .

In one aspect there may be a direct link between human and animal reaction: few species seem to relish captivity and take their freedom at any given opportunity, then when they have achieved freedom they do not quite know what to do with it and often seek to return to captivity – which indicates that all species can become institutionalised.

Maybe I have an affinity with captive animals because I know the feeling myself: I have graced some of the finest, most renowned nicks in the world. Penitentiaries the mention of which sends a shiver of fear down most men's spines – Siberia, would you believe, and a spell in 'chain gang' country in the Deep South of the United States . . . nothing but the best, no squalid little obscure prisons, big league stuff only.

A period of rest as guest of the authorities of the Union of Soviet Socialist Republics in their penal establishment in Igarka, Siberia, came after one of those idiot adventures when imminent poverty and the promise of quick salvation money tempted me to sign on for another rough sea trip.

This timber boat was going North to that place on the map where all the lines of longitude get narrower and narrower and start running to a point; where there is a dotted line on the chart marked Arctic Circle and an inscription saying *limit of ice (spring)*. The dreaded North Cape and Barents Sea were nothing to this old tub, she liked her bottom well frozen so only the Arctic Ocean would suffice. She kept going North and further North still until the point was almost reached that whichever way she steamed was bound to be South. And she kept going until she arrived at the Yenisei River – some people spell it Yenisey because most Russians I have ever met never seem to know their 'eyes' from their arses, they are so drunk the best part of the time.

One look at the Yenisei and you ask yourself: 'Why did teacher make all that fuss about the Volga?' The Volga is a vulgar little upstart of a river compared with the mighty Yenisei. The Yenisei starts its spartan life a frozen continent away on the very borders of Mongolia and makes its tedious way across thousands of miles of barren, icy wastes until it flows into the Arctic Ocean.

And the tough little timber ships plod a weary 500 miles up it to Igarka: on the port side, thousands of miles of Mother Russia stretching to Alaska; to the starboard, more thousands of miles of Mother Russia extending to Poland, East Germany, West Germany . . . warmth, bright lights and colour, everything this interminable grey monotony is not. Only after giving up all hope of ever reaching anywhere ever does Igarka loom up out of the tedium.

A lot of people go to Igarka, many more than you would think which is surprising because it is not the sort of place people talk about in the vein of: 'Where d'you go on yer 'olidays?' 'Igaka, s'nice there. Siberia, lots of the old crumpet an' that about, plenty of booze, s'luverly.' But so many people do visit that many signs are written in ten languages. Which goes to prove that there are more masochists in the world than head-shrinkers would have us believe.

Seamen are shepherded to the International Club, a

place where the dreariness of Communist life ends abruptly at the door with a quick flash of hard currency and decadence, Western style, is abundant in exchange for D-Marks, Dollars, Francs or Stirling notes. Champagne, no less, vodka of the finest quality Russia could provide, exceedingly beautiful girls, the infatuation of powerful rhythmic music, laughter and dancing: a dreamlike quality such as would happen in a way-out spy film when the KGB is softening up the hero with luxury and sex before slamming him into the dank cell and the company of guards with chopped-off rubber hosepipes.

We loved it, my Norwegian shipmates and I. 'Come on,' we yelled, 'let's have a bash at this Cossack dancing, grab a couple of the black-eyed, raven-haired beauties and off we go'.

The bar downstairs, the dancing upstairs and between the two was a large multi-lingual notice: 'It is forbidden to take drink into the ballroom'. But who cares? Let's have a ball. Well, the Russkies cared. They did not like alcoholic beverage in the ballroom; they did not care all that much if it was inside a dancing reveller, three-quarters of them were as wobbly as Sauchiehall Street, Glasgow, on a Saturday night, it was its external presence in bottles that upset them.

We were loathe to leave our champagne bottles behind, so we argued the point, but to no avail. Unfortunately, in the heat of the argument, a few Russian policemen were injured; not badly, not stretcher cases or anything like that, but enough for Mrs. Natasha Olga Nikolayevski to say to policeman hubby Joseph Vissarionovich Nikolayevski: 'Oh, Jospeh Vissarionovich Nickolayevski, where did you get that beautiful shiner from?' So they put us in the cooler.

Five of us, two Norwegians, two Finns and me, appeared before the local Commissar charged with causing an outrage to public decency and did the right thing by pleading guilty. Not out of any noble George Washington attitudes of 'I cannot tell a lie', but because the consul had warned that if you pleaded innocent, thus casting doubt on the probity and authority of the local gendarmerie, and if they had to prove you guilty they were liable to add an extra two or three years to the

sentence for fibbing and wasting the Commissar's valuable vodka-tippling time.

'Ninety days', said the Commissar.

'Ninety days', said the interpreter.

'Ninety days', repeated the consul's representative, and
he beamed a smile at the Commissar, 'less than I expected,
good, first rate, splendid.' But he wasn't going to the
labour camp.

It didn't worry any of us: I have never worried about
being sent to prison, I have counted it an experience and
I have never regretted it after coming out. Nothing is
more humiliating and annoying than these lads who
smuggle drugs to foreign countries, or go on the booze in
dry Muslim states, get sent down and then their mothers
appear, weeping on TV and their MPs protest involving
consuls and embassies who should have better things to
do. Put them away, lock them up, it does them good and
I have seen it work from the inside. They should not be
indulged in the outlook, 'I'm English, I can do anything
and my Mum and MP will kick up a rumpus if I'm caught'.
If you play the game, you take the consequences laid
down by the country you misbehave in.

The Norwegians shrugged their shoulders and winked;
the Finns thought it was as good as home – better than
home, they needed it, it gave them the chance to dry out.
Actually, the whole establishment proved to be something
of a drying-out clinic where most of the Russian inmates
could, for the first time in a long while, see a sunset
through sober eyes.

It was a big labour camp, a village on its own surrounded by a fence and housing a couple of thousand
miscreants with its own farm. Breakfast was black bread
and gruel, work started at 6.30 a.m., lunch was black
bread and potato or beetroot soup, the evening meal was
black bread with beetroot or potato soup, not a choice,
you understand, just variety in the diet between noon
and sunset.

Our task was loading potatoes on to a cart and here the
Russian economic and agricultural system worked mar-
vellously to our advantage. Try as they will, they do not
manage to grow all that many tons of potatoes per acre
– or all that much of anything per acre, so the actual

labour was not all that backbreaking, and the inmates were a cheerful lot by Russian standards. They seemed to think that it was better inside than out in many respects.

Ninety days on the dot and we were freed having gained an insight into the Russian lifestyle and character which very few people have the chance of observing. Certainly the circumstances were curious in the extreme, but I found a lot to like about the maligned Russians, so much so that I would not mind going back – I would not view it with horror. They have excellent zoos there.

Halfway across the world is the Gulf of Mexico, and the ports of Houston and New Orleans. The cultural gulf that divides them from Igarka is ten times as wide as the Arctic and Atlantic Oceans put together and infinitely deeper; a sailor ought to be in a permanent state of cultural shock from the different environments he is called upon to absorb in the course of a year's work.

Now Houston is a great city for a young seaman to jump ship in; put another way, it is a city with temptations enough to make it difficult for easily led young seamen not to jump ship.

New Orleans is such another place only more so, a city on its own out of time and out of place in modern America. Or so it appears through the eyes of a stranger though the inhabitants see it as an all-American town and do not recognise their highly individualistic approach. But if you mix French, Spanish, British, Mulatto, Creole, Creek and Choctaw Red Indian influences together in one great hotchpotch then top if off with all that Negro slave jazz and soft-shoe shuffle, something exciting and special is bound to come out. Where else would you find a beautiful Cherokee Indian girl barmaid in the Squirrel Bar who, out of the kindness of her heart and sympathy for the underdog, would keep two near destitute British seafarers plied with free drinks all day and most of the night?

We had missed the ship, money ran out. A daily visit to the shipping office to collect five dollars a day subsistence allowance was not the lifestyle we envisaged for ourselves in this city of delights, so we took jobs on the black economy; no visas, no green cards, no permits of any kind, there was nothing else we could do. Ron became compere in a strip show and I was the tout outside

164

drumming up business; as a sideline I sold tortillas and hot dogs and life was quite good. Somewhere along the line we had made the acquaintanceship of three delightful ladies who had invited us to share their flats, which was a very charitable thing to do.

Then the bastards in the shipping office found us a ship and we were escorted to Houston to join her and it looked very much as if our lotus eating days were over.

The *Regina de la Mer*, she was called and from our arrival at the dock gates our hearts sank. *'Regina de la Mer?'* the gateman queried in the tone of voice which immediately raises suspicions.

'Regina de la Mer, you joining that hell-ship?' bystanders asked, givings us funny looks. All the way along the quayside was a straggle of coloured seamen all coming off the *Regina de la Mer* and offering advice to us like: 'You fooey?', 'You crazy, man?', 'You mad, fella?'.

By the time we reached the gangplank we had formed the distinct impression that the *Regina de la Mer*, fine ship though she might be, was not a popular berth for any qualified seamen no matter how broke they were. The suspicion sneaked into our minds that it was a devilish ploy by the bums in the shipping office to extract retribution from us for the five dollars they had been issuing daily over the weeks to allow us our lives of luxury and indolence.

In crisis, firm decisions: 'Get aboard', said Ron, 'cop the signing on money and a sub, 'ave a quick shifty, don't like it – scarper'.

'Good thinking, Ron,' said I, leaving my kit bag hidden behind a bollard so that this time it would not disappear over a far horizon with me ashore.

'Hi, boys,' the girls shrieked in delight when we returned to the flats, 'isn't this just swell, pass the liquor over, we'll mix the drinks. You fellas got a few bucks? That's just swell, we'll have fun.'

And fun it was, fast, furious and exhausting until, WHAM! the door burst open without knock, ring or by your leave. 'Hit the wall, arms wide out, legs apart, no reaching inside shirts, no pockets, just stare at the pretty wallpaper, hands up, up, UP, keep still, look cute but don't move and everything's gonna be fine.' The police lieutenant must have apprenticed as a tobacco auctioneer to judge by the speed and monotone of his instructions. Backed by a pack of what looked like retired university American footballers, he was clearly a winner so there was no point in opposing him. Be charming and reasonable, I thought as snap, jingle, click the handcuffs went on.

'Take it easy, don't mess about, we won't give any trouble,' I said with an ingratiating smile and, since I was genuinely mystified, 'how did you find us here, how did you know where we were?'

'We find all the missing sailors in these flats. The captain reports two sailors missing so we come right on round to see the girls and the missing sailors are always here, we need never go no place else.'

The girls said: 'Hi, lieutenant, hi, Jacko, hi, Buster, hi, everybody – you'all have a little old drink, yeah?' The policemen tipped their hats and put their guns away. They had stormed the flats with more weaponry than General Andrew Jackson had used to beat the British at the Battle of New Orleans in 1815 – so we kept on being nice and polite.

The judge said: 'Waal, George, boy . . . you come from li'le ol' London, England . . . I sure know that li'le ol' place . . . sure do . . . that's one mighty nice li'le ol' place, London, England . . . you sure one lucky fella comin' from li'le ol' London. Now, George, boy, I have the bad noos for you . . . it's gotta be ninety days, ain't nuppin I can do about it, that's what it's gotta be . . . now you be sure and say hello from me to li'le ol' London when you get back there, George, you be sure to do that . . . you sure one lucky ol' fella coming from li'le ol' London . . . ninety days, that's what it's gotta be.'

Like thirteen is a universal unlucky number, ninety days is a favourite short, sharp reprimand for minor offenders in many countries, a good round number. And since we had already been nicked once before in the Squirrel Cage Bar for illegal entry – into America, not the Squirrel Cage – the only inconvenience resulting from which was a night in the can until they registered us with the shipping pool, the judge was quite generous.

Actually, Ron Yoe was a little more inconvenienced

than me during the first arrest. He was obliged to spend the night in a cell with a convicted murderer, a psychopathic strangler; he told me that it was like watching the late night horror movie on TV, only for real.

'Hi, George. Hi, Ron. You boys like a snort and chew the fat a while?'

'Hi, Captain,' all the warders were addressed as captain, 'sure would like a snort.' So it was drinks and candies in the guards' room in the Paris jailhouse, New Orleans.

Making corn sacks and, of all things, combs, you could earn 8 dollars a week. 'More than you get outside,' said Ron enthusiastically, 'we'll have 100 dollars clear when we get out.' And that was quite a lot of loot in those days.

Quite a comfy prison, the Parish – if you were white. But heaven forbid going in if you were black. We saw the black prisoners only from a distance and a miserably wretched crew they looked dragging around shackled and reduced to the status of subhuman. Passing the end of a corridor one night, I stopped and shouted out excitedly: 'Hey, there's a chimp, down there, whose is it? I used to look after chimps.' I bounded down to look at it and, of course, it was a negro manacled to a fixed chair, slumped and stark naked. He had the complete posture of a chimpanzee, the humped, slouched crouch, everything human had drained out of him, he saw the world – the walls of that corridor – through unseeing eyes.

The guards guffawed. 'Hey, chimp, d'you hear that, Alvin? D'you hear that, Ike? You wanna take him back for your zoo, George? This guy George is one big comedian, he sure is a funny guy . . . hey, chimp. . . .' They rocked in their mirth and slapped my back at a great joke.

'You too late, George, boy. You sure too late. He's for fryin', he fries real good tomorrow mornin'. Fried chimp for breakfast, George boy.'

Igor, a deranged Russian wandered through the prison playing an imaginary violin tucked under his chin. 'You gonna wear out that cat gut on that li'le ol' fiddle, Igor, have a candy. C'mon, you caint chew candy with a fiddle under your chin.'

'Hi, Catfish.'

'Hi, Captain, sir.'

'Now that Catfish, George, he's jest a li'le ol' country

boy come up to the city, good as gold, 'cep'n he gits real mean when he gets mad, real mean.'

Catfish was a Bayou boy who had committed crimes of terrible violence. His family did not know he was in jail. Catfish said: 'Hey, George, you'all go back to England, Europe, when you git free? I done wrote this letter to my gal down'n Mississippi, you post that goddam letter for me from England, Europe. I told her I gotten a big, big job in England, Europe, and I'll be sendin'fur her to come soon as I can, sureashell I will.' I worked it out that that would be in about seventeen years if be behaved himself in prison and did not let his mean streak out.

Came the day when the captain told us: 'We gotta git you boys deported, fast. When you quit the jailhouse, you gotta be on one aircraft, fast, going someplace, any-place so long as it is a long, long ways from N'Orleans. Now the Governor he don't want you hanging your asses out in some hot cat house around the town, you gotta GO. Sureashell I'll miz you, George, and you, Ron, sure-ashell will.'

'Now, I've bin readin' the book an' 'seems you boys can be deported to any goddam country in the world, any goddam country you elect, that's what the book says. I figure that for li'le ol' England . . .'

'Hang about, Captain,' we said in unison, 'did you say any country?'

'Sureashell did, boys, any goddam country. . . .'

'I rather fancy that South America,' said Ron, 'I never bin down South America.'

'Good idea,' I concurred, 'I fancy that South America as well.' My mind filled with romantic visions of black-eyed beauties dressed like Carmen Miranda at a carnival.

'How's about South America, Captain, that will do nicely.'

'South America,' mused the captain, he fixed his spec-tacles and perused the schedule, 'Argentina . . . Bolivia . . . Brazil . . . Chile . . . Columbia. . . .'

'That Argentina's said to be a bit tasty,' said Ron.

'So is Brazil', I chipped in, 'they say it's quite nice in Brazil.'

'Mexico, Central America,' said the captain, 'now that

Mexico City, that's one-hell-uva-town, sure is, if I was you boys, I'd think about that Mexico City.'

The captain read on. 'Colombia . . . Ecuador . . . now I don't know too damn much about those goddam places and they don't read good to me. Paraguay . . . Peru . . . Uruguay . . . now those damn banana republics ain't no good to no man, no how, they just one big heap o' trouble, yes, sir.' His eyes lit up: 'Venezuela, goddam it, Venezuela. Now my buddy has bin in Venezuela and he tells me that Caracas is one hell of a town. . . .'

He picked up the telephone and called his buddy. 'Hi, Howard, you tell me that Caracas, Venezuela, is one hell of a town? Yeah . . . yeah . . . yeah . . .' his eyes glistened, 'you don't say . . . gorgeous tail in every bar . . . godammit . . . yeah . . . oh, boy. . . .'

He replaced the phone and said: 'That Caracas is *one* hell of a town'.

So we sat in the captain's office in Paris prison like privileged customers in a Thomas Cook's travel office discussing an exotic holiday while, back in London, my Mum had telephoned the American Consul, having heard that I was in jail. Poor old Mum, she got the impression that I was in a chain gang in the deep south and having seen the chain gang films and read the books, she was in a state of acute terror.

The captain, enthused by the idea of South America for two of his customers, set the wheels of officialdom and diplomacy in motion and overcame enormous problems – like why should South America welcome two American jailbirds of British nationality who had requested to be deported there in preference to home?

'Gee, boys, I'm sorry,' he would say, 'we've gotten a li'le problem an' the State Department say its gonna take a li'le time to work this out, but it's gonna be OK, it gonna be jest fine, sureashell it is, if you boys will jest be a li'le bitty patient.'

'Sure thing, Captain,' we would reply, adopting the local vernacular as best we could, 'we ain't going anyplace . . . yet.'

Freedom day minus four and the apologetic captain said: 'Gee, boys, I hate to tell you, but it's gonna take some more time to git you all to South America, if those cocksuckers in the State Department would only shift there asses . . . UK, great, go tomorrow, first plane, but South America, that's gonna take some time, maybe a week, maybe a month . . . you can stay here while we make the deal, OK?'

Freedom day minus one we told him not to worry about South America anymore, but thanks for trying, and we would settle for the UK option. 'Gee, boys, I am sorry, I'm real sorry,' said the captain. So the following morning we arrived, handcuffed as the law required, to board the New Orleans-New York flight; up the boarding steps, down the alleyway to our reserved seats and the cuffs were taken off. 'Sure gonna miss you guys,' said the captain, and to an astonished open-mouthed stewardess, 'now you look after my boys real well. Solong, fellas.' Several passengers looked nonplussed too.

We began to get drunk using all the lovely corn sack, comb money in our pockets; we told the stewardess and everybody else who was listening how we were illegal immigrants being sent back home. How we had stowed away to get to the land of the free, and how we had sweated and laboured once we had arrived until some fink had let us down and betrayed us. How we were desperate to stay. There was hardly a dry eye in our section of the cabin and the drinks rolled in. We landed in New York totally drunk with 99 per cent of our jail money intact.

It was then that the impossible happened, or at least one of those remarkable coincidences that are so improbable that they seem unreal in the telling: I fell down the steps from the aircraft into the arms of the immigration officer waiting to take charge of us and escort us safely and surely to the next London flight, looked up into his face and recognised an old, old friend. He had been a mate of mine in London years before. I did not even know that he had emigrated to the United States let alone become a naturalised citizen.

We stood together just repeating each other's names in the idiot fashion people who haven't met for years do, shaking hands, slapping each other on the shoulder, shaking hands again, repeating names and laughing. A little crowd of curious and utterly bemused passengers from the flight gathered round. They stood at a respectful distance and muttered between themselves about the absurdities of life: convicts boarding a respectable flight, prison officers giving them a tearful send-off and 'Jeesuus, this guy gives him a big hello like he was the president of the corporation'.

Scotty, the immigration officer, said: 'There are four hours to wait for the London flight. Either we wait in the can or I can take you round the World Fair. The World Fair is a great show, you ought to see the World Fair. If you'll be good, I'll take you.' We let him persuade us. We visited every bar on the site and those we couldn't take in, I am sure didn't matter. Four hours later, happy, drunk and still rich we were on the BOAC flight to London.

It was the most civilised deportation I have ever suffered.

Chapter 15

Rats, or when to leave a sinking ship

In case you are thinking, by now, that I am a fly-by-night in the jobs business, let me tell you that no stigma attaches to having a lot of different jobs. Classically skilled German wood craftsmen and stoneworkers were forcibly sent packing by their respective guilds to walk, dressed in their funny wide-brimmed black cowboy hats, white shirts, knee-britches, white stockings and buckled shoes, from places like Hanover and Cologne through France and Spain, working in every major city they came to, and back again to the Fatherland before they were considered experienced enough to set chisel to a precious piece of teutonic oak or granite. They clocked up a few jobs en route. It is the same with animal keepers. I went to gain experience with a big British animal dealer who had strong show business connections. I quite fancied a bit of show business – all those glamorous people. But it wasn't as simple as all that . . .

If Sean Connery and his cronies had decided to stop and reshoot the scene once more, they would have achieved yet another James Bond spectacular in *From Russia With Love* and turned black into white, but this would have been one stunt director Terence Young and producers Broccoli and Saltzman wouldn't have been enamoured of. They were busy cocking up the shots in the great dramatic sewer scene in the film and also cocking up my carefully laid plans.

The trouble was that every time he missed the cue or misquoted his script, like every film actor does under pressure from time to time, or the lights were wrong, or the sound was bad, or somebody muffed something and

172

the director called 'CUT', all tough man Sean had to do was to sit and re-read his script or hang about while the technicians sorted things out. Whereas I had to round up 600 scurrying, squealing, slippery rats rooting them out from the corners, nooks and crannies of a film studio, prodding them from under complicated, heavy equipment, chasing them from the top of sets, beams and rafters in the roof and collecting them altogether again for yet another attempt at the scene.

All you can expect from the film world is madness and this was sheer lunacy: film producers and directors think that a film contract automatically gives them a licence to suspend and defy the laws of man and nature. Defiance of the laws of man incurs predictable penalties but it can be much costlier to buck nature's system.

The deal had been fixed by Clive Desmond who ran a dealer's business at Colindale in London. He rather fancied cutting a dash in the film world and showbiz as much as he undoubtedly fancied the big profits in it. By way of normal business his company, Zoorama, did not handle much big stuff but a volume of small mammals and birds which is why I was working for him since I was interested in them at the time. He had supplied animals for a couple of television shows which had given him a taste for the bright lights and smell of greasepaint, though he fancied himself more as a big wheeler-dealer fixing deals in the background while mixing with film moguls, producers, directors and glamorous stars. So when the call from Elstree studios came he said in his best big-business voice: 'Rats? Five or six hundred? No problem, I'll send down my man George to sort that out for you.'

Terence Young, the director, was explicit about his needs and painted a graphic, dramatic picture: James Bond and Daniela Bianchi down a stinking sewer fleeing from terrible danger. At first a few rats scurrying around to inject menace into the scene, then – as the music swelled to drama pitch – the sewer is filled with hundreds of rats stampeding along, scuttling round Bond's shoes and trousers, clambering over Daniela's peek-a-boo toes, brushing against her shapely legs while she pressed a diminutive mini-skirt firmly against her clenched thighs in the traditional pose of a woman frightened by a mouse

173

– all women seem to suffer from the dickory-dockery-dock syndrome fearing that a tiny, frightened mammal will scurry up their exposed legs and cause them acute embarrassment. The whole idea quite got me going – sexy. Then I thought about it and stopped in my fantasy tracks as quickly as I had started: it isn't as easy as it all sounds, you cannot give rats a script to read and they are not trained to follow stage directions.

Meanwhile, back at the ranch, Clive had been doing a bit of post-euphoric thinking. The euphoria had come with the thought of all that lovely film money – visions of marching from Elstree to Colindale like a latter day Pied Piper of Hamelin followed by a swarm of rats each with a fiver in its mouth – the let-down was thinking about how we could possibly do it.

'Sewer rats!' Clive expostulated, 'it's illegal, we can't buy them, we can't *deal* in them, there are strict laws against it, they are vermin.'

We had no rats. At a time of crisis like that the final problem tends to be forgotten, in this case how were we going to get them to do what would be required on set, and you concentrate on the immediate problem which has sprung up and that was to acquire sufficient *legal* rats which would look the part and not bring down the wrath of the Department of Health gestapo on our heads.

A cable was sent to an Asian dealer who worked in the Cameroons, West Africa: 'PLEASE SEND URGENTEST (FIGS) 1,000 (WORDS) ONE THOUSAND GAMBIAN POUCH RATS STOP'

The reply came: 'AM NOT UNDERSTANDING YOUR ESTEEMED ORDER STOP IT IS NOT POSSIBLE FOR ANY PERSON TO REQUIRE ONE THOUSAND GAMBIA POUCH RATS STOP PLEASE CABLE CORRECT NUMBER STOP'

London to Cameroons: 'FIRST FIGURE CORRECT STOP REQUIRE IMMEDIATELY ONE THOUSAND GAMBIA POUCH RATS STOP FIVE HUNDRED INSTANTLY WILL SUFFICE TIME BEING STOP ORDER VERY URGENT STOP'

Cameroons to London: 'IMPOSSIBLE COMPLY SUCH STRANGE REQUEST STOP DO NOT HAVE POUCH

174

RATS IN STOCK STOP DO NOT HAVE SUFFICIENT RODENT CATCHERS STOP'

London to Cameroons: 'PLEASE SEND MAXIMUM NUMBER POUCH RATS AVAILABLE STOP NOTIFY CONSIGNMENT NUMBER STOP'

Cameroons to London: 'HAVE ONLY ONE DOZEN POUCH RATS FOR IMMEDIATE DISPATCH STOP WILL TWELVE BE A SUFFICIENCY STOP'

The thought of arriving at Elstree to face that lunatic host and producing a ridiculous twelve rats before their beady eyes numbed me a little. How could you explain to them? Everybody knows that rats are a plague the world over. There are billions of them in our own back yards; all the film crew wanted were a piddling 600. I could see that it might be difficult convincing them that something which ten thousand Rodent Officers up and down the land spend their working days fighting a losing battle trying to exterminate was in short supply.

Mrs. Desmond, washing her hair upstairs, had the brainwave: She rushed down, hair in a towel and clutching a bottle. 'Hair dye,' she yelled, 'black and grey hair dye. There are thousands of white rats on the market.'

I raided the local Woolworths store and cleared the hair dye counter. A large fish tank was filled and the brew made as per instructions on the bottle, but dying a rat is not as easy as tinting a lady reclining in a crimper's chair: rats squirm, wriggle and bite when you try to dip them into the dye. Mass production was the answer. We put our entire stock of white rats into keep nets and, to get even more done at a time, into pillow cases. Then we immersed the pulsating sack into the mixture holding it under for exactly thirty seconds.

They came out pefectly dyed, the fur took the dye as if it had been made for it, they were faultless. So we toured all the dealers and pet shops of London. 'Buy all your white rats,' we said, and many a queer look we got in return. But the looks we got from animal dealers were nothing to those from hairdressers when we bought up their entire stocks of dye.

Terence Young was delighted: 'Fantastic,' he exclaimed, 'come along and I'll introduce you to Sean Connery.' But I was in a churlish mood and becoming rapidly disenchanted with the film world, film people, film sets, film technicians, rats white, black or pouched, so I said: '**** him, let's get on with the job.' At the back of my mind that niggling doubt about whether we would be able to get the rats to do what was required was now beginning to emerge and loom large. I looked around and thought: 'Six hundred rats in the turmoil of a film set with the lights, shouting and commotion, they'll be more temperamental than the stars themselves.'

Note the phrase 'let's get on with it'. It is the last phrase that should ever be uttered on a film set, it is the last thing that ever happens on a film set, it is the ultimate final thought in anybody's mind on a film set. There has to be a committee meeting equivalent of the General Assembly of the United Nations to move a camera ten sprockets along a reel: 'Get the rats ready,' 'Stand the rats down,' 'Let's try it with a dozen rats.' So it goes on hour after hour – sorry, day after day. It took us five full, rat-infested days to get the scene (two minutes?) in the can.

The first takes were not too bad – except that they were a *minor* disaster. A dozen rats were to scurry round the stars' feet in the sewer so the taps were turned on, water began to drip from the walls and roof of the sewer, the lights were arranged to the director and cameraman's satisfaction, the rats were released in the right place, the clapperboard clapped, cameras whirred . . . and they didn't like the way Sean Connery said his lines.

Through it all again . . . sorry, Sean, they didn't like it again, or he didn't like it. Anyway it was 'CUT'.

My poor little rats were beginning to show the strain of being popped into and dragged out of the watery sewer. They began to look as if they were ageing visibly before our eyes and going grey. The dye was washing out; another few takes and they would be white enough for a washing powder advertisement and definitely not the right shade of black for the sewers of Istanbul. At that stage we had plenty of spare black rats, 588 in all, but what if the takes and retakes were repeated during the main scene and they all turned white?

It was vital, as I saw it, that Sean Connery should be persuaded to get it right so apart from 'M', I'm probably the only mortal ever to give James Bond a bollicking – I made a few remarks about Sean Connery's acting ability at the same time too. Then I telephoned the shop to warn them to have a standby fish tank of dye ready as a precaution. (How ridiculous can you get? Have a tank of rat-dye ready, love, all the rats are going grey.)

Then, at last, it was time for the BIG action, the power-house drama: Bond and his horror-stricken leggy companion trapped in the dripping sewer when suddenly the floor is alive with rats flooding down the tunnel like an evil tide: I yanked the cord to open the cage doors simultaneously and, thank God, it worked, I shook the cages to make the rats run, the cameras whirred. . . . But the rats did not run: they hopped out of the cages, stopped, blinked at the lights, sniffed around for food, no luck so they squatted on their haunches and cleaned their whiskers. One or two of them even curled up for a quick snooze when they found a warm spot under a concealed light. Try again, and again, and yet again – no good. My rats were not going to run for anybody. Being essentially domestic rats they liked the home comforts of their cages too much. The thought of venturing out into the big, strange world outside did not appeal to them.

This was not at all what the director had in mind; he did not require fat, contented rats taking their ease in front of his cameras on his hyper-expensive film set, he wanted a-c-t-i-o-n. A laconic cameraman yawned and offered the advice: 'When you open the cage doors, make like a sinking ship, man, rats always run from a sinking ship.'

For sheer inventiveness and fecund ingenuity a film set can hardly be matched. There is no shortage of ideas and the people are so technically skilled that even the daftest notions can often be made to work. They came up with the idea of a clear perspex chute to be placed inside the tunnel. 'We'll coat the surface so that nothing will be able to stand on it, then we'll pour the rats down it, they'll slide along on their bellies, on their asses, sideways, everyways, it'll look great, it's gonna be really dramatic all skidding and pouring down the sewer in a tangled mass, great, really great. . . .'

In the way of film studios, say no more, let it be done and the technicians had a hey-day working out the inclines and the *piste* of the surface. On a trial run with inanimate objects it worked like a dream. But the bloody-minded rats treated it as a challenge and tried their damndest to run up it with the result that they jammed in the middle with the stars stranded in the melee looking very disconcerted, and not at all photogenic.

Failed again.

As the animal 'expert' it was, I gathered, up to me, but a rat trainer is definitely what I am not – but I had an idea, the simplest of notions, they are usually best.

Problem: what will make an idle, lazy rat jump?

Answer: a terrier dog.

Question: what is the best breed of ratting terrier at the moment?

Answer: Jack Russell.

I suggested: 'Let's put a couple of Jack Russells out of sight at the end of the sewer tunnel, muzzle them, put them on leads and let them lurch at the rats when I release them. The rats should fly down that tunnel.'

A man was sent out to find and hire Jack Russells and two hours later he returned with three of the sharpest, keenest, most aggressive Jack Russells known to the breed, all tail-wag and eager sniffs while tugging at their leashes. 'Brilliant ratters,' said the proud owner, 'absolutely fantastic.'

'Can we make sure they don't yap?' the sound recordist queried, clearly with thoughts of a noise like the baying of the *Hounds of the Baskervilles* intruding on to his sound track. I quickly brushed the question aside.

The dogs were made ready with muzzles and lurching leads and put in place; the cages arranged, taps turned on to make the sewer drip, Bond and the girl stationed . . . lights, cameras, ACTION! Connery got his lines right first time, I opened the cages just in front of the dogs, the Jack Russells strained and lurched like good 'uns drooling at the mouth, the rats took one look and scooted down the sewer leaping and tumbling over one another in their haste to flee the threat of the dogs; the whole effect was of panic and mob hysteria in a mad rush to get away from some awful danger.

I could imagine it all through the cameraman's viewfinder, concentrated into that tight, restraining oblong it would be terrific and terrifying to watch.

Being at the despatching end, I missed the real drama at the receiving end, but it was told to me in graphic detail: the cameraman's lips had curled back into a strained smile for the first time in days, it was all working brilliantly at last. Then his expression snapped from relaxed to pained shock so sharply that it could have been recorded on the sound track; for suddenly, round the bend and smack into the middle of his vision and the action in the sewer, flying like a hot favourite out of trap six on Greyhound Derby night at the White City, came a Jack Russell trying desperately to snap and furiously frustrated by its muzzle, lead whipping the air while he thrashed and lunged at the scattering rats, slipping on the wet surface, scrambling up again and having a marvellous time – C-U-T !

Following the dog and covered in embarrassment came a stage hand explaining volubly: 'The little bastard tripped me and slipped the lead, I'd no idea he could pull like that'.

By now there was a touch of exasperation in the call: 'Round up the rats and start all over again'.

That is a short description of how it took five days to put two minutes' film in the can. It felt like five years to me.

When I telephoned Clive to tell him that we were finished and ready to come home, he said: 'Don't bring the bloody rats back here, we've nowhere to keep them. Lose them somewhere.' Thank you, Clive. Where do you 'lose' 600 rats? Somewhere between Elstree and Colindale we found a convenient, secluded wall and dumped the lot over into somebody's garden hoping that they would lose themselves – which they would. Ah, well, let's move rapidly on from that incident.

Life with Clive was seldom humdrum and usually too lively by far. I should have been warned by his business card which was emblazoned: 'Quality, integrity and a full personal service', the sort of slogan and claim which usually puts me off like it puts most people off.

'George, I want you to sleep at the shop tonight, there's

179

a chimp coming in and it is wanted on the film set first thing in the morning,' he told me one evening.

The chimp had been hired from another dealer to fulfil a film contract. Clive could not bear to admit that he hadn't got a particular beast in stock and, if it was a film or TV job, he would grab it immediately.

'What kind of a chimp?' I asked very suspiciously, knowing a bit about chimps and their propensities. 'I hope it isn't too big and I hope it isn't frisky, otherwise we will never control it.'

'Not at all,' Clive cut me short, 'it's a big one, that's what the film company wants, but I know the owner well and he assures me that it's as steady as a rock, docile. Handles like a baby, nothing to worry about *at all*, believe me, George, ever so steady.'

I have heard that sort of old guff too often to take much notice. The chimp arrived in its crate and, of course, it was massive; I thought: 'You can stay in your crate until morning, matey. We'll get you out on the film set.' I pushed in food and water, turned out the lights and bedded down. Mrs. Desmond was upstairs and Clive was out and about his businesses; he had fingers in everything. At the time he was closely associated with John Bloom in the Rolls Razor washing machine shambles which was then peaking to success before inevitably, like nemesis, financial disaster caught up and took them all to the cleaners and J. Bloom Esq. to the fraud courts.

In the middle of the night, as I had half suspected would happen, the crate began to heave and sway accompanied by sounds of breaking timbers; the chimp wanted walkies. I had made my emergency plans for such a possibility – like a quick dash to the stairs leading upstairs to observe developments from a vantage point with a substantial door nearby to be slammed if necessary – and sucks to Mrs. D's sense of the proprieties.

The crate crumbled and the chimp emerged from the wreckage looking like King Kong appearing among the skyscrapers of New York. He was a big fella, a *very* big fella indeed, and I decided – since we had not been formally introduced – not to tangle with him or impede his progress. We had lodged him in the dealing section of the establishment which was behind the shop fronting on to

180

the pavement. It was only a small shop but crammed with a wide variety of stock, dozens of parrots, tropical birds, small mammals, reptiles and fish plus the paraphernalia for keeping and feeding them. Such a glittering array through the dividing door attracted our friendly monster; chimpanzees are notoriously inquisitive apes which are always intrigued by novelty, so what else than that chimp should lumber along to investigate the cheeps, chirps and tinkling bells next door?

What he found fascinated him, so he ripped each and every cage from the walls, toppled the tanks, sat on and squashed other cages and finally squatted among the bedlam of screeching, hissing and squawking livestock, part of which was trying to gobble up the other part while the remainder squabbled vociferously for any available safe perch and the shop shuddered when chimp made an occasional leap to a better place.

'Your pal's ever so steady chimp,' I could not resist remarking to Clive when he returned, 'could register seven on the Richter Scale if he snored in his sleep.' Surveying the wreckage, Clive nodded disconsolately.

Crates were not a problem. We had plenty and we soon knocked up a robust one. Then I had to make friends and influence the chimp with a basket of fruity goodies and a lot of soft talk to get him back in his cage. I jumped into the crate with the goodies with the objective of jumping out again before he could and slamming the lid down, but he was quicker than me most times and thought that it was the greatest game invented since swinging in trees. We were in and out of the crate like a Jack-in-the-box on amphetamines until he got greedy and went back for a second helping of some fruit I'd dropped and we dropped the heavy lid. Normally we would have given him a good hiding with a heavy object and left him to it, but he had to be unmarked and happy for the morning's work. I hope that doesn't shock you too much, but a good wallop often works wonders. It is not, by any means, all done by kindness.

He was wanted for another TV job, this time to play the part of Vincent Ball's pet in the series *Compact*. He did three takes beautifully until he got bored, then the studio manager got bored with him after he pulled down three great lamps from the wall and showeted the set with sparks.

Still Clive could not resist the lure of the limelights and the disproportionate money that went with it. A call from the tinsel world blew all semblance of reason out of his mind, he just could not say no. The day the BBC next telephoned I was present when he took the call. I heard the BBC voice say: 'I understand that you are an expert in handling several species of dangerous animal, Mr. Desmond'.

'You could say that,' Clive answered preening himself, 'there isn't much I haven't handled,' he added with modesty.

'We need a king cobra, a big one if it's going to look good in the scene we have planned,' said the BBC.

'It just so happens that one of my men here is one of the world's experts in handling these big poisonous snakes,' said Clive with a smile of absolute confidence in his voice. 'I'll send him along, you couldn't have a better man.'

'Who's that?' I asked intrigued to know. 'I would like to meet him, there's a lot more I'd like to learn about snakes.'

'It's you,' said Clive, 'don't argue, there's a fiver expenses in this for you if you'll get a king cobra across to Shepherd's Bush studios. They'll just want it to wriggle about a bit, dead easy.'

I stopped outside the door and listened while he called back to the BBC. 'My man's on his way to assess the situation. It will be rather expensive since he is such an expert, at least £20 a day . . . plus the charge for the snake.'

Of course, they are charming at the BBC, lunatics like film people, but charming. They explained the scene: they were filming a series about the Crusades. There was a sword fight: one of the combatants had lost his sword, his adversary's blade was at his throat when over the adversary's shoulder there loomed a cobra. The actors played through the scene. It all looked so dicey to me that I said: 'Why not use a papier mache model, or even a stuffed cobra? You can make them look very real.'

'No, no, no, it must be absolutely authentic, we want

182

the snake's movements and the tongue darting in and out – there've been some wonderful shots like that in films.'

Clive was aghast at the suggestion that he should persuade the BBC to use models or even our eight foot python, lethal looking but harmless.

'No,' he insisted, 'they want the real stuff. They won't pay for substitutes.'

I played my trump card: 'But we haven't *got* a king cobra . . .'

'Nonsense, George, there are dozens of them about. I'm sure you can find one.'

So it had to be the zoo man's grapevine again, the way so many things habitually happen in the animal world. I went to see my pal at a reptile house, slipped him a few quid and borrowed a magnificent 13 foot king cobra in prime condition.

'Don't mess about with him,' he warned, 'they can be very tricky, watch it, and I mean *watch* it. Don't let any half-baked idiot pull any silly strokes with it. I don't want somebody dead from snake bite and the coroner demanding to know where it came from.'

That was the warning of a man who had spent most of his working life tending all the known reptiles of the world. He loved the things but treated them with the greatest respect like most reptile men do and he had reached that highly satisfying stage of feeling that he was beginning to understand them.

Since the great surge of interest in wildlife was stimulated by television, the general public has been told so often about the true nature of snakes that they must be tired of hearing it; yet though they know that snakes are not slimy, deceitful, evil creatures but rather very beautiful creations there is still no great rush to keep them as universal household pets. The irrational fear of the serpent is too deeply ingrained in human nature to be changed by well-founded knowledge. A colourful, decorative snake in the house would be as good a mouser as a cat without the disadvantage of caterwauling felines outside the door or stinking Toms inside – now here is a confession from a professional animal man – I am not a great lover of domestic cats. I can take them or leave them and I prefer to leave them.

I have kept innumerable snakes as pets in the house and I have grown fond of them; by and large snakes are only dangerous when they are annoyed, frightened, disturbed, interfered with, excited and generally messed about – just like human beings except that snakes do not go round mugging innocent people.

Television studios are not, as a rule, oases of tranquility. If you take all those names which run interminably at the end of every television programme on the credits list and assemble them all together on a studio floor, you have a crowd. Put a king cobra among them and you have an excited and annoyed snake.

Please do not ask me why they wanted a king cobra, a hamadryad, in a film which was, presumably, located in the Holy Lands when the hamadryad is an oriental species except that they wanted a big one and this species grows to almost twice the size of the common or garden Asian cobra, call it producer's licence.

With trepidation I took my basketful of venom to the studio. 'Have you got a fridge handy,' I asked, 'I want to put him in for half-an-hor or so.' The pretty girl assistant looked quizzically at me and asked: 'Why do you put a cobra in the fridge? Surely reptile houses at the zoo are heated to near tropical temperatures?' I was on the point of telling her when I had second thoughts. Not wishing to spread panic and alarm, I lied through my teeth: 'It brings a shine up on their scales, they look much better.'

The real reason is to cool them down and make them less frisky, particularly after being lugged around London in a basket, a chilled cobra is sleepy and lethargic compared with one which is heated up, so much the better.

They are too sharp, these TV cuties. 'You could oil it, that would make it shine,' she insisted.

'It doesn't like oil,' I snapped.

When later I tipped it from the basket on to the floor and uncoiled it there was a gasp, surprisingly few people have seen a big snake in the flesh. 'When does it put its hood thing up?' the director asked. A cobra's hood comes up when it raises and pushes forward its long anterior ribs stretching the skin over them to form the broad disc which is called the hood; other snakes inflate their windpipes and expand their necks.

184

Seeing all sorts of problems ahead, I thought it best to give it to him straight so I told him and the assembled crowd: 'Its hood goes up when it is bloody annoyed and looking for somebody or something to kill – and it moves quicker than lightning, so keep a respectful distance.'

'Ooooh, how thrilling, how hairy,' somebody in the audience gushed. Ignorance is bliss and if you don't know, dicing with death can seem fun.

They arranged a run through of the action so that camera angles and such like could be fixed. The two sword-fighting actors were nice lads and very cooperative. Lads like that earn their money, which isn't actually a lot, dressed in their armour and putting everything they could into the action to make it look good. Under the studio lights it was like having a strenuous workout wearing a tracksuit in a sauna bath.

My little reptilian pal was beginning to thaw out in the heat of the studio and looking distinctly more active; I was desperately trying to think how to control him in whatsoever eventuality should arise. A king cobra is not a thing you can train to do things in a few easy lessons; the more I saw, the more foolish the whole enterprise began to appear.

Sweat pouring off him and running in streams down his face and neck one of the combatants grinned and asked: 'Is this thing poisonous – really poisonous? Has it been 'doctored' or whatever you do to make them safe?'

I answered him in reverse order: 'No, it has not been doctored, you cannot do that. Yes, it is one of the most poisonous snakes known and its bite is extremely dangerous. In India several thousand people die every year because of cobra bites.'

'Holy Jesus,' said the actor. 'Jeez-zuz,' echoed his mate.

I pressed the point to an audience which had retreated quite a few feet back from the now undulating fellow on the floor. 'It is a proteroglyphous snake which means that it has fixed poison fangs set at the front of its upper jaw. In all proteroglyphous snakes the venom attacks the nervous system and its action is much more rapid than that of other types of snake whose venom acts on blood corpuscles, which is relatively slower.' It was the quietest I have ever heard a film or TV set and the crowd of on-lookers thinned out noticeably.

A curious thing is that when you do talk about the dangers of wild creatures of any kind, there is an under-current of incredulity, if not disbelief, about what you are saying. Listeners think that you are piling on the agony probably unnecessarily just for effect and to frighten them. There were such looks of disbelief in my audience though I did have two listeners paying rapt attention. 'You're joking, of course,' said one of the actors, 'I mean, there are things which you can take to counteract snake bites.'

So it took a little more blinding with science: 'Yes, in the case of viperine and opisthoglyphous snakes. Adder bites are treated every year in this country but there is not as much vaccine readily to hand as you might imagine. People get very poorly and some die from adder bites even now. There are antivenines for cobra type bites but they have to be given hypodermically and immediately. Really we should have a doctor standing by with a hy-podermic syringe.'

Actor one said: 'Excuse me, I think I'll have a word with my Equity representative'.

Actor number two said: 'Yes, I think I'll come with you'.

Heated conference. Then a smiling director approached me: 'I think we've solved this problem. You can stand in for the actor, since you know all about snakes, and we can film over your shoulder.'

Calmly, it may have been coldly, I said: 'How am I to control him if he is behind my back and I can't see him?'

We seemed to have reached a degree of mutual disen-chantment so I packed my snake in his basket and went home – feeling considerably relieved that it was all over and two crusading knights were still around to tell the tale and fight again another day.

If ever there was a boom industry which kept its success secret it is that of performing animals. It happened with television and exploded with the advent of commercial television but those involved prefer to keep a low profile because there are so many animal welfare societies with money in the bank, influential friends and loud voices when they consider animals are being misused. It is the sort of attention neither television companies nor advertisers relish. But if proof was ever needed of the pulling power of animals it lies in the use made of them by commercial advertisers: a wide range of goods from oil, petrol, and paint to teabags and toilet rolls is sold by them.

The public adores them when they appear in the finished, polished advertisement but might take a wholly different view if they were aware of the technicalities of making the films. Patience and persuasion are the two principal elements in getting animals to perform a specific act, but what might be thought of as technique by animal trainers might well be seen as cruelty by the public. There is a great deal of cruelty used by some people in training performing animals and what would horrify most onlookers would be the extent to which fire is used, fire in all its forms from burning torches to red-hot iron bars used as a threat or corrective. The inescapable fact is that an animal trainer has got to show who is boss and keep showing it; if he doesn't dominate the animals, he loses them.

I have handled dogs, cats, lions, cheetahs, tigers, chimpanzees, elephants and bears among many species for television advertising. I have even handled fish; it can be a wearing, sickening, dull business of unbelievable, unremitting boredom. Talking dog sequences, and there have been any number of them, are the ultimate in tedium for film crew, handler and animals alike when everybody concerned sits for days at a stretch waiting for the dogs to yawn or open their mouths in the correct order so that the words can be convincingly dubbed in. That is all you can do, sit and wait . . . and wait . . . and wait, try all the little dodges you know to make the dogs react, but they will only do it when they are ready. In the end it is all down to the dogs.

When animal stars did hit the headlines in the national media often it was not in a favourable way: Arthur, the famous white cat which ate its food by lifting it by paw from tin to mouth, was said to have had his teeth extracted to force him to do it that way; then he was alleged to have been stolen and there was a legal dispute as to his ownership. The squabble became very messy and did not enhance the cat food product's image.

But when animals hit the jackpot of popularity, they became as valuable as pop stars: Molly Badham put Twycross Zoo on the map when her chimpanzees scored a notable success in Brooke Bond tea commercials. She made a lot of money and a grateful Brooke Bond built a new chimp house at her zoo, complete with all mod-cons and closed-circuit television, and the public flocked to gawp at her TV stars romping about their cages. Life was good and beautiful in the Badham chimp camp while the fame and adulation lasted, but, calamity, such things are fleeting and the public is fickle. Molly's chimps were homely little fellows, lovely but with limited talents, whose act was becoming just a wee bit stale and along came a bunch of swarthy, dago Italian interlopers. The chimps from the Italian Circus Togni were full of monkey tricks even to the point that they could ice skate. They were so exceptionally talented that they won the contract and poor Molly's troup got the 'don't call us, we'll call you treatment'.

The Esso Petroleum tiger is now a full international star. He lives in America and is filmed there but the commercials appear universally and his fame is spread on posters and a mass of promotional material distributed by Esso.

The regimented penguins in the 'Pick up a penguin' chocolate biscuit advertisements all come from Edinburgh Zoo and, if you will excuse the phrase, help to keep the wolf from the door of that august establishment.

But bears, once again they are the problem animals in that they will insist in growing. So the lovable, cuddly little cubs in the Sugar Puffs commercials outgrew their usefulness and were shot.

One famous and successful bear was Andy Robbins's now famous big, brown bear Hercules who hogged the headlines when he escaped to go walkabout on his own in the Hebrides Islands. Hundreds of people hunted him and the owner offered a £2,000 reward for his return, well worth the money since he stars in the Kleenex tissues ads.

Guinness's toucan lives on the South Coast and makes a good income for his owner. The fortunes to be made for the lucky owners of exceptional animals are summed up in the value of a Cruft's champion: if your dog is voted champion, from that moment on he's worth £50,000 in advertising and breeding values.

But the profligate spending by television producers was a boon to many of us hard-up animal keepers. The order came in: 'Send one fish tank with tropical fish for use in a domestic drawing set'. And it added the instruction: '. . . plus handler'. The studio electricians had to plug in the tank and set the thermostat while I watched, because union regulations said so. I checked the thermometer in the morning and evening, tipped in a packet of fish food and spent the glorious relaxed days drinking tea and chatting up the good-looking cuties they always have as part of the furniture around television studios – all that and £15 a day too.

James Bond – filmed in black and white.

Chapter 16

. . . but did you see the kitchens?

When my love/hate relationship with Howletts and Aspinall was in its H-for-hate-it period, I travelled and worked in other zoos and safari parks. It was great experience for collecting a gallery of clowns, buffoons, eccentrics and imposters . . . human, not animal. Parliament was told during the debate on the Zoo Bill that only 25 per cent of zoos reached a required minimum standard in hygiene, safety, administration – everything. It is difficult to squeeze fun out of squalor and stupidity but we managed a few giggles. The Royal Society for the Prevention of Cruelty to Animals and other examiners saw the zoos after they had been cleaned up for inspection, front of the house stuff: my friends and I worked behind the scenes. We wanted to change things for animals and humans alike. There is no misery like a misery shared with a miserable animal. But it wasn't as simple as all that . . .

Life with Clive was a little too hectic and uncertain even for me with my predisposition for variety and excitement: excitement there certainly was but with a lack of substance which made it feel that if you shook it the whole set-up might come apart at the seams; plus the fact that it appeared to attract disaster as a way of life when its ambitions soared above its capabilities.

As it happened when the *big one*, the deal Clive had dreamed about for years, came along: 'Hundreds of thousands of pounds in it . . . money no object . . . spend what you like . . .' he enthused, 'a Tarzan-type animal film to be shot on location in Africa . . . all the big stuff, lions, rhinos, hippos, giraffes, gorillas . . . you name it, they need it. . . .'

'The job will be *director of animals*,' he rolled the phrase off his tongue as if he were The Monarch proclaiming, 'Arise, Sir Clive.' Eyes glazed he repeated: 'Director of animals . . . the opportunity of a lifetime . . . terrific, it will make us all for life. . . .' But it fell terribly flat when the would-be magnificent entrepreneur in a safari-suit explained: 'My wife won't let me go'. Then in conspiratorial tone he went on: 'It would be perfect for you, George. You go down there to Africa. I'll run it from this end, do all the organising, that's the really hard work. You'll have all the fun in the sun, all those dusky maidens and sexy film actresses. You'll have the time of your life, George.' He let the phrase roll off his tongue again with relish: 'Director of animals. . . .' In his mind's eye he was watching the credits roll at the opening in the Empire Cinema, Leicester Square.

By this time I had had dealings with quite a few film producers, directors, film actors and actresses, studio technicians with their hangers on and the motley crew of argumentative, indecisive and cantankerous supporters who make up an average film set in action and something deep down inside me – like a well-developed instinct for survival – told me that after a few months with such a shower under the hot tropical sun and in dank, steamy jungles the chances were that I would end up swinging in the trees with the monkeys. And with Clive 'organising' three thousand miles away the chances were even greater that I would prefer to take a swim with the crocodiles. The potential for disaster was unlimited so I told him: 'Not no, Clive, but Hell, no!' And he stared at me in stunned shock.

Perhaps my view was coloured at the time because we had just suffered one of the little daily contretemps which were so common to our working days. A huge consignment had arrived one evening and we spent the night unpacking, caging and bedding down hundreds of monkeys, parrots, tropical birds and so on. At lunch time next day we went to the pub to slake a thirst well-fired by excessive sweating, straw-dust, saw-dust and the dusts of South America left in the packing cases; driving back we found, to our astonishment, a great crowd collected outside the shop window. They were elbowing and shoving to get a better view. 'There is something bloody wrong here,' we exclaimed together and screeched round to the back entrance.

The monkeys had got out. Naturally, having been just uncrated and seeing real daylight for the first time for weeks they were excited and ebullient. A monkey will get his fingers into anything so a cage is not much of a deterrent once his curiosity is aroused. Then he lets out everything else in sight.

Many species are as natural enemies as a domestic cat and mouse; given half a chance they eat each other. So there was a python in the window strangling one monkey and a second python eating another; monkeys had killed birds and dead stuff littered the floor.

While we were thinking – deeply – about what to do the R.S.P.C.A. arrived, appraised the problem and commented: 'You've got a pretty tricky situation here. What do you suggest we do?'

We said: 'Go in and grab what we can and get them back into cages. Get the tricky stuff first, leave the rest until last, a lot of things will not hurt each other.'

The inspector said: 'I'll go to the car and radio for the proper catching gear. We shouldn't start without it.'

Minutes later an R.S.P.C.A. van arrived and, to the cheers of the crowd, two R.S.P.C.A. stormtroopers, looking like German riot police in full gear of visors, helmets, leather jackets, gloves and boots, tumbled out to begin the round-up – not a sight you often see in the Edgware road.

The stark truth is that most animal dealers are a shambles and in many cases a positive disgrace. Zoorama was assuredly one of the better ones, but there are very many which are fit only to be shut down as an affront not only to the animals unfortunate enough to find themselves incarcerated in them but also to the dignity and integrity of the human race which professes a regard for animals. Exactly the same remarks and criticisms apply to zoos of which only a few are worthy of the name zoological garden. Most commercial zoos and safari parks, entertainment centres, are little more than hell-holes for both animals and staff.

If there is fun and laughter in the animal world, there are tears too.

Respectability is an insidious and deceitful attribute which sneaks up on a person and ensnares him in collar, tie, shiny shoes and clean fingernails: it nearly happened to me. By God, it nearly happened to me and the thought still sends shivers down my spine.

London Zoo is regarded by many as the seat of all learning in zoology and, certainly, the expertise instantly available within that expert society is phenomenal. It isn't the best zoo in the world, not by any means. Several American and Continental zoos can knock it into a cocked hat and other zoological societies are equally progressive and, if anything, probably more adventurous. But it remains one of the great animal institutions of the world. Everybody and anybody, professional, amateur or curious, inquisitive public can learn a great deal from London Zoo.

There are usually not all that many jobs going at London Zoo. Staff tend to stay: after all it is a very good job, rather like being a member of the staff of a great cathedral and you do not get vergers and such ilk at St. Pauls nipping to the Dean and saying: 'The geyser down at Westminster Abbey has offered me an extra two nicker a week and double sippers of communion wine. What 'you going to do about it?'

However, one job always seems available: assistant keeper in the insect house. Nobby Ashby, now retired, ran the job for nearly all his life; he had a very special strain of dedication. The insect house is an essential and vital part of the zoo and on paper sounds quite fascinating. I took the job and learned a lot, indeed, everything there is to know, about window cleaning. It really was the best apprenticeship for window cleaning there ever was; every morning – bucket, squeegee and wash-leather to wipe the sticky fingermarks off the cabinets and clean the glass. (As a result I am now one of the world's most accomplished window cleaners . . . and there aren't many about anymore, as you know.) And that was the excitement of the day, followed by the feeding round carrying a little tray with a few live crickets for the scorpions, cotton wool soaked in honey for the butterflies, a teeny-weeny bit here and a morsel there.

But London Zoo breeds prodigious numbers of insects to feed its birds, fish and other insects. The locust breeding houses are below ground under the parrot house and in the summer you work there in temperatures of 90 degrees Fahrenheit without ever a glimpse of daylight, feeding them specially grown grass free from pollution by spray or chemical – tropical bird fodder; then make up the feeding trays like a nurse preparing hospital diet trays, 20 insects in one, ten in another.

Red ants provide the highlight of the experience: they will not propagate so a thrilling expedition is arranged to Burnham Beeches to dig up a few ants' nests and get bitten to pieces in the process.

The whole enterprise numbed me and, apart from that, I felt that I needed a rest from praying mantis, predatory females and a quick injection of ozone into the lungs, so – oh, you guessed – back to sea again. Not to make a meal of it this time, just a short, sharp dash and splash, a quick financial injection best achieved on the fishing boats and the best place for that was out of Stavanger. We know our geography, us footloose-and-fancy-free lads. We have to to find our ways home again. There is a marvellous underground-intelligence in the Black Economy which tells where the quick money is to be had at any given moment. All the old, familiar faces turn up.

Six months of drinking, fighting, suffering the indescribable weather and storms of those bitter northern fishing grounds: day-long greyness and black ice, towering black seas with the only warmth the thought of that thick roll of Kroner building up and waiting to burn a hole in your pocket; it is purgatory while it lasts and only good to look back on after you have stepped ashore, collected your wad and can look at the world with a sense of freedom the money will buy you.

Even now I cannot look into a fishmonger's shop without feeling colder than the fish on his slabs. Have you ever thought why fish look so sad on the marble slab? It is because of the terrible places they live in when they are alive.

Ashore again, spent up and needing a quick berth, God

forgive me, I went to Chessington Zoo, the most money-orientated zoo in the business and the biggest money-spinner. It is superbly situated from a commercial point of view with a catchment area of all the thickly populated, wealthy western outer suburbs of London which are just about far enough away from Central London, and on the wrong side of the City, to make a family visit to London Zoo an expedition rather than an outing. It has everything going for it.

Since I was at Chessington, the zoo has been sold to a new management, Madame Tussauds, and tremendous changes and improvements have been made. Though I reserve the right to say that they are not necessarily improvements which all zoo people like because they have had to stress the commercial side of the business in order to keep the enterprise viable. I think that they were courageous to take on a zoo and try to run it profitably, zoos have a tendency to eat fortunes away – quite literally, the profits often go down the animals' mouths.

Sincerely, I wish them the best of success. At least they have the commercial know-how to make it work and it has the potential to be one of the finest zoos in Britain.

They won't mind me saying that they bought a headache.

Yet you will not find a genuine zoo man who, at the time I am speaking of, could find in his heart one good thing to say about it from any aspect: animals and their conditions or staff and their subhuman conditions. I met a man at Chessington, a pitiable specimen, who had lived in an old banger of a car in the zoo car park for three years. He got up at six o'clock in the morning and did whatever ablutions he could from the boot of the jalopy. He had one outfit of clothes which had become biologically integrated with him. He looked after the sealions and he stank. If only he had been the exception there might have been some excuse, but he wasn't.

Harry Snazell had his office in an old mansion called Burnt Stubbs, which they said was so called because it had caught alight once or twice. He had been a catering manager who had worked his way up to run a zoo though he had no zoological qualifications. It was a big zoo with a lot of exhibits though, as time went by, it could more properly have been called an amusement park with animals – the dodgems definitely took precedence over the deer park and the primate house keeper would be rapidly seconded to run the ghost train if the need arose.

The office was furnished with polar bear rugs and leopard skins on the walls, made from former inhabitants. Harry sat behind an impressive desk. 'You look a likely lad,' he greeted me, 'and you seem to have done quite a bit, quite experienced really. Can you handle men? Well, you're big enough to, shouldn't have too much trouble in that area.' He appointed me head keeper on the spot just on my own say so about what I had done and how I looked.

The order was: 'Start now, as soon as possible.' So I collected my gear and made my way to The Black Hole of Chessington which was to be my home.

'There it is,' said the gateman pointing to a shabby concrete block with a cracked and battered door and a couple of brown-stained windows, 'that's the bunk house.'

'Bunk house?' I queried somewhat taken aback by the appearance of the place, 'it looks more like a bunker to me.'

'That's right,' the gateman exclaimed giving me a surprised look. 'How did you know that? Have you been here before? It used to be the old coal bunkers. They had 'em swept out and a few beds put in, the lads live there now.'

The walls may have been swept at the time of the change of use but never again. There was no sign that paint had ever been used on them; the same applied to the concrete floor the only covering of which was a layer of yellowing, torn newspapers littered with used baked beans and soup tins. An old nissen hut stand-up stove with a bare pipe through the roof provided heat and cooking facilities, a covering of coke-dust covered the metal plate the stove stood on and coke-dust footprints led from it to all parts of the room. Around the walls were two- and three-tier bunks each with a horse blanket, one of those was your bed and bedclothes complete. At the far end of the room was a lavatory with no door surrounded by sheafs of torn-up newspapers. In a corner

196

was a sink stained brown with black streaks with the original white showing through around the top rim. The air was rank with a mixture of sweat, bad breath and carbon dioxide fumes from the leaky stove-pipe; the sharp blade of a penknife could only scratch a streak of light in the stain on the windows.

A bedraggled shambles of unshaven humanity, squatting on a lower bunk near the stove, gave a yellowed smile and said: 'Grab a mug, help yourself to a coffee'. The first Nescafe tin was empty so he threw it toward a cardboard box and missed. The tin rolled clattering across the floor until it struck a Heinz baked beans tin with its jagged lid protruding. I tried to drink the brew without the mug rim touching my lips. Another staff member bustled in, hurried to the lavatory, took a tightly folded newspaper from a pocket, dropped his jeans and sat on the pan calling out the runners at the afternoon's race meetings. ' 'a fancy that bastard at Lingfield that bloody Lindley mount the bastard that let us down last Sat'dy din'na yews Alex?' He said in a broad Glaswegian accent.

Alex could only respond with gutteral grunts which could have meant yes or no or don't care. His grunts were matched by those of the man on the throne going about his natural functions completely unself-consciously.

Squalor, pestilence ridden filth, degrading and dehumanising conditions, those were the living standards of the staff at Chessington Zoo; conditions which would have been intolerable in the worst days of the Glasgow Gorbals and would certainly have been unbelievable to the affluent housewives of the neighbouring salubrious Home Counties suburbs driving past the gates to drop hubby at the station en route to his respectable City job and uniformed children at the gates of their private schools. Had they known but half the truth they would have treated the place like a leper colony or razed it to the ground.

The animal superintendent was Eddy Orbell who is a respected man in the business, recognised as knowing his job, but to me – and to many who subsequently were trapped into serving a period of time in the wretchedness of Chessington – it was apparent that he was completely constrained by the overweening money-grubbing approach of the organisation. The philosophy was to squeeze the public till the pips squeaked then put them through the wringer to extract the last drops.

Without reservation we in the serious zoo fraternity condemned Chessington, but it raises other disturbing questions. What was the local authority doing at the time? What were the medical officer and his health department about? Include in those questions the Environmental Officer, Sanitary Department, Planning Department and the rest of them employed at fat salaries to protect the public's interest.

I put that as a question to them. Local authorities do not like being criticised or called to question, but the whole time I was at Chessington, I never saw any evidence of them doing anything to improve the conditions.

So I criticise them because I had to live under the conditions I have described . . . and I think that gives me the right to question. To a great extent it must have been their responsibility that they allowed humans at Chessington Zoo to live like pigs in such conditions that if a pig farmer had dared to house his herd in a similar way, he would have certainly been prosecuted.

If they kept their people like that, imagine how they kept their animals. They were mostly in little boxes with iron bars – and that was the 'respectable' part the public could see, behind the scenes was awful. There were no facilities for locking off animals while cleaning and maintenance work was done on the cages so the system was to stick a hosepipe through the bars and squirt out as much muck as you could. Hosing by itself, as any housewife who has cleaned a yard or husband who has washed a car will tell you, does not get things clean. And how could you expect a bunch of degenerates such as were employed there to keep animals hygienic when they could not keep themselves clean?

The staff: we had the man who had not changed his clothes for three years and who had seen nothing more than a running tap for his occasional wash; an ex-porno filmmaker on the run from the vice squad; two others who were on the run for offences they cared not to discuss; a couple of diseased male prostitutes; an ex-convict just out of Wormwood Scrubbs and sundry others for whom the description deadbeats filled the bill. Many of them came from the twilight world of travelling fairgrounds and the small circus. The calibre of the workforce was shown when the police paid a visit, which they frequently did, nine-tenths of the staff would just melt into obscurity. They were nowhere to be seen. About four people could be classified good, conscientious workers who could be relied upon to keep the show running.

In such circumstances the death toll could only be heavy and stock was lost at a sickening rate. At the best of times, with top-class staff and good housing, it is tricky to keep animals in good health. They are living artificial lives and have to be watched with great care. Here they just gave up the ghost, laid down and died.

Our degenerates were as quick as the management to see the chance of making a fast, cheeky buck. I wondered why the job of feeding the sealions was so popular: the lads fought to get it and a rush of volunteers for a cold, slimy, smelly task was out of character until the truth was revealed. A sharp-eyed money-man had thought up a scheme whereby the public could be persuaded to pay for the sealions' food on the guise of having an extra bit of fun. Buckets of herrings were taken to the pond and sold to the public to throw to the sealions at the so-called feeding time, so-called because feeding time then became anytime a big enough crowd was gathered and there was money to be earned, the public paid their pennies for the thrill of tossing a portion of fish into the pool and watching the acrobatic sealions catch it.

The opportunities for fiddling were endless. The attendants chopped up the fish into small portions and charged the full amount for them; it was easy to extract more than the ration from the cold store, sell it and pocket the money; waste from local fish and chip shops was collected and put into a keeper's secret storehouse to be sold to the public at the right time: whatever profit the management made from the deal, the keepers quintupled it for their own benefit. The management need not have worried had they known, it all went back over the bar in the cafe.

Never were there so many overfed, bloated sealions in

199

a zoo pool and when the time came to clean out the pool the folly of the enterprise was revealed.

It was cleaned out once a week and the bottom of the pool was inches deep in a covering of rotting, decomposing fish, which had accumulated because hundreds of people a day were chucking fish in.

Let me give you a couple of examples of the sort of thing that happened witnessed by a number of us: Ben, the hippo, was a great favourite with the public, a good crowd puller. So it was decided to make him more comfortable and coax him out to his outside quarters even when it was a bit too chilly for his taste. A fine scheme was set afoot to give him a heated swimming pool and the zoo staff installed it themselves.

The great opening day arrived, the heating was switched on, the pool warmed to the desired temperature and old Ben plunged in. He loved it, he wallowed, snorted and blew and clearly considered the arrangement a great improvement on previous conditions. It suited him so well that after a few minutes, he began to play his favourite hippo games which included great barrel rolls, which he always did when he was pleased with the world. A few tons of hippo barrel-rolling in a confined space is spectacular and delights the crowd. But on one of his more enthusiastic spins, poor old Ben got entangled with one of the electric cables and wrenched it away from the wall. It broke, there was a blue flash, a puff of smoke and the pool was electrified. End of Ben.

A family of four in the gorilla house got an even bigger shock. Mum and dad and their two children were watching a big gorilla indulging in one of most gorillas' favourite pastimes, leaping with tremendous force against the plate glass window which forms a side of the cage. Many zoos now have these windows which show off the apes to far better advantage than having them behind bars.

You can see them used to great effect at Bristol Zoo where the display can be quite spectacular. They are popular and usually very safe and the gorillas love them, they get as much fun from watching the public reaction as the public does from watching their antics.

You cannot blame Chessington Zoo for what happened

this day, they were following a tested and tried technique in the best of faith and for the public's better enjoyment.

The gorilla made a spectacular leap against the glass, the family of four cringed in a thrilled reflex action. Wallop! The gorilla hit the glass and CRASH! It shattered and the gorilla flew straight through.

Pandemonium broke out.

There were shrieks and screams. The family scattered. Other visitors dashed in all directions, there was a mad rush to the doors.

The gorilla was the most shocked of the lot. He was terrified and stunned. It was the end of his safe, secure world and he thought the whole thing a dirty trick and wanted nothing to do with it.

So he made for the door as well, quicker than the public. Being elbowed out of the way by a frightened gorilla is a demoralising experience when you are shocked and shattered yourself. So a trembling, frightened group stood shivering outside the gorilla house while a trembling frightened gorilla leapt around the flower gardens. He was reluctant to go back and sat in the flower bed clutching his keeper's hand.

The British public is incredible. They all went to the manager's office to check that they were all right . . . and they all laughed it off as a big joke.

Chessington, in my time there, was a hell-hole for man and beast providing conditions unacceptable in any modern society. The bunker was simply unfit for human habitation, insanitary, disgusting and a hazard to health. The local authority as much as the then management should be condemned for allowing it to exist.

To be fair and accurate, things did improve over the years but only marginally. Julian Buffery worked there after I had left. He describes his living conditions in the mid-1970s: 'When I arrived I was shown my room, a wardrobe and a mattress on the floor were the only pieces of furniture in it. The previous occupant must have been either eccentric or deranged, the wall and ceiling were covered with thousands of little red arrows all pointing the same way and crawling like a swarm of beetles over every inch. The wardrobe door was hanging off and the floorboards were bare. There was one slopping pit be-

201

tween seven people, one loo with a leaking cistern, a cracked sink and a leaking roof over our heads. But my conditions were good compared with those of a mutual friend of ours, George Gissing. He lived above the aquarium between the water tanks in a space infested with mice to plague proportions.'

As I said, Chessington has changed under the management of Madame Tussauds, the world famous waxworks exhibitors. The bunker dormitory has gone, new accommodation for staff and animals has been built. The incidents I have described happened before Tussauds bought the property. The new management talk of great plans for improvements and everybody wishes them great success, in fact, prays for their success. But they must forgive a degree of scepticism on zoo men's part. Realistically, keepers believe that all animals' voracious appetites have a habit of eating away all commercial owners' best intentions. No slur is intended upon the owners, it is just a fact of animal life that the costs of keeping them usually make a zoo totally unprofitable. Parliament, in considering the problem of animal welfare in zoos, could have done a service to all by considering what can be done about the problem. Commercially it is virtually insolvable.

The capital now needed to keep a zoo running is phenomenal; as officialdom and the public become more aware of the animal problem in zoos, increased safety precautions present an enormous bill to owners. It could easily become a charge which no private or commercial owner could possibly sustain, or be expected to. The World Wildlife Fund, Greenpeace, Friends of the Earth and the burgeoning conservation societies throughout the world have succeeded in instilling the plight of the world's wildlife into the public conscience. There is now a strong public revulsion at the uncontrolled slaughter of wildlife and unnecessary cruelty to animals, and public opinion is the most powerful factor in forcing change and improvements. It could easily happen that through the public conscience, public interest and instruction in wild animals may have to become a charge on the public purse since private pockets will not run deep enough.

In buying Chessington, Tussauds came up against the hard facts of owning a zoo and making a profit. They promised, and made, many improvements to the actual zoo part of the complex. For instance, a magnificent new bird garden.

But, and nobody blames the owners of Chessington Zoo, they had to concentrate on expanding the money-spinning sides of the business. So they put up new gift shops and a huge new slot-machine shed. Then a massive new carpark which the *Observer* newspaper – that ever aware journal in zoo matters – described as 'having all the alluring qualities of a lunar landscape'.

In all honesty, they ought to rename the place Chessington Amusement Park. Soon after they took over, Tussauds' new management toured American zoos on a fact-finding mission. On his return, the General Manager, Mr. Ian Richardson, lectured the staff on the management's findings. It was significant that animal keepers were told about:

Litter: how to handle it cheaply.
Novelties: how to sell more of them.
Ice-cream: how to push more of it to the public.
Car parks: how to use them profitably.

All, without question, perfectly legitimate commercial points but the animals were accorded only five minutes of the whole talk.

The sadness of Chessington in the past has been that it is the best situated of all British zoos, better even than London Zoo, with a catchment area of millions in the thickly-populated west of London area, plus good access by rail and road. A natural born money-spinner, a great crowd puller, by all standards it should have been one of the finest zoos in Europe with all its advantages of potential paying customers and cash flow. Yet it was run in the way I've told you. Imagine, if you can, conditions in the other 75 per cent of establishments the R.S.P.C.A. has classified as substandard, when they can hardly scratch together an income.

The answer to the problem of substandard zoos is to open the cage door and let out a scandal of horrifying proportions: let out the filth, the squalor, the health risk, the danger and let out the cruelty which would scandalise the nation.

If many zoos are bad, which few will deny, they are paradise compared with safari parks which, in two decades have proliferated throughout the land.

Let me take you on safari. All you will need is your binoculars, leave your gun at home, we will not be shooting anything – not even safari park proprietors. So leave the gun at home, if you have it with you temptation might prove too much.

A safari park owner had a huge aviary which was an acute embarrassment because it was empty and members of the public were complaining that they weren't getting their money's worth.

That saddened the safari park proprietor because, in the rush of novelty, cars were queuing for miles along the roads outside his establishment anxious to pay the two, three or four pounds entrance fee. He had never seen ready cash like it before in his life. (Not all of it went to him. In those early, terribly disorganised days many gatemen worked on the principle of one for him, two for me, or in generous mood, two for him, one for me.)

The proprietor did not like complaints which, he argued, might affect the rush of customers. He ordered: 'Get some bloody birds in *quick*. No, I don't give a twopenny toss what kinds of birds, just get some bloody birds in. As long as they flap about and tweet, that's all that matters.'

Dealers were telephoned. A consignment of diamond doves from Africa had arrived at a dealer's in the Midlands. The safari park bought the lot and they were hurriedly transported by lorry. When they arrived, the proprietor ordered: 'Get them in the bloody aviary. I want 'em all in there by the time the punters start coming in tomorrow morning.'

Untrained staff hammered, axed and crowbarred open the crates and released the terrified birds into the open aviary. It was spring and the early morning frosts were severe; in the morning the aviary floor was littered with the corpses of eighty per cent of the consignment.

The proprietor telephoned the dealer: 'Those bloody ducks you sent me weren't much cop, mate. They've all bloody died on me. Get me another bloody load down in a hurry.'

The dealer explained that the consignment was virtually one year's supply for the whole cage bird trade. They came from a particular forest and he couldn't obtain any more for months.

Livid at being thwarted the proprietor fumed: 'I want those bloody birds. If you want to do any more business with me, you'll get that bloody forest cleared and them birds in my park.'

Still on safari, I spent some time at Windsor when it opened. The staff who opened Windsor Safari Park were such hard cases, so tough, so wild, so brutal and sinisterly arrogant that the desperate management ordered: 'Get rid of them. They are terrifying the public and frightening away paying customers.' But nobody dared to dismiss them. Nobody would risk the consequences of walking up and saying: 'You're fired, collect your wages and your employment cards'. Other ways had to be found to ease and winkle them out.

They were physically immensely strong and mentally hard-minded men with no respect for authority of any kind except that which could lay them flat in an argument and that was because of their training and their lives. They were travelling men who had followed the touring circuses and fairgrounds and were used to throwing about several tons of heavy equipment every other day, who even performed as strong men, tumblers, acrobats, boxers in fairground booths; men of considerable physical prowess but essentially men who had always been on the outside of society and who had, almost as a routine, punched and fought their ways out of successive trouble spots all over the country. The public labelled them gypsies. Some were genuine Romanies but most were just travellers who knew no law because they were always on the move and one jump ahead of local police. A vicious punch-up in Huddersfield one night could be forgotten because the following day they would be in Suffolk, miles away, and two days later in Bedfordshire and the police could never catch up.

This is not to suggest that they looked for trouble – usually they didn't – but the word gypsy, whether truly or falsely applied, is so emotive that trouble sought them out.

That was the atmosphere I walked into. The management knew that I had been around animals for a long time and was thrilled to find somebody who had at least a modicum of knowledge about livestock. Exactly the same criteria applied as at Chessington, the first consideration was: 'Can you handle men?'

Can you handle men, did he say? Gorillas, lions, tigers, hippos and elephants, yes, I'll take them in my stride. But handle this lot! If you said to them: 'Nice day, you're doing a great job', they looked at you as if you were some sort of con-man nutter and you could see the thought going through their minds, 'Should I duff him over now, or should I leave it until after the tea break?'

The management issued them with rifles. They actually gave them guns and ammunition: ·303 ex-army rifles powerful enough to knock over a horse at half-a-mile. Yet these men had no arms training and most had no idea how to use the weapons should they be required to. But the men loved the effect of being so well-armed, it satisfied their egos; they lounged around smiling knowing, leery smiles at the girls while twirling their rifles like John Wayne doing fancy things – one-handed – with his trusty Winchester while sitting astride his horse. Meanwhile the innocent, unknowing public, with its multitudes of offspring in tow, trailed around the park secure in cars and in the false belief that, should an animal escape and go berserk, they were safe with trained marksmen guarding them, alert, attentive and every one a crack shot.

When the weapons had to be handed in to the gunroom at night there were always bullets missing. Nobody quite knew who had bullets or how many; who didn't have bullets, who should have had bullets or who shouldn't. Arms issue at the park was an army drill sergeant's nightmare, if anybody had cared about spare ammunition floating around unaccounted for.

Such was the character of the inmates of the place that I had a theory that some of the real toughies bit off the heads of the bullets and chewed the gunpowder when they ran out of baccy.

Our immediate job at Windsor was to release forty lions into the park – and that is easier said than done – it is not possible to turn out a pride of lions like a herd of pedigree Jersey cows. Account must be taken of the lions' natural territorial imperative; each group must be allowed to stake out its own territory and then trained to stay in it. Lions fight if one trespasses into another's territory. We lost a number through fighting over this. But there was a quarantine area attached to the park so in the dead of night we switched the corpse for a live and kicking lion from quarantine. It was virtually impossible to check the identity of a switched lion even if anybody suspected that they had been changed, which they never did – or if they did, they never raised the matter. One lion or lioness looks pretty much like another to a busy, bustling veterinary surgeon and he isn't too concerned about them when his fortune lies in treating pet poodles for wealthy widows.

The staff at Windsor, apart from the heavy-mob of yobbos, was bizarre: my assistants were a dentist's son who had just finished university and either could not find a job or decide what he wanted to do, a nice enough lad – lion keeper, BA (Sociology), and a convicted confidence trickster who had just finished a five-year stretch in prison. These two, inexperienced and grassy-green as they were, steered clear of trouble but two very experienced lion men were badly mauled. There was Carlos, the head lion keeper, who was himself disembowelled and wanted to subpoena me as a witness to his injuries. I was saved from a court appearance when a settlement was reached out of court.

The fun came when worried managers began to realise that the 'wild bunch' out among the crowds in the rolling acres were beginning to intimidate the public and frighten them. A look from one of these lads could be as scary as a snarl from a lion. 'Get rid of them,' the management said, 'they've got to go. Get rid of them.' Me? Not likely, not that lot. Instead of telling them, I whispered into a few ears that they were paying double the money down the road at so-and-so's park and there was a free beer ration in the refreshment rooms after work. Soon we had a shortage of staff.

No matter how strongly aristocratic proprietors and circus showmen protest their passionate love of wildlife, the motivating passion was profit. Fortunes were won, and not only for the lucky owners who coined money quicker than they could bank it in the days when it was new and fascinating and public interest intense; contractors who built the installations and erected miles and miles of high, tough fencing grew rich on the boom.

At first doubters had sniggered at the Marquess of Bath when he announced that his vast stately home, Longleat, in Wiltshire, was to become a safari park. Lord Bath and his lions became a standing joke in pubs, clubs and holiday camp variety shows. Then, after the first Bank Holiday weekend he was open, came the photographs and newsreel coverage of cars queuing for miles to get into Longleat, cars with their drivers clutching folding money in their hot, sticky little hands desperate to pay to watch nature's glories running free and untrammelled in a natural habitat. 'Keep all doors locked, close all windows, do not get out, Danger, Danger, Danger' vivid notices proclaimed – all part of the new thrill the public flocked to experience.

Nothing motivates the British aristocracy more than greed and nothing inspires them to instant action more than the smell of quick, big profits. The eccentric, wise old sage of Longleat smiled among the priceless treasures of his great house as he listened to the clink of safari park gold dropping into his coffers while every impoverished nobleman with a mortgage on his property, a bank overdraft and an encumbrance on his assets hot-footed to his bank to raise the money to fence his estate and buy exotic wildlife to put into the enclosures. The animals got a very rough deal. In most cases the way animals were treated was little short of scandalous in a country of so-called animal lovers.

Safari park owners and zoo proprietors are in legitimate commercial business. They break no laws, they infringe no statutes. They are good, honest businessmen out to make a profit and if the public pays to buy what they offer, honour is fully satisfied. Huff and puff as they may about their integrity and dedication to the cause of conservation, it is only a part of the sales technique to bring in paying customers; public interest in conservation and the preservation of wildlife is good for business so they support and encourage it. But this is when they begin to be a little bit morally dishonest with the public since profit is their motive, not the protection of species.

The plain facts are that, wholly legal though they may be, conditions for animals in the parks are often deplorable to the point of being reprehensible. A hyena arrived at a safari park in a crate, the top was partially opened to see what it was; there was nowhere to put it. The animal was left unattended and unfed until it began to eat its own limbs, it chewed its own legs and had to be shot when this was accidentally discovered by a passing employee who was curious as to what the crate contained.

Horror story piles upon horror story in the remarkably short history of safari parks. Genuine keepers are shocked to tell them. And criticism of conditions in safari parks leads to a thunder-blast of denial and protest from park operators; it is a hugely PR and publicity-orientated industry and consequently anything that comes out of a safari park information office is suspect. I have worked in them, I have earned my crust in them, I have taken my personal profit from them; I confess to shame at the part I played, but I reserve the right to criticise and question the owners' intentions.

Not all shambles in zoos come about through conditions, people often cause them. Funny people, crazy people, nice people and many as daft as brushes but it is all part of the fascination of the job if you can stand the pressure. If you put a group of unpredictable animals with a group of equally unpredictable human beings together in a confined space all you have to do is to wait until the mixture explodes. Then you pick up the pieces. I have picked up a few pieces myself in my time, as you may have gathered. To be fair, I have been picked up in pieces myself on quite a few occasions also.

The trouble is that there is an awful lot of amateurism and shamateurism in a business which, in consideration of the creatures we are caring for, should be highly professional.

I did not stay long in safari parks, I didn't like them. They had all the disadvantages of a craze where people had rushed to cash in while the craze was hot and a lot of people who should never have been allowed within biting or kicking distance of sensitive animals jumped on the bandwagon. The pity being that *they* didn't get bitten or kicked, while the public and animals did.

So, with wife, two toddlers and assorted animals and pets, I went walkabout again. In the usual way of the business, I met a man in London and took a job on the spot at a zoo I had never seen and didn't know a lot about.

Cricket St. Thomas was the prettiest of zoos, fresh as an old English country garden, bright with colour, tranquil and inviting. It was run to all intents and purposes by the sort of benign old gent who might well answer the door at the end of the path through that old English country garden. He was Mr. Hugh Taylor, retired pig farmer and father of Mr. John Taylor, one of the zoo's directors, and his attitude to zoo wildlife was summed up in the phrase: 'Now, if that was a pig, I'd do so-and-so . . .' Conversation went thus: 'Er, Mr. Taylor, one of the Asian green broadbills in the tropical birdhouse looks a bit dickie this morning. It's off its food and shedding plumage.'

'Oh dear. Now, if that were a pig I'd give it so-and-so. . . .'

They had an elephant which had won itself quite a reputation as becoming an unmanageable menace to keepers so I went to look after it. Not that I fully appreciated that she was the nasty, ill-tempered beast she was, when I took the job. Twiggy, she was called and it suggested a fun creature with a giggly personality like the model-cum-filmstar she was named after. But this Twiggy had a black nature. Let me digress for a moment about bad elephants.

When an elephant goes bad, it goes the whole way, it can seldom – I would say never – be redeemed. Back in Hannover Zoo, my hero Wolfgang Rhanin has a rogue bull, the biggest elephant I have ever looked after, a full six tons of venom. He had killed six keepers: one he had trapped between his tusks on the ground, rolled him and, as elephants always do, knelt on him. The man was turned to a jelly. They had to sweep him up. There was nothing left. Another he had speared with his tusks, the tusk went right through the keeper and protruded from his back; he was in his death throes on the tusk while the elephant walked round picking up apples in its trunk and eating them.

Wolfgang was the only person who could control it, but he was special with elephants. 'Lie down,' he would order the brute, and it rolled on to its side like a sheepdog responding to its master's commands. Two hours later it would still be lying there waiting for the instruction to get up. But only for Wolfgang.

Twiggy picked me up in her trunk as soon as I walked into her cage and chucked me on the ground. Then she tried to kill me. I had learned a lot from Wolfgang in Hannover, like how to get out of the way of an elephant with murderous intentions. It takes two ingredients, fear and agility and the first breeds the second. I moved – fast. And from that moment on it was one continuous battle of wits with me keeping well out of her reach. Even when in close proximity to her, I approached on her blind sides, leaving plenty of get-out-quick space around me and keeping the elephant goad always ready to prod her sensitive parts, while she got meaner and meaner in determination to get me.

She had maimed her two previous keepers and it was clearly folly to keep her in a small family zoo where, should she feel like it, which she would one day, she could do untold damage and even put the public at risk. The only suitable place for her was a big zoo with staff and ample facilities to control and look after her, so she was sold. But even that course failed: she injured a couple more keepers who, though they had been warned about her evil habits, had, unfortunately, not been quick enough to dodge. They shot her.

That wasn't the only thing from Cricket St. Thomas that managed to get shot. Among all the prettiness and charm lurked an ugly incident waiting to happen: every beautiful rose in the garden had more than its fair share of doubly-sharp thorns, the place was accident prone – but some of the accidents were less accidental than others.

One of the best and most expensive shoots in the West Country was organised at Cricket St. Thomas. It was very exclusive and all the big guns of the county came down for it. There were five beats a day, up one field, down another, with plenty of good stuff to shoot at. In the evening came the highspot of the day – the mallard; excitement mounted, the keenest guns could hardly contain themselves, they hurried to their positions. Normally the mallard landed on a lake in an isolated part of the zoo grounds and the beaters went out in a boat to put them up and bang, bang, bang – honour was satisfied, congratulations all round, 'Wonderful day's shooting'.

But this evening they had landed in the duck paddocks in the main part of the zoo. The paddocks were in a small valley which ran through the grounds; in some of the paddocks were deer and llama and then compounds of ornamental duck, flamingo and the like. Quite a lot of them were pinioned, but many weren't. Half a dozen furtive figures appeared at the top of the valley loitering around and awaiting a signal. 'What are you doing?' I asked.

'We're going to beat down the valley, Old Man Taylor told us to.'

I spotted the old boy lower down the valley and thundered towards him. 'The ornamental duck, the flamingos, the deer and llama,' I gasped.

'That'll be all right,' he said, 'only the mallard will fly.'

Too late! Much too late. The whistle blew, beaters moved purposefully forward with the precision of a well-drilled infantry platoon their approach filling the evening sky with squawking birds and the rush of beating wings; the guns were sharp and in fine fettle: crack, crack . . . crack, crack, crack . . . crack. Llama and deer bolted at the din; the thrashing of wings reached a crescendo as more birds fled in wild panic and pinioned ones scrambled frantically trying to get airborne. The guns cracked on and acrid whiffs of gunpowder drifted on the gentle breeze; birds were falling like rain from the skies, ornamental duck, crane, mallard, expensive rarities and common or garden geese all mixed in together.

'Brilliant shoot, marvellous,' the jubilant guns chorused as happily they tramped back up the hill.

212

In the first light of morning I took the grub down at feeding time, but there were far fewer than the day before. Misfortune dogged Cricket St. Thomas and Michael, who was in charge of the reptile house, would have made a perfect mascot for the zoo; he had written a book about reptiles and keeping them as domestic pets, but as a practical, working zoo keeper he was utterly jinxed. He too was dogged by misfortune and he could spread it like a contagious disease. If Michael crossed my path in the morning followed by fifty jet black cats all meowing and rubbing round my legs, I would still think it wiser to go back to bed and stay there for the day such was the luck he attracted. He had been bitten, clawed, kicked, butted, trunked, stung or damn near pecked to death by every living creature in the zoo; he had only to cast a passing glance in the direction of an animal and it would savage him.

Arm in arm, two gossipy old dears came out of the reptile house smiling happily in a mock-shocked way as if they had received an improper suggestion and were really well pleased about it because they imagined they were past it.

'That young fellow with the snakes is a bit bold,' said one with a semi-bashful smile, 'he tried to frighten us. I'd be terrified to touch those snakes but he's not a bit frightened. Tell him it's very naughty to try to frighten two old widow ladies – merry widow ladies,' she added with a giggle.

'Frighten?' I asked. 'How did he frighten you?'

'Well, he didn't really. I've seen it all on the television before, so we weren't really scared,' the old dear continued, 'wrestling with that big snake and falling about all over the floor. Oooh, I mean, really grappling with it, he did it very well.'

We found him on the floor of the reptile house completely encoiled in the grip of the reticulated python and showing all the symptons of imminent asphyxiation, his colour had gone with his breath and his eyes had a faraway look. Uncoiling a reticulated python, a really big one, is quite a tricky job and needs considerable persuasion. Afterwards he said: 'I can't think how it happened, the damn thing had been asleep for a fortnight'.

Michael's embarrassment was just one of many incidents. I walked around that floral paradise expecting disaster to spring from behind every hydrangea bush. The jinx spread to the inanimate as well as the animate. The zoo was keen on publicity and jumped at opportunities to lecture to Women's Institutes and similar organisations. They sent me to talk to a group in the village hall at East Parrock, or some similar sounding place – very Somersetish.

'Take the projector and film and just talk over it as it's running. Talk about the animals as they appear, you know them all, it's dead easy,' said Old Man Taylor when I protested that I hadn't seen the film and knew nothing about it.

I followed somebody who had been talking about flower arranging and was so knowledgeable that she overran by half-an-hour and still hadn't got it all in.

The film began to run and I could not recognise a thing on it. I said: 'Hang on a minute . . .' The ladies waited expectantly. New but still strange views. 'I don't know anything about that.' More changes of scene and still not a familiar view or animal. I said: 'I don't know anything about that.' I got tired of saying: 'I don't know anything about that.' So I gave them a chat about shooting crocodiles, it was the only thing I could think of at the time.

It was a beautiful little zoo and they had spent a lot of money, care and thought on the tropical bird house. As well as elephants, tropical birds are a passion with me. The tropical bird house had fountains, waterfalls, luxuriant growths of tropical flora and some very good exhibits indeed, as well as plenty of space, plenty of room for the birds to fly about without undue restriction. This was how birds should be kept and displayed. In the lush, humid conditions aphids and insects thrived as well, and the house was plagued with greenfly. I suggested that a bunch of small greenfly eating birds should be imported, which is what most zoos do to control insect pests and it works – good for the zoo, you have a captive dinner for your stock. But instead, horticultural experts were called in. They arrived and went into action with commendable efficiency. One man came with a huge tank on his back. It had to be plugged into the mains to work the fan;

214

another man with a variety of sprays to reach every nook and cranny of the building.

'This will shift every greenfly in the place. You'll have no more bother with them,' the head de-infester smilingly promised. They fastened up their protective clothing, pulled on their face masks and moved in belching a fine mist before them as they slowly traversed the length of the aviary.

A fine, penetrating, lethal mist.

Ten minutes later there was complete silence in the house, birds in a tragic mockery of their brilliant plumage, lay cold and dead on the floor. The plants thrived.

It was far too expensive to replace that splendid stock: some of the exhibits were valued at more than £300 each. To fill the empty house a batch of budgerigars and zebra finches was rapidly bought. They ate the plants and paradise was transformed into desert.

But that is the story of the modern world in a microcosm: science and nature have become incompatible; throughout the length and breadth of the land whole species of magnificent birds of prey have been brought to the brink of extinction by scientific farming techniques, if not poisoned directly, poisoned in the food chain from insect to small mammal to bird.

Yet at Cricket St. Thomas we enjoyed one of those wonderful once-in-a-lifetime experiences: we watched a life come back from beyond the dead. It caused us to suffer all those heartaches and terrors of new parents with a first-born child, the sheer dread when it seems ill, the fear when it doesn't move – but there is no Dr. Spock book to turn to for leopard cubs, only panic and prayer conquer.

Jaharti was an accident. She had virtually used up her ninth cat-life when we took her on; she should not have been alive – technically she wasn't. Her mother, an African leopard, was having great difficulty with the birth so the vet was called in to perform a Caesarean operation. Quite clearly the little mite was dead and she was put on one side while the vet began to stitch up her mother.

There is a great sadness at such a time. The vet is disappointed, and usually they cannot hide their disappointment under their professionalism. Success and they are laughing, failure and they are silent; everybody else is miserable.

I have a theory that it says something about the human race which would be worth a psychologist's study: we are the world's most prolific killers and yet we are deeply saddened by the failure of life. We hate to see a tiny creature seemingly cheated of its chance for existence; all our instincts when we witness it contradict everything else we do in other circumstances.

The vet had brought a party of students with him to give them experience of exotic animal welfare and it was tragic to introduce them to the subject with a stillborn cub. One of the students picked up the diminutive ball of fluff of a carcass and rubbed it with a massaging movement. He put it down and there was a flicker of a twitch. He rubbed again and there was a definite glimmer of life. The vet stitched double quickly, finished, and began his own massage with a look of incredulity on his face. Nobody dared to interrupt his concentration until he smiled, his face cracked in half, he beamed. 'She's alive,' he said. 'I've got a heartbeat.'

The cub was lost in a shoebox. Joanna, my wife, and I kept it by the bedside under infra-red lamps. It was almost too fragile to pick up by hand and opening its mouth to insert a fountain pen filler teat was an ordeal of nerves. Once an hour, every hour, day and night we wakened or watched to feed a few drops of milk into that reluctant mouth. Was it getting enough? Was the mixture too strong or too weak? There is no way of knowing. There are no guide charts for leopard cubs, and sickly ones at that.

We used a Dutch milk called Humana, which we had found very successful for other creatures we had hand reared. But the mixture *must* be exactly right or it won't work and the little thing will die. However, it is strictly a matter of trial and error. A human baby has a cast iron constitution compared with a wild animal cub born out of its natural habitat.

So you feed in the mixture, watch for diarrhoea or a gain of weight; at a sign of the first, panic; at the second, elation. The cub takes over your lives completely. Its welfare dominates your thoughts, it could be worth £5 or £500 or even £5,000, it doesn't matter. The battle to make

216

it live is all that counts. And you are becoming tired, tireder and nodding off with exhaustion but terrified to sleep in case a crisis erupts.

The natural mother licks her cub like a cat licks its kittens and this provides an essential biological necessity: she licks round its tail and this stimulates the cub's natural functions, without it, nothing happens. So the licking must be simulated using coarse tissues with a surface as near to the mother's tongue. The natural mother is in attendance all the time, a human foster-mother must completely take her place and allow the cub to develop a total attachment.

Suddenly all seems to be going well: the cub's strength is increasing, she is gaining weight. You watch the scales with the same anxiety as you watch them when your own baby is being weighed. The cub becomes frolicsome and ever more demanding. Play is an essential part of its development and since it becomes active and mobile so much more quickly than a human infant, it is the more exhausting. Most people know the damage a kitten or puppy can do to the house – soft furnishings torn to shreds, carpets stained. Multiply that tenfold to allow for the added strength – and destructive inclination – of a *wild* cat and you will be able to judge the havoc created.

A wild creature cannot reasonably be house trained, nor should it be if it is to return to its wild state, even in a zoo. All the time you are hand rearing it, it is becoming too humanised and too reliant on domesticity; unavoidably, and the time will come when it has to be broken of its habits.

But first the shock. No matter how many wild creatures you personally rear by hand, it always comes as a shock. One morning you will waken to find a bald cub in its cage by your bed; naked, emaciated and vulnerable to the slightest draught. About ninety per cent of hand reared animals shed their coats in this dramatic, frightening way. You agonise about the diet, you wonder what vital element can be missing, worry nags you that the poor mite will catch a chill and die of pneumonia. It writhes and struggles to shake off the wrapping you tenderly tie round its exposed body and you wait looking with desperation for signs of new fluff growing. Nobody knows why it

217

happens in hand reared animals, it doesn't in the wild. Zoologists are now working on the theory that it is prevented in nature by the mother's constant, non-stop licking of her cubs' coats – which looks to human eyes to be an expression of maternal love. The most probable explanation is that something in the mother's saliva, a trace element or perhaps an acid as yet undiscovered, stimulates the growth of the coat and keeps it in condition during early days of life. Bald cubs do recover their full coats and have no further trouble with them. Someday we will discover the answer.

Remarkable discoveries often come about by accident or somebody following a hunch. Gerald Durrell, a pioneer in this field, instances many such enlightenments in his books. Zoology is an ancient science, practical conservation in zoo keeping is astonishingly new; it really only began to happen through Gerald Durrell in the late 1950s and early 1960s when he set up his zoo at Les Augres, in Jersey. That was the first 'Thinking zoo' as opposed to the 'lash-up jobs' which exhibit animals to the public for commercial gain only.

The 'big boys', the well-established and famous national, municipal and society zoos will dispute it, but the proof is in the number of previously accepted wisdoms and laws which have been thrown out of the window since Durrell brought his mind to bear on the subject with the facilities and premises to put his theories into practice.

One astonishing discovery was made by a young keeper at Howletts, Angus Scott-Knight. An unlikely zoological pioneer, not trained as a professional zoologist, coming from a typical middle-class background, his mother was the Mayor of Canterbury, it was strange that he was working as a muck-shovelling keeper in a zoo anyway.

Among the most difficult species to hand rear are deer. Now that sounds a contradiction in terms. They should be easy: their offspring are like calves or lambs, they are grazing animals and they have been around the human race since man got on his two hind legs. By experience we ought to know a great deal about all species of deer. We have kept them in herds in special parks, hunted them in forest and glen and eaten them.

Certainly, the exotic breeds might seem to pose more

problems. There are obvious differences in climate and fodder, but we know a lot about that and for generations we have coped with keeping them alive and well.

But the fact remained that out of every ten fawns abandoned by their mothers and attempted to be raised by hand, only an average of two survived. It was frustrating and heartbreaking. Following the rules, you took them inside, you kept them warm, you fed them hourly and two-hourly; you watched the milk mix with the critical appraisal of an atom scientist adding heavy-water to his nuclear concoction, a millimetre more, a grain less. They would appear to thrive and then keel over and die on you.

'What are you doing with that feeder?' somebody asked Angus.

'I've got a couple of day-old fawns. I'm taking it out to them.'

'Where have you put them?'

'I left them where I found them in the deer compound.'

'In this weather? You must be bloody mad, they'll be stiff.'

Every two hours, day and night again, he put on his waterproofs and wellies, packed his feeding gear in a little box, and trudged across to the paddock, rain or shine.

'He's a bloody nutter,' the boys said. 'Angus and his alfresco nursery,' they joked. But they admired his persistence. After a few days, sympathetically but with a touch of sarcasm, we asked him: 'How's your fresh air brood?'

'Fine,' he replied, 'thriving.'

They were. After another couple of orphans thrived and grew strong, we were questioning him in a different tone of voice.

'What is the idea behind it, Angus?'

He explained: 'They do not survive and live indoors. Warmth doesn't seem to help them, maybe the environment is wrong. Maybe it is psychological and they can't get over the shock of being deserted by mother and cut off from the rest of the herd. Or it could be the stress factor of being brought into a room and warmth. Perhaps they suffer from claustrophobia. I don't really know, except that something was wrong in bringing them indoors so it was worth a try raising them in the open where they had been born. Another point was that you reduced the risk of them picking up a virus or other man-carried infection.'

After he had successfully raised a notoriously tricky black buck, an axis deer and a hog deer, we began to take Angus very seriously. Following his technique, the infant abandoned deer mortality rate has slumped to negligible proportions.

That is thinking zoo keeping, and caring zoo keeping too.

Accident-prone Michael wrapped up in the job.

Chapter 17

Cry wolf – and holler it out loud

For animal-hater Julie Buffery a home in the middle of a zoo made the hours of darkness sound like living in the middle of the London Philharmonic recording Mussorgski's 'Night on the Bald Mountain' – every trill, tremolo and crescendo of noise struck terror into her heart. This is Julie's story and it is also her husband Julian's story though we were all involved the night the wolf pack broke out en masse. Everybody employed by the zoo turned up to help put them back into the compound. But it wasn't as simple as all that . . .

It was to be a relaxing evening of blood, terror, the odd heart cut out, suspense and cider for Julian Buffery after he had put his elephants to bed at Howletts. And that meant a Hammer horror film on the television plus a few jars of strong cider – the stuff they had nicknamed 'mind-blower' which, being cheaper than beer, was easy on the pocket but with a lethal potential. Not quite so good perhaps, as genuine Devonshire scrumpy, yet with almost the same paralysing qualities. As the night wore on it became clear – or hazy – that something was wrong. The tele seemed to have gone stereo and banshee wails and howls were hitting the ears from several directions, not just from the box.

'A marvellous sound effect,' thought Julian, 'so real that it's like when a telephone rings on the box and you think it's your own bell going.'

Then it became odder and odder. The howls did not coincide with the script; he could have sworn they were coming from very close outside. So he told himself: 'I'm going to pack up this mind-blower rubbish. I'm sure the old sod at the off-licence doctors it with meths, or something.'

But was that particularly piercing howl really on the box? Or was it outside, like it sounded? He went to the window, drew back the curtains, wiped the condensation from the pane and peered into the hazy moonlight. There seemed to be shadowy forms slinking in the yard. 'Wolves,' he thought and, quickly dropping the curtain, he murmured to himself, 'Christ, I really *must* give up this mind-blower gut-rot – but it'd be a pity to waste that last bottle.'

Julie his wife came in from the kitchen and said: 'There's a pack of wolves on the doorstep.'

Quickly Julian reasoned: she's heard the howls on the tele, she's seen me peeping through the window, she thinks I'm pissed, which I am, therefore she's having me on.

So he replied: 'Yes, I know.' Then he added: 'I think I'd better go to bed. I'm becoming tired and emotional.'

There was a touch of tetchiness in Julie's voice as she insisted: 'There's a pack of wolves howling on the doorstep.'

'O.K., O.K.,' Julian replied, 'let's go to bed – they might have gone away by the morning.'

Julie was distinctly acid as she said: 'I am not going to bed with a pack of wolves outside the front door – no way!'

And in emphasis she added: 'No-way-at-all . . . DO SOMETHING ABOUT THEM!'

Julie, and it is very regrettable for a zoo keeper's wife, is unfortunately terrified of wild animals, even in the strongest cages. She thinks it would be a wise precaution if all attendants were compulsorily armed with loaded Kalashnikov 47s and stick-grenades as part of normal duty. No zoologist has ever yet been able to convince her that wolves cannot climb like bears or leap like cougars. When they produce the evidence of centuries of observation to prove their point, she replies: 'They're clever, they do it when nobody's watching.'

Julian is basically an elephant man and the closest he had ever got to wolves was on the other side of the wire,

222

but he had heard that wolves have been known to have nasty habits on occasion.

'Do what?' he queried.

'Well, you are the expert animal man,' said Julie, 'do something, anything, but do it quickly.'

He could see that Julie was becoming very tense and he sympathised with the fact that she was afflicted with a basic fear of animals which a lot of people suffer from. Many women are frightened by mice and positively terrified by their lovable little aerobatic brothers, bats. Others, men included, will not pass a yapping dog – there is no shame in it and such people are wise to keep away from animals because their fear has the effect of making the animals nervous as well.

Julie would not answer the front door of her house in the zoo unless the creature outside had assured her at least three times that it was human, articulate, and, for Christ's sake would she open up. She might have felt more secure married to a steeplejack and living in a cradle atop of Salisbury cathedral spire.

'Chicken,' said Julie, nearly in tears.

'That's what I'm afraid they might think if I go out there,' Julian answered. 'They might mistake me for a tasty morsel of Colonel Sanders' Kentucky-fried takeaway. . . . I can't just open the door and say, "Shoo".'

Then the awful realisation dawned of what could happen if the pack suddenly decided to move away. There were nine wolves outside. They were loping round the yard with that peculiarly meaningful, menacing gait of wolves on the prowl, stopping only to lift their heads, open wide gaping jaws and utter that prolonged, banshee howl which has struck fear into mankind since time began. (Where the breath comes from to sustain such a wail of terror for so long is a mystery, it must be enormous lungs and a controlled emission of air.) If they decided to move down the drive they would be in the public highway through the village in less than two minutes. A pack of marauding wolves loose in the lush farmlands of rural Kent would not be welcome and would cause some consternation to the public, police and council officials, shepherds, farmers with prize dairy and beef herds,

223

shepherds and sundry others such as newshounds from the national media.

What might be the reaction should they chew up the odd sheep or cow – or possibly person – sent shudders through Julian and sobered him remarkably speedily.

Once away they could be very difficult to recapture: a wolf pack in the wild will comfortably travel 30 miles a day, often more. They are among the hardiest and most adaptive creatures in the world, renowned for their cunning. The potential for damage, which would mostly come from the hunters in hot pursuit, not necessarily the pack, was immense. So Julian organised a posse . . . by telephone.

The zoo's wolf men made a midnight reconnaissance on tiptoe to discover that the escapees had chewed through the chain-link fence to gain freedom. The thick wire had been broken and twisted, more than human fingers could ever do.

'My God,' said Julie, 'if they can bite through that, they could go through this door as if it were candyfloss.'

At the side of the main wolf compound was a smaller pen, still intact and secure, which would be the only place to keep them until the main run could be repaired. But how to get them in on a dark night, with the moon now behind cloud, a hundred or more copses, spinneys and bush plantations providing ample cover and the only point of recognition, a pair of gleaming eyes flashing momentarily in headlights. The posse decided that driving the pack was impossible, temptation was the only answer.

Like a man, the way to a wolf's heart is through its belly or, put another way, wolves who eat together, meet together. Carcasses were fetched from the store and a juicy one used to bait the side-pen. Then the other dripping bodies were dragged behind a Land Rover in great arcs, starting from and ending at the gates to the pen, encircling – it was hoped – the roaming pack, other trails were laid from the arc to the pen gates. It was a giant 'scent net' spread across half-a-mile of the park with the idea that the delicate nostrils of members of the pack, now dispersed because of the unavoidable hubbub, would pick up the scent, and hunting instincts and greed would assert themselves and the hapless beasts would lope along the trail in search of the quarry in the pen. Then, hey presto, snap! The gate would drop and wandering wolfie would be caged again.

Posse members deployed themselves up trees, astride high walls and at various vantage points and tried, with straining eyes, to pierce the darkness for a sight of a slinky grey form against the uniform blackness of the undergrowth.

Sure enough, the first to come were the younger, lesser members of the pack, those at the lower pecking-order and therefore the hungriest. With hardly a deviation they followed the prepared trails, fell upon the carcass, sinking great incisors into the flesh and tearing ravenously at it. They came in dribs and drabs and were so intent upon their feast that they failed to notice the thud of the falling gate and the squeak as it was pulled up again to await the next arrival. But somewhere out in the darkness were the top dog and top bitch, presumably wondering where their faithful followers had disappeared to, but they made not a sound; and only the sound of their own heartbeats and breath in their nostrils disturbed the still of the night for the watchers. Slowly the minutes slipped into hours until dead-of-night was threatening to become crack o'-dawn with a slight lightening of the sky in the east. It was now possible to discern a movement across the grass or against the bushes but a waving branch or blowing leaf could easily mislead.

Suddenly the top pair appeared cautiously slinking along one of the scent trails. They did not rush their approach but trod carefully, ears pricked, nostrils aquiver and nerves tensed, not liking one little bit the silence and the strange, unaccustomed smells of the night. Being boss dog and bitch of the pack they were also the brains of the pack and used to unquestioning obedience. They were near enough now to know that there was meat about and that their pack was wallowing in it, but something did not ring true and instinctively they sensed a trap.

For an agonisingly long time they sniffed the air outside the pen and every concealed watcher felt an almost irre-sistible urge to cough, sneeze or clear his throat, but daren't. Then the bitch sprang and loped toward the carcass, her underlings backed off; for a further five minutes the wary old dog hung about outside until he tentatively moved in. Thud! The gate was down and they were back in captivity. Number one dog and number one bitch were the crux to the problem, with them back with the pack the trouble should have ended. But it didn't.

The natural social life of a wolf pack can cause great problems to zoos keeping them in captivity. Wolves, far more so than most other species, are nature's wanderers knowing no territorial limitations. Or, if there are territorial limits, they are on a vast scale covering hundreds of square miles. They live and survive in the world's most inhospitable areas where, in fact, survival would seem impossible.

There is, in a way, a curious similarity between a wolf pack and a bee-hive – but it should only be taken as an illustration.

In any wolf pack, be it 300, 30 or thirteen – and the latter numbers are the more likely since stories of packs of 200 to 300 strong rampaging across frozen Siberian wastes are probably Russian old wives' tales or figments of Ivan's imagination after sledging home from the local vodka jag – only the number one dog and number one bitch will ever mate. Perhaps the Russian travellers' tales *could* be true, there are an awful lot of wolves in Russia, but they drink an awful lot of vodka as well. Yet even so only the top two will ever breed; so the pack consists of the current breeding pair, the breeding heirs apparent who don't do it until the older couple have moved on, say the equivalents of Queen Bee with the rest of the pack the equivalents of drones and workers who get no fun at all except in rustling up the grub. (Funny, then, that a lecherous male is dubbed a wolf which, in truth, is a gross calumny of a wolf's sexual proclivities.) So nature ensures that only the fittest, strongest and best specimens reproduce to guarantee the survival of the species in the worst possible conditions known to mankind – bitter cold, sparse flora and sparser fauna, the White Hell of the far North.

The problem with wolves in captivity is that when the bitch comes on heat and the breeding season begins, the top dog and bitch also begin to feel an irresistible territorial urge: they crave space and privacy, the wanderlust comes

226

heavily upon them and where they go, the pack will follow. It is then that they are prone to bite through the toughest fence and surmount the most daunting obstacle to be free and fulfil their overpowering instincts.

This must have been a compelling season for our couple. Nothing would keep them in the spacious compound which had been their home for a number of years; the morning after the night escape they were out again with the pack following. Then again after each successive escape they became more difficult to recapture and more wily and resourceful in their efforts to stay free. It was clear that the situation was building to a local catastrophe and a possible dangerous threat to the public. The desperate decision had to be taken to shoot them. Then the pack settled down peacefully with its new leaders.

There is a great deal of sadness in a zoo man's life and you never quite get used to death, though it is a common, everyday factor with wild creatures who live by it.

Wild, fierce wolves at bay in the country lanes, imagine the panic. It happened once before some years ago and the great wolf hunt became a national excitement in the press and on television. Kentish maidens – and men – weren't much about after dark while it was going on and there were notably fewer dalliances in lovers' lanes and sweet-smelling corn fields while it was happening.

We ran around the county like madmen following up each alleged sighting and carrying irons, nets, cages, dart guns. . . . Then an ancient crone a few miles away telephoned to say: 'I think I've found your dog thing. You know, the one that's been on the tele, the one that's missing, will you come and collect it.'

We rushed to the spot with all the clobber and asked: 'Where is it, Missus?'

'It's in my front parlour,' she told us, and we *knew* we were on another stumour but decided to humour the old dear. We went in and there it was. A great brute of an old dog wolf about filling her tiny front room . . . drinking milk from a saucer on the floor.

'How did you catch it?' we asked the 71-year-old lady.

'I just made a few clucking noises and said, "Come on chuck, come 'ere, 'ave a saucer of milk," and it walked in.'

227

Those wolves . . . they became the stuff of horrific nightmares for Julian, producing murderous thoughts in his mind. Like they explain on television, there are scenes of an explicit nature in the next sequel and people of an ultra-sensitive nature are advised to skip a couple of paragraphs.

Julie had been assuaged and softened. She had almost forgiven Julian for bringing her to live smack in the middle of a park full of wild, predatory, man-eating potential killers and, like people do after a great emotional crisis, they were engaged in the loving process of kiss and make up, the second courtship, honeymoon and all that old guff. At the very instant of consummation of this newly restored passion Julie froze, her pliant body stiffened, her soft caressing fingers clutched and her nails dug sharply into Julian's flesh, her lips dried and she uttered a gasp of terror.

'What the hell . . .?' Julian expostulated, his mind being fully concentrated on the matter in hand. And only then did he hear, right under the bedroom window that spine-chilling ya-whoo-hooo-ooo-ooo-whoo, the wolves were out again. 'This time,' he swore, 'I'll shoot the bloody lot, if I don't strangle them first.'

Shooting the top dog and bitch had not worked, the pack had got the wanderlust and nothing could keep them in the compound. The zoo staff was organised into shifts so that a twenty-four hour watch could be kept on the wolf pen but still they managed to escape. Then what everybody feared would happen did happen, they escaped from the zoo grounds into the surrounding countryside and the alarm was spread to the police, emergency services and the media.

Then a motorist driving through Littlebourne village crashed into one in the village street. And that situation could in itself produce a few unexpected problems: a wolf is not something you expect to see every day in a quiet English country village high street, and thus a law-abiding motorist, complying with the regulations and reporting such an accident to the police, runs certain risks.

'Excuse me, sergeant, I've just knocked down a wolf. . . .'

'Oh yes, sir . . . a wolf?'

'Yes, a wolf, a dog wolf, it ran under my wheels. . . .'

'Very good, sir, would you just breath into this little bag, merely a routine test, sir, you understand. . . .'

It could be very tricky.

After twenty comparatively trouble free years, the wolves were becoming a problem. Once the pack goes 'bad' there is little that can be done about it. They want out and they will get out. So it was decided to sell the whole lot and send them to the Marquess of Bath's safari park at Longleat where a change of environment might cool them down and turn them into docile stay-at-homes again.

Crates were prepared, nets fetched – all the catching and safety paraphernalia prepared and the troops mustered for the great round-up. The technique is to entice them into their earthen underground lairs by baiting them with meat, then block up the entrance, dig a small hole through the roof and administer a slight sedative so that they can be lifted into the nets and carried into the crates.

Mark Aitken dug through the roof of a big bitch's lair, popped in the sedative and, in a couple of minutes gave a confident OK: 'She's stone cold,' he announced, 'let's dig her out.' The hole was widened, Mark grabbed her back legs and heaved. But the wily old bitch had only been lying doggo. The instant she was in the fresh air she was very much alive, snarling, kicking and full of the indignity of being held by her back legs. So, once again, young Mark was doing his wheelbarrowing act round the compound yelling: 'What shall I do? Give us a hand.' With the rest of us sitting comfortably on top of crates, smoking, swigging tea and advising: 'Hang on to her for a bit while we think of something.'

Another curious but unconnected incident happened during this time: I was sitting out the midnight vigil when the zoo secretary came running across the paddock to say that Herne Bay police had telephoned to say that they had found a small animal which climbed trees and made prodigious jumps. Could the zoo send somebody to help? They had put the animal into police kennels at the back of the station. It was a coatimundi, a small mammal with a long, pointed snout and a long, ringed tail. As soon as

I saw it, I knew the owner, a friend of mine called Peter Taboni, a private collector.

Peter had probably the finest collection of parrots in Britain, 500 to 600 of them which he keeps in 20 acres at his home in Blean, near Canterbury. He breeds from them and does a considerable job of preservation and conservation, having made himself into an expert on the species. He also keeps a few small mammals, including three coatimundis.

Odd things have happened at Peter's establishment. Vandals have broken in and caused havoc. Twenty of his birds were stolen but, at the same time, the doors of all his cages were kicked in or ripped off their hinges – all for no obvious or discernible reason except sheer bloody-mindedness. This was the latest in a series of worrying incidents, somebody had stolen his coatimundi and then released it twenty miles away.

At last the wolves saga was finally ended, they were either safe under our feet by the fireside or secure in Longleat. But for incredible endings to escape sagas nothing beats the tale of the wandering tiger.

We had lost a Bengal tiger cub. It had escaped into the surrounding countryside, and we were seeking it in quiet desperation when an old Kentish farm boy arrived at the gate in a battered pick-up truck, the type very popular with smallholders, a sawn-off 1100 saloon with the back seat space used as a carrying platform, canvas sides and top and drop down sides and back. A tiny utility for those who cannot afford a bigger, more expensive one. He was typical of the type: squattish, cloth cap over a weathered face, a short-stemmed pipe in his mouth, grubby fawn raincoat once, long ago, used for Sunday best, cord trousers and boots with thick soles, metal toe-pieces and metalled heels. A quiet, pleasant man who would stand in the bar of a real country pub saying nothing while others prattled on.

'Marnin',' he said in a thick local dialect. He sucked his pipe reflectively while he eyed the premises. 'Nice place 'ere, well kep' an' thaat. Must cost 'im plenty, cost of feedin' stuff an' thaat,' he pointed the stem of his pipe at the mansion to indicate that by 'im he meant Aspinall. 'Can't say oi sees the point of it, just chuckin' money down 'ungry throats an' no return. Still, each to 'is own, live an' let live, thaat's what oi says.'

Country style, he squatted on the step, pulled on his pipe, adjusted the contents of the bowl, lit and prodded, prodded and lit again, sucked, screwed his eyes against the sun and nodded at us in a friendly, confidential way. We gave him a cup of tea and asked: 'What can we do for you, Dad?'

'Oi were cummin' to thaat,' he replied, indicating his pick-up with his pipe stem, 'oi reckon oi've got summat o' yourn there in the back of the truck. Oi spotted 'im down the road an' oi thought, "That yonder must belong to they fellas at thaat zoo place, stands to sense it can't belong anywhere else." So oi put 'im in the back there an' oi brought 'im ere.'

He undid the securing ropes of the canvas, flung back the covers – and there was our male Bengal tiger cub which we had been frantically, despairingly searching for since the escape; for which sophisticated schemes were afoot to find and trap.

He dropped the back-flap of the small truck and said: 'Come on, boy, this is where you get out.'

Delighted and laughing we turned round . . . but the old boy had driven off without a word of thanks from us, without a mention of the reward which was being offered just for information leading to its capture. We have never seen him again from that day to this. We never discovered what we would dearly have loved to know, how he got the enormous, great beast into his truck in the first place, how he kept it there during its bumpy run to Howletts and a lot of other things. So, Dad, if you ever read this, do please come back and tell us, we would love to know.

Chapter 18

Bring on the clowns

We decided to join a circus, just like that, just for fun. Sitting in front of the tele one evening, marvelling at the skills and artistry of circus folk, we said: 'Wouldn't it be fun to join a circus. A bit lovelier than plodding old Howletts.' Lots of people join a circus like that. I met a girl who used to work at the Osram light bulb factory, in Oldham, Lancashire, until Billy Smart's circus arrived in town. Bedazzled, she joined them and left town with the rolling wagons. Three years later she was back in Lancashire – a member of the internationally fabled Flying Merrilees flying trapeze troupe – starring at Blackpool Tower circus. From examining filaments on a production line to triple somersaults on the high trapeze is quite a step. 'How did you do it?' I asked incredulously. 'Well, I was always quite good at gym at school,' she explained. I thought I could be quite good with animals in a three ring circus and I thought I would look well in spangles. It wasn't as simple as all that . . .

Circuses to us are animals and people, not amphitheatres, buildings, tents or the material things, but animals which can do remarkable things and people with consummate skills: the astonishing people who deserve to be called so because they live to astonish others with their feats, dexterity, strength and bravery; people who can make animals, wild and domestic, behave and perform for them in ways which defy nature and are incomprehensible to the average man. The fascination of a circus must be not in the wonders which are performed before your very eyes but in the application, patience, discipline which have supplied each and every act; the training, aches, bumps, bruises, breaks, fatigue and fear which have gone to make it work; the skills of jugglers, tumblers, slack-wire, high-wire and flying trapeze artistes do not come overnight or painlessly. And animal trainers are not flash-in-the-pan people.

Some circus people joke: why are there so many midgets in the circus? Because they have to find jobs for the high-wire artistes who fall off when they are training.

The work involved in becoming a circus artiste is horrifying, like it is in just being in a circus; the backbreak and heartache behind the flashy smiles and spangles in the ring would destroy the average person, and most average persons in my sort of rough and tumble life know a lot about hard physical graft. But a circus is something else: a working day is from four o'clock in the morning until midnight, not just occasionally but all the time the circus is on the move. It is the only life I have experienced where a cat-nap is rated worth a week's wages.

A typical day: four o'clock, muck out, water and feed the animals; eight-thirty, clean and repair gear; ten o'-clock, two hours' practice and animal training; twelve noon, clean and repair yourself. One-thirty, start hustling, cover the car parks, gates and cash-desks; two o'clock, afternoon show; four o'clock, prepare for evening show; six o'clock, evening show during which prepare for night show; eight-thirty, night show; eleven o'clock, clean and bed down animals; midnight, clean and bed down yourself . . . except on the third night when the routine changes: nine o'clock, begin to strike the animal tents, food tents, service tents, stow all gear into trailers; eleven o'clock: 'Hurry up, lady, had a nice time? Enjoy the show? We've 'ad your money, off you go. . . .' Get the bastards OUT, don't let 'em dawdle; strike the rings, get the high-wire down, get the trapeze down, stack 'n' stow the seats, strike the big top, stow those tons of canvas, miles of ropes, pegs, poles, wires and lights; midnight, hit the road; only 100 miles tonight, great. Does anybody know where the site is? Is it signposted? Will the trailers go down any tricky sidestreets? Four o'clock, unpack the trailer, put up the animal tents, unload the animals, water them, park the caravan, put the jacks down, cuppa tea, cat-nap; what-the-hell-is-the-time? Does it matter? Unpack the trailers, start pulling on the ropes, get the big top up; clean-feed-water-groom the animals . . . what day is it, does anyone know?

So what is Joanna, former beautician trained at the Innoxa Salon, in Bond Street, London, nurtured in the plush, expensive sweet-smelling quietness of the Steiner Salon in the Royal Garden Hotel, doing here in the middle of a cold, wet, windy night, broken-nailed, with an eye-shadow from lack of sleep not cosmetic, mud-caked and up to the neck in horse shit? Well, she married George Jacobs, silly girl, that's what she's doing here: at this moment she is putting up the tent for nineteen horses which is a big tent and heavy with it.

A tent for nineteen horses is a big top in itself, so it is heavy, gut-tearing work . . . and it's wet, and the ropes are soaked and slippery; the only good thing is that the kids are sleeping through all the noise and commotion.

Life now is a little different for Joanna from those lazy, hazy, gin-washed days in the Steiner Salon aboard the Cunard Flag Ship, Queen Elizabeth II, and the lotus-eaters' existence of sheer sun-kissed bliss as hostess aboard a luxury schooner cruising out of St. George's, Granada, for a fortnight's pleasuring via Tobago Keys, St. Lucia and all sun-spot points West. And eight Liberty Horses, four Shetland ponies, two ponies, Bandit and Patch, a massive Shire horse called Oliver, once owned by film star Oliver Reed, a magnificent dressage horse, Bobby, the donkey and two bad-tempered zebras need much more attention than rich dowagers, actresses and socialites aboard luxury liners.

'George, this guy rope's tangled and it's cutting my wrist.'

'Can't help you, love. I've got four elephants, four llamas and a bloody-minded camel going berserk.'

Thinks: 'She can give me a quick manicure before we turn in this morning. I want to look pretty in the ring tomorrow.'

'The circus,' we had said at some moment of boredom and disenchantment with life at Howletts, 'that sounds fun, exciting, plenty of travel, fantastic people. Besides, I've always fancied doing it just for the experience.'

Gerry Cottle was delighted to have us. Gerry is delighted to use anybody who has experience with animals; running a circus nowadays is a constant battle with staff, costs and officialdom; it is not a trade, nor a profession but it is a vocation – a calling as strong as an archbishop's calling to the church. Whatever circus people do, they never really quit the circus. Of all human endeavour a circus must be the masterpiece of improvisation. A circus is a moving scrap yard with bright paint on it. What is junk to everybody else is gold to circus people; miracles of engineering and craftsmanship are performed as a matter of course. If the new gear won't fit into the trailer, re-shape the trailer to fit the gear. 'But it will. . . .', 'No buts, get on with it, do it now.'

Who needs a workshop to repair 40-ton juggernauts and keep them rolling? Not a circus which is a constantly moving, never resting mechanical M.A.S.H.; do it now, instantly – procrastination is unknown in circuses . . . except when it comes to pay and pay rises. Money was part of the world you left behind when you joined the circus. Even zoo pay began to look good on circus rates, £40 a week for two of us working full time never less than 100 hours a week – and bring up your children in your spare time. 'Oh . . . are they old enough to lend a hand? Not yet, pity.' You have to adore doing it or you couldn't last a day. Many people spend a lifetime in the circus, they could never leave, the world outside is far too bland a place for them to contemplate. And children thrive in the atmosphere, they are schooled well, a school now travels with the circus, they learn a multitude of skills and crafts just by living in the tight circle. Above all they feel welcome and loved – circus people are one of those breeds of people who worship and value their children.

Improvise: 'So there's no Road Fund Licence on that Lorry – stick up a Guinness bottle label . . . nobody will notice.' Joanna and I have travelled the length and breadth of Britain on a Guinness Label. Did you ever notice that Arthur Guinness – founding father of the great dynasty – could not spell his own name? He signed himself 'Arth Guinness' and that is how the famous signature appears on all Guinness products to this day. That is the sort of thing you notice when travelling 200 weary, slow miles at 20 m.p.h. towing a trailer laden with heavy gear plus a caravan hitched on behind with only the back of a Guinness bottle label to stare at during the tedium of the journey. Creak, squeak, groan, splutter, every twitch and rattle of the vehicle sends a shudder of dread through your nervous system. The circus 'firemen', knowing the propensity of the transport to break down, patrol the convoy – it may be twenty miles long depending upon how quickly each section packed and moved out of the last site – ready to leap in and improvise when a truck gives up under the strain. The rule is never to leave them on the road, in the first instance, their loads are urgently needed at journey's end otherwise the show cannot go on, and secondly too many nosey-parkers may be tempted to probe the vehicle's credentials . . . move it on – fast.

Police forces cooperate wonderfully, not only in Britain but the world over, and not out of love and admiration of the circus tradition or the pleasure it brings the populace; police chiefs act on the single premise: 'Circuses are poison, get the bloody shower off my patch, get it out of my territory as quick as can be done'. They smile only when the last trundling, garish vehicle crosses the boundary of their domain and becomes somebody else's worry.

Six of Joanna's liberty horses formed the main equestrian act, the other two were in training, and the dressage horse was used by principal trainer, Carlos McManus, to school daughters Clare and Carol. Their mother came from a famous Scottish circus family where trick riding ran in the blood, so life in the saddle was second nature to the children and Carlos taught them in the exacting classical art of dressage.

The zebras were the bad lot, they always are. There has not been the zebra born which wasn't mean, evil-tempered, highly strung and untrustworthy. They are another of the few species which hide a vicious nature under a pretty exterior and they are so nervous that they spread nervousness to every other creature around them like a virus epidemic. My theory to explain their constant state of stretched nerves is that they are forced to live in perpetual fear of retribution because they know that they have been so vile to everything in sight. They are, of course, related to the horse family and the best way to

236

think of them is as pure white horses, the black stripes are where the Devil's fingers have etched their characters.

Each show started traditionally with a 'Parade of the exotica': comprising an impressive column of elephants, llamas, horses, zebras, acts in full dress, brasses jingling, spangles sparkling, band playing and whips cracking. Sam, the trickiest of the zebras, would lead the parade at a high pitch of nervous tension: all the old-fashioned razz-matazz of 1,000 years' history, all the smelly, snorting, touchable excitement which has set hearts pounding through the ages. Live and living entertainment now all but killed off by motion camera trickery, faked exploits, antiseptic, second-hand thrills on flat cinema screens. So often, more often than you would think, we would play to full houses at all nine shows in a three-day stand; other times, quite inexplicably, we would die in an echoing void of a dozen watchers – seven was the lowest I can recall. There are no nights in the cinema when it goes brilliantly and everybody is on top form; there are no nights when it is catastrophic and disaster breeds disaster. So there are no moments of supreme elation or inquests after which you go to bed hoping you will not wake up in the morning.

Zebra Sam, the intractable, awful, maverick Sam, bane of Joanna's life, was leading the parade when he farted, frightening the wits out of himself. It came out PHUTT! and startled him so much that his whole body tensed. Ears pricked and nostrils quivering, he bolted from the shock and, with the effort, farted again and yet again: phutt, phutt, phutt, phutt, phutt, phuttphuttphutt – each little staccato blast adding to his nervous terror. By now he was up to a collected trot and working toward a canter with Joanna's legs whirling like a trick-cyclist's on a one-wheeled cycle: Llamas, elephants, horses and ponies all gathered speed to keep pace, the camel's legs splayed but once he got them straight and underneath himself again he was determined to outrun the lot. Sam was now but-ting the backsides of the horses at the rear of the parade and they accelerated to get out of his way; the band, lost for a moment by the unexpected increase in tempo, were catching up with the action and playing at post-horn gal-lop speed. Animal attendants gave up trying to keep abreast and clung on to their charges their toes kicking up little bomb-bursts of sawdust when their feet touched ground. Faster and faster the stampede whirled round the ring. The audience roared its approval. They clapped and shouted spontaneously, and we watched the flash of smiles as their faces creased with pleasure.

But this living impersonation of a mad fairground merry-go-round of prancing animals had lost its brakes. The rides were running the engine and gaining momentum with the risk of flying off in all directions. Our engine was the ringmaster in the middle and he was visibly over-heating: his usual imperturbable elegance in top-hat and red frock-coat was fraying at the edges and his rising pulse rate showed clearly in pounding veins in his temple which were not usually visible.

Now we were beginning to spin like a catherine wheel, the first initial splutters and spurts were over and we were travelling so fast that colours were merging in the eyes of those trapped in the whirling circle in the ring. Something had to give and it was Patch, peppy little heroine of the Wild West act, who decided that with elephants pounding, camels blowing and zebras champing, enough was enough. So on her next circuit she made a dash for the entrance tunnel and the rest followed her to come to a halt in a plunging, bucking, rearing melee outside.

The audience gave an ovation and some local big-wig, who was guest of honour for the night, yelled: 'Bravo, encore'. He leaned over the side of his box to tell the pale, numbed and shattered ringmaster: 'Quite the most exciting first act I've ever seen in a circus, first rate, old man, first rate, congratulations.'

Outside the atmosphere was strained as artistes, attendants and trainers mopped themselves down and struggled for breath. Angrily the trainer demanded: 'Who let that zebra fart?'

There's no answer to that. As Joanna remarked, you can't turn a zebra on its tummy and pat its back until its wind comes up, like you do with a baby, before you go on. But you have to try to stop it happening with the elephants before they go into the ring. Windy zebras are the light ack-ack of the circus's armoury, elephants are

238

the heavy howitzers and might cause the audience to bolt not just the other animals.

It is an earthy world in the circus and animals tend to treat natural functions just as what they are – natural functions. But they do have a habit of performing just at the crucial moment when they are in the public eye. How often does the winner of the Victor Ludorum at great international horse shows lift his tail and let it all go at that very moment the television cameras turn on him when, full of honour, his proud rider is receiving his coveted sash and cup?

Nor is royalty immune. Those patient, brilliantly schooled mounts, which negotiate long and complicated routines on high ceremonial occasions without putting a foot wrong or turning a hair, wait until the climax of events with the eyes of millions of them to plop, plop, plop the parade ground either in a gesture of unconcerned mastery of the drill or contempt for the whole charade.

Elephants could cause technical and physical hitches in the show if they were allowed to spoil the ring: a flat race for the liberty horses following on could become a Grand National course with formidable obstacles.

So in the terminology of the circuses, they are raked before they appear, in the way that children are chided: 'Do you want to go to the toilet? This is your last chance. You'd better go. Well *try* even if you don't feel like it.' The attendant puts the elephants facing a wall, stands them on their hind legs by making them climb the wall with their front legs. This, in theory, should force anything inside them through their very simple systems and deposit it in neat piles out of sight of the sensitive public; if it doesn't work, the attendant inserts his hand and rakes out the elephants' insides – a manual enema, no worse than what a hospital does to patients.

We had our Jumbos in Gerry's circus magnificently potty-trained. I would rear them up against the wall, place a wheelbarrow under each one and bellow: 'Now!' or whichever four-letter command seemed appropriate. And, hey-presto, four barrowloads of steaming, rich manure. 'Half a nicker a barrowload, bring your own sacks,' I told the locals, 'grow your cucumbers like marrows, grow your marrows like barrage-balloons, marvellous stuff.'

Sometimes it didn't work and that resulted in the continuance of one of the longest running feuds in circus history between the elephant keeper and the lighting manager: after an elephant had misbehaved, I have slunk into the ring in every conceivable disguise, even crawling on hands and knees dragging my bucket and shovel in the shadow of the ring fence, to remove the offending pile as quietly and unobtrusively as humanly possible. But the lighting manager considers that, no matter whatever else is happening in the ring at that moment, he has a right and a duty to perform so suddenly your neck is sliced in half by the shaft of the spotlight, the supertrooper, trained full on you as you begin shovelling; it usually stops the show. And afterwards the lighting man always says: 'I thought I'd better give you a bit of light to help you see what you were doing, mate'.

Circus people, even though living as a tight-knit, inseparable family, readily accept the intrinsic social structure and its pay differentials: the artistes, the high-wire, trapeze and stunt men are the aristocracy commanding vast fees and most workers not only agree that they should be paid so much but are proud that they are getting the money. In Cottle's circus Mr. Universe, Christos Montez, 'The Human Canonball', was paid £1,000 a week; animal trainers are paid less because, usually, the animals belong to the circus, the trainers present the acts, but they are paid a relatively handsome fee for prancing around with anything from half-a-dozen to twenty big cats or bears for twenty minutes a time, three times a day. A trainer with his own animals earns much more.

So on through the hierarchy to animal keepers like Joanna and me until the circus hands and tent hands are reached. Indispensable, they are as much a part of the circus as anybody, but roughnecks seldom come rougher or tougher. When you hear those dreaded words 'good as gold at heart', 'salt of the earth', 'rough diamonds', you know to expect trouble. They do not cause trouble except by inviting it by their presence: they are so intimidating that every would-be tough feels that he must set upon them to prove his potential.

Tinker stock, Romany stock, travelling men, they have been ostracised by society for generations so they are wary of it, and the trimmings of organised society such as Social Security, insurance and health cards look to them like devilish official ploys to ensnare them, so they steer clear of all that jazz.

Kelly was the tentmaster, a barrel of steel with two sledge hammers for arms and hands. Kelly what or who Kelly? 'Kelly, that's enough, who needs know more? You call me Kelly and I'll know who I am and who you are talking to.'

Kelly would ride a day ahead of the circus to the next site and order 50 labourers to help erect the big top at six o'clock the following morning, £5 a man. They would turn up in the grey dawn, as unpalatable a bunch of deadbeats and layabouts as could be dragged from any gutter. At the end of the back-breaking, bone-cracking, hand-blistering session, Kelly would bark to those who had not yet fled from his wrath: 'You're not worth a wank, any of you, more of a bloody nuisance than a help. Here, I'll give you a couple of quid each as sufferance money, now piss off.' Then he would call his regular travelling gang together: 'Come on, lads, we'll have a drink on the "overs".'

Members of the public, affronted by the circus hands' general demeanour, termed them layabouts and dropouts; if half the real layabouts in Britain did one tenth of the work this lot did before breakfast every morning, Britain would be top of the world prosperity table.

Drivers are always in short supply. So tent hands drove from site to site. The trouble was that they usually did not have driving licences. Standard procedure if stopped by the police was: licence? Left it at home. Insurance? Haven't got it with me, see the boss. Address? That of the next site. When the police called round, if the circus was still on the same site which wasn't often, the explanation was: 'Charlie Brown? Never heard of him. He must have been one of the casual drivers we hired back there. Our own bloke was sick at the time.' Insurance was a little more difficult to explain . . . but not, by any means impossible . . . I mean, well, a circus is comprised of

241

sleight-of-hand men, jugglers, part of the job is fooling the public.

Animal trainers keep themselves aloof from the staff and the animals; they do half-an-hour's training in the morning, only if necessary, three shows a day and that is that. Out of the ring the animals belong to the keepers. Trainers do not see them, get to know them, pet them or even bother much about their welfare; the boss is the boss is the boss every time and all the time and over-familiarity with animals or keepers does not happen. In the circus code, it is not done, trainers comport themselves with immense dignity.

Captain Sidney Howes was a famous trainer of the real old school, highly respected and valued by every person who knew him. Pity the brash youngster who chanced his arm with a cheery: 'Good morning, Sid.' 'Captain Sidney, if you please,' the old man would retort in such tones that the familiarity never happened twice. But he was a marvellous old man, a great teacher willing to pass on every ounce of his experience to a willing pupil and, providing the relationship was never breached, one of the dearest and best friends anybody could ever have.

He was famous as the 'fastest breaker' of animals. He could school and train big cats and bears quicker than anybody then working in the circus world. There was something in his natural *commanding* bearing which influenced both animals and people; I stress commanding because he had that undefinable natural attribute which literally commands people and animals to take notice, a quiet approach, a gentlemanly consideration and yet total authority.

A lion can be trained in three days, though it may, in some cases take three weeks or months. The newly arrived, wild creature is put into a round cage – it must be round so that there are no corners to back into. The first stage is purely psychological, the natural instinct of a lion is to back off from the unknown, and as a rule it is only if it is cornered that a big cat will attack, if there are no corners to be trapped in the animal has a false sense of an easy escape route. It feels the availability of a way to evade its pursuer. That is not an anthropomorphic assessment of a lion's thinking, it is the way it works in

242

practice. You do not walk into a lion cage unless you have a reasonable idea of how it is going to react.

So the trainer goes into the cage for one-to-three minute spells time and again during the day, the more often, the better. Sooner or later the lion will stop retreating. Even a lion will tire of walking backwards in a circle realising that there is no profit in it. The cat has been kept hungry and a morsel of meat will be fed to it from a spike on the end of a long pole; the pole serves two purposes, either to reward or admonish.

The fact cannot be escaped that cruelty is always a part of animal training but much depends upon the definition of cruelty: caging an animal is cruel, whipping an animal is cruel, starving an animal is cruel, factory farming an animal is cruel, vivisection on an animal is cruel, over-feeding a dog is cruel; the question of degree depends upon your conscience.

And the plain facts of training wild animals as opposed to the domestic variety are mostly unpalatable and even downright offensive to fireside animal lovers.

Fact: as an almost invariable rule the trainer will have to thrash the animal to begin with to establish supremacy. Animal men know and accept it, they may not approve, they may detest it, but they acknowledge the fact. And they regard with deep suspicion and disbelief those who protest that such treatment never happens.

Fact: the principal system used in training wild animals is universally known as fear and reward which means that fear is first instilled into an animal and assuaged by reward. The crack of a trainer's whip and the chair in his hand are constant reminders of that initial fear.

That is the way it is done. That is how it has been done since man first felt the compulsion to bring wild animals under his control; that is the way it will continue to be done because no other system has yet been discovered to work.

Forget *Ring of Bright Water*, forget *Born Free*. Such brilliant experiments and observations, such fascinating adventures which trigger human emotions so effectively and make the heart warm to the wild are not in the catalogue when it comes to wild animals in captivity.

The basic purpose of any animal act from a flea circus

to a masterly performance by the greatest animal trainers of all time, Gerd Zimmermine and Ditte Gabor, is exactly the same.

Zimmermine, maestro of the Swiss circus, ended his act with six tigers, six elephants, six horses and six Shetland ponies all together with him in the same ring: twenty-four animals performing their routine simultaneously. Quite an act.

Gabor attempted – and succeeded – to disprove that tigers go mad at the smell of blood, which is supposed to excite them at feeding time in a zoo. In the circus ring he carried a dripping carcass on his back through a double line of twelve tigers sitting on pedestals, chopped it up while they waited and threw each one its ration down the line. They did not budge until they got their allocation.

Flea circus proprietor, Zimmermine and Gabor are each simply showing man's supremacy over the wild and the watching public gets a vicarious exhilaration from the display.

In that small, round cage in the very beginning, man is exerting his supremacy in physical and pyschological ways: the lion has stopped retreating and is confounded by the situation, so he stands; already the simple logic of fear and reward is beginning to work, he has been rewarded for compliance and suffered sharp rebuff for refusal. One major factor weighs in the trainer's favour, that is that animals learn more quickly through pain, however slight, than do human beings. At that point the animal is a baffled and confused creature and in the trainer's eyes, he is ready for contact. The trainer walks up to the animal and places a collar and chain round its neck. He secures the collar, then secures the chain to the cage bars.

For the first time he walks within reach of tooth and claw and, by any man's standard, that needs nerve, ice cold nerve, and courage; the trainer's nerve as much subjugates the lion as the spiked pole. That implement has to be used sparingly, the trainer does not want a scarred or maimed animal on public display.

There is usually an assistant in the cage to handle props and pass rewards at the appropriate time, but the trainer may complete the whole operation single-handed, a

244

one-to-one, face-to-face confrontation from which he must emerge the winner – or he won't emerge at all.

Then the lion is prodded, poked, cajoled on to a pedestal and rewarded, off the pedestal and rewarded. The crack of the trainer's whip is as much a reminder as its sting. Often it is as quick to put an animal with the rest of the troupe and they will teach him. Animals are rarely asked to do what is not natural to them: they walk narrow planks, they walk tree branches in the wild; they climb, leap, roll and balance in the wild so they adapt with remarkable ease to a circus routine. A man of Captain Sidney's calibre will have a new recruit schooled in days.

Disapprove of his art and skill if you must, but do not disparage the man. It is a dangerous job and men like Captain Sidney are brave men to do it; some men need constantly to test their own courage in order to live at peace with themselves. Sometimes the test does not work and the trainer ceases to live. Captain Sidney's personal tragedy was that his son had been killed by a big cat while working in a circus in Ireland: grief stricken, his family had pleaded with the old man to give up working with cats. To mollify them, he agreed. For a while afterwards he toured the circus with a small chimpanzee act, but the heart had gone out of him. He was still loved and respected but he had lost himself. When he eventually retired to Bournemouth, he faded away. In the old-fashioned way, he did not die, he just gave up living.

But in his time he could work those cats as well and fast as anybody I have ever seen in a circus ring: he had them snarling at him, attacking, disobeying and moving at speed all the time. He worked the rogue cat routine to perfection when one lion is clearly disaffected, always turning the wrong way, snarling and slashing at the trainer – all part of the act, of course, but still stopping hearts in the audience. I cannot recall his latter days, they seem to be obliterated from my memory. I remember him only in the ring with his cats, or in dignified composure in his caravan, the boss, gently correcting the errors of our ways and advising.

The circus is an exacting task-master, it takes its toll of the second-rate. A group of Spanish trapeze artistes arrived, billed as a Magnificient Flying troupe. They were all dramatic Flamenco gestures, Castilian bravado, flashing eyes, black shiny hair and voices rattling like machine-gun fire in a perpetual ferment of anger. Standing outside the big top you soon recognise the subtle difference between shrieks of delight, astonishment and thrill and shrieks of dismay. Shrieks of dismay rent the air far too often. Gerry Cottle covered his ears with his hands, rolled his eyes to the heavens and bewailed: 'Oh, my god! It's the magnificent *Falling* troupe again. Blessed be the man who invented safety nets. They'll have to go. It's bad for the circus to have trapeze artistes tumbling out of the skies all the time, the public pays to see them . . .' he pointed his fingers skywards, 'up there.' He reversed his finger to point to his shoes and added, 'not on their arses down here.' A laconic circus hand lolling against a post worked it out. 'I know what's wrong,' he confided, 'the geysers put their 'ands in the chalk all right, then they rub their 'ands through their 'air, they're always doin' it, just watch. So their 'ands are covered with Vaseline 'air tonic or olive oil or something and the girls slip through.'

Yet real talent abounds. Barry Walls was a man of remarkably varied talents and smiling and self-effacing with it. For weeks I thought he was the sign-writer, and a first class one too. He painted those beautiful, ornate circus rolls and scrolls in the age-old style; a style which came back into fashion in the arty, glossy colour mags in the late 1970s and still continues. Visitors would photograph his work, historians and antiquarians questioned him about it, he was master, it seemed, of a dying art which, when it was nearly too late, people had come to recognise as an art form.

'Where did you train?' I asked.

'I didn't. I just picked it up,' he told me.

Then I discovered that he worked in the ring under the name of El Hakim, lying on a bed of sharpened nails with members of the public standing on his chest, swallowing swords, eating fire, doing acrobatics in the Wild West act as a red Indian chief.

Social contradictions in circus life are fascinating: through generations the pecking-order has been firmly established, respect and discipline have become self-en-forcing. It is a much inter-married community, family life is paramount, promiscuity does not happen within the group and morality is revered with Victorian fervour. Yet circus women have for generations displayed themselves as revealingly as the belles of St. Tropez; they were into bikinis when flappers were wearing frilly bathing costumes on Brighton beach to the scandalised reproof of the citizenry.

Humour, however, is crude and earthy. Barry Walls' part in the Wild West act was to rush on at a crucial moment clad in his fearsome warpaint. Before his dash into the ring he took a great gulp of spirit from a bottle left at the ring entrance and arrived in the middle of the ring belching a great fire-ball from his mouth. Some wag substituted a bottle of urine. . . .

No matter how much the circus envelopes you in its undoubted magic, nothing can disguise the fact that the animals are kept in abominable conditions. By force of circumstances they are kept locked up in cramped quarters for twenty-three out of every twenty-four hours in the day. The beast wagons are converted railway stock and four big cats will share one wagon, the horses and other stock must suffer similar confinement; the travelling circus is a working unit, the animals slot into the work schedule at their ordained moment in time and then return to their quarters. In the case of big cats this may not be as hard as it may seem: cats spend 90 per cent of their time asleep anyway. Lions, in particular, are naturally idle. Their life is sleep and lazing, only hunger galvanises them into action in the wild. But it is tough on tigers which are a more active species and even tougher on bears which are busy little creatures by nature.

Occasional diversions break the monotony for the animals and, as far as can be told, they revel in them. As a publicity stunt, my four elephants opened a new lorry wash in Birmingham. They got under the water jets and did not want to come out, leaning against the spinning rollers and splashing about frisky as toddlers in a paddling pool.

Yet the animals are kept in magnificent condition, glowing with health and fitness, the bloom on their coats testifies to their wellbeing. They all receive almost continuous grooming throughout the working day; their feet are pedicured, teeth and mouths given minute attention. Cats are cleaned three or four times a day; they are cosseted with loving care. Life for them lacks nothing except space, light, air and freedom. And it is anthropomorphic to presuppose that those things are essential to them since they thrive and live long lives under the conditions they are kept in.

Conditions for men are no better, they hardly can be. Families have their own mobile homes and the luxury of the circus proprietors' and principal artistes' accommodation is well recorded. They live well as befits the managing directors and top executives of any commercial enterprise; Joanna and I with the two children, Gayle and Georgina, had our own caravan (which I did my unwitting best to incinerate one night) but the hands and unmarried artistes lived in buses and lorries converted into dormitories; The Cottle's Hilton they were nicknamed, silver-thin compartments with hardly room to turn – cramped, but unavoidably so. The art of the circus is to pack as much as possible into the smallest space.

Gerry Bean did not take up much room. He was the smallest man in Europe. In his mid-thirties, he had long since reached his maximum height of 33 inches. He had been christened Gerald Buttery but changed it to Bean to suit his size and sound better in promoting his professional life.

There may never be any more Gerry Beans or anybody like him. They have now discovered a cure for dwarfism, which is a much more widespread disease than is ever imagined by normal-sized people. A disease sufficiently prevalent for great drug companies to run intensive research projects into its causes and cures. The good news is that laboratories like Calbiochem-Behring Corporation, of La Jolla, California, now market a drug derived from pituitary glands which means that people born with the disease no longer have to carry their affliction through life.

Though people like Gerry carry their burden with remarkable stoicism and fortitude, most of the time they just want to forget it and for other people to forget it. But the human race has never been noticeably kind to what it thinks of as freaks. Where does a dwarf find work except in the circus? If any work is available, it is menial and shockingly poorly paid. There is one instance where a dwarf has been given the opportunity to do what is usually considered a 'man's job': the British Post Office employ a dwarf as a postman, providing him with a specially built pair of stepladders to reach high letter-boxes. He does a splendid job and has won a place in the local community he serves.

Gerry had won his place in our circus and in our affections. He and I became great mates though an incongruous couple we looked together, me at six-foot-four-inches and him standing two-foot-nine. I used to carry him on my shoulders down to the betting shop. I carried him because the affliction means that dwarfs cannot walk too far, and if we had walked there at the speed his legs took him over the ground the last race would have been over with the runners tucked up for the night in their stables. Our children, I think, will accept freaks much more readily than we do – freak is an accurate word but it carries nasty overtones which it should not – because of sci-fi and space epics which have accustomed them to the unusual and taught them not to judge entirely on appearances.

Gerry was one of us, so much so that we failed to notice his size except when strangers were clearly taken aback by it. When we went boozing he came with us, though when he got drunk one night it did pose a problem. He went to the loo to be sick, leaned too far over the pan and toppled in.

His home was the driving cab of one of the lorries with a specially made three-foot bed, a matching wardrobe, dressing table, drawers and chair, which made him the most comfortably accommodated man in the circus.

Little Gerry, what a lad, what a friend, he was splendid. If he couldn't match the rest of us in size, he certainly could equal any of us in style, outrageousness and the ability to spring surprises. We had arrived in Peterborough and it was one of the rare occasions when we had an evening off which we made the most of in the hospitable pubs of the town. Gerry was with us and joined in the fun of chatting up the local girls. That was when he

249

decided to spring his greatest surprise. He fell in love, head over heels in joyous love.

And the lady was obviously very attracted to him. She was a very good-looking blonde lady but – and isn't it always the way? – she was also a very big girl. Tall and with a well-endowed figure. They were obviously enchanted with each other and in no time at all a very intimate understanding had developed between them. She laughed at his jokes; she listened intently to his talk. She had eyes and ears for nobody else. And they wanted to be alone so much that they froze out everybody who tried to interrupt them. She came and stayed with him at the site. The week in that Anglian town was a highlight in Gerry's life, it changed him. It seemed an extraordinary relationship to all of us watching, but it made him an ecstatically happy man.

A helping hand is the rule of circus life, travellers will move heaven and earth to assist each other. It was a long haul to the next site and we chugged along through the night until the grey of dawn was filtering into the eastern sky. My caravan was hitched behind the trailer and so out of sight. Six miles from the destination, rounding a long corner, in the driving mirror I saw clouds of smoke billowing from behind the trailer; if I went faster they disappeared, when I slowed they rolled out across the road again. You dare not stop a monster truck like that on the main highway, so pull up in the first lay-by, which, thankfully, was nearby. The wheel of the caravan was red hot and glowing, the tyre had long since burned away and the caravan was running on the metal wheel gouging a deep rut in the surface of the road. It was a big van with a wooden floor and the wood was charred black and smouldering, flickers of flame broke out as the light breeze fanned the embers.

It would have to be a night when I was travelling 'tally' on a Guinness label and hope. I dreaded the police arriving. I dreaded the caravan suddenly going up in flames. It was my own and my only home, and the horrible thought intruded that they would charge me for damage to the road – they do, you know, if you knock over a bollard or lampost, you foot the bill.

Relief. The trouble shooters came round the corner and a frantic roadside emergency conference was held.

'We haven't got a spare, so we can't change it.'

'We dare not leave it here because the police will be sure to arrive.'

'You can't drive it because the van will catch fire.'

'We've got to move immediately otherwise the early morning traffic will be flowing.'

'Nip up to the site, get the circus fire engine.'

We dragged the last five miles with the fire engine playing a cooling jet on the caravan wheel – it worked.

When the time came, it was a hard decision to quit. We were beginning to be ensnared in the magic of the circus and its people; six months more and the likelihood is that we would have stayed for life, because a circus is life which is why its magic is so strong and has lasted for so long. But the children were growing up and reaching that crucial age when school becomes all important. They were sadder than we were to have to leave.

Chapter 19

Hannibal Jacobs

If I could get elephants out of my blood, I would do something else with my life. But I can't and nor do I want to. I am a jumbo junkie, I need my daily fix of them and when I do go away from elephants I suffer withdrawal symptoms. To me there is one last great adventure to be achieved: to follow in Hannibal's footsteps and take a troupe of working elephants across the Alps and relive Hannibal's triumphs. Fantastic. But it won't be as simple as all that . . .

Sometimes a wild, mad ambition surges through my veins and tickles the soles of my feet. I think: 'What the hell am I doing here? Approaching forty and still shovelling shit; on the breadline, no prospects; working for a pittance and surrounded by an ever swelling army of plum-in-the-mouth buffoons: The Buck's friends and appointees all brought in to run the zoos now that they are public. And their idea of running a zoo is to strangle the soul out of it.'

What they are supposed to know, only The Buck knows. What we, the men with the shovels in the cages, know is that they do not know animals and never will. Contempt for the so-called abilities of 'management' has crept into the zoo; the keepers assess each newcomer on to the staff: 'Brilliant man with a chit, not so hot shifting shit'.

The media rumbles on incessantly about recession, monetarism, interest rates, productivity, the inability of the British – and now the German, Dutch, Belgian and even American – working man to work hard enough and produce. But the advent of Mrs Margaret Thatcher as Prime Minister of Great Britain, and the introduction of her Iron Maiden fiscal policies proved, among other things, that huge areas of British 'management' were hopelessly inadequate and had for years relied upon the good-will and indulgence of the working man rather than their own skills. And nowhere is that point more dramatically illustrated than in Britain's zoos. But for the tolerance and patience of a few highly dedicated workers they would stop and die in their tracks tomorrow. Like a farm, a zoo goes on happening for twenty-four hours a day, seven days a week, three hundred and sixty-five days a year, and only the good will of the workers keeps it going.

If I say baldly that British zoo management is a culpable disaster, then you might think that the managements of those British zoos which are rightly ranked among the foremost in the world would bristle in anger. They won't, they know that it is a disaster and they have been urgently pressing that it should be radically changed and that standards should be enforced.

That is why it became a matter of urgency to get an Act of Parliament on the statute books. When the matter was debated in the House of Commons it was stated that seventy-five per cent of British zoos were substandard – and shockingly substandard at that.

The good zoos want it put right. On those quoted figures alone, which mean that three out of four zoos are bad, anybody is justified in saying that British zoo management is a disaster.

The managements talk at conferences and seminars, zoology is a fashionable occupation greatly enhanced by the exposure it gets on television; the glamour and prestige generated by knowledgeable, intrepid and personable star nature-men on television rubs off on a squalid, money-grubbing sector of society. They look clean, white and impressive on the conference platform, they look terrible from cage level. They are a MESS.

Hardly a man, woman or child in the civilised Western world is unaware that whole species are in imminent danger of being wiped out, and once gone they are gone for ever. There is agreement that the wholesale slaughter and obliteration of wild life should and must be stopped.

Whales, seals, elephants, tigers, deer, antelope, all are in danger. We are at the bottom of the wild life barrel, and everybody knows that the bottom of the barrel runs out fifty times more quickly than the top.

Now we are becoming afraid of what we are doing or allowing to be done. We do not know what side-effects and harm the destruction of a species may produce.

It is a salutary thought that the saving of the wild – and possibly the saving of the world – is left in the hands of a largely uncaring, unskilled and often downright disreputable group of people who have hitched the magic word 'conservation' to their commercial bandwagons. They destroy in a greater ration than they conserve: they kill more than they create.

Disillusionment spreads through the conservation and animal keeping world like an outbreak of foot-and-mouth disease. From my own small group, the list of defectors is alarming: Aspinall wrote in his book about Paul Ottley: 'He has agreed to work out his life with the elephants and when the four resident bulls reach adulthood he is prepared to face the necessary risks to get a birth.' Paul has quit. It all became too much for him, the hours, the pay, the accommodation, the bloody-minded idiocies of management. He jook a job with Canterbury Parks Department and is enjoying life.

Kurt Paulich could take no more. He re-married, packed up and went back to live in Austria where public service in the care of animals is better respected and rewarded.

Richard Johnstone-Scott is the only really happy fellow; he went back to Gerald Durrell's zoo in Jersey and Durrell has always inspired affection and loyalty.

Derek Rushmere runs a fish-and-chip cafe in Folkstone and does not suffer ulcers any more.

Nick Marx bought his couple of acres in the West Country and went self-sufficient; Harry Teyn went to Edinburgh; Brian and Bob – killed.

The list is sad reading: all devoted animal men, happiest when handling animals and all gone from the business. So of the 'best and bravest keepers in the world', in Aspinall's words, only one stays. As for me – I get this mad, wild ambition to do something better with animals; sometimes I find it difficult to suffer fools gladly; so I go walkabout. Big walkabout: Russia, India, America, South America, Africa . . . and I always end up shovelling animal shit.

Too many of my friends put too many ideas into my head and arouse my jealousy: they go to work the *schwartzerarbeiter* market in Germany and return with pocketsful of crinkly 'brownies' and 'blueies'; they work 'on the lump' in the building trade and get very rich, very quickly and I become envious.

I went to work in a local factory which was paying very big money at the time. The first morning, on the works bus, my neighbour said: 'I think I recognise you. You got me in dead trouble. You're the bloke who took two tigers round to see your Mum in Canterbury.'

He was right. Mum had moved from London to Canterbury to be near her gypsy offspring and persuade him to take a respectable job. I had taken two tiger cubs to visit her.

My companion went on: 'I lived next door. I was just arriving home from the pub that lunchtime and I said to my wife, "There are two tigers in the next door garden, come and have a look". She went wild and said, "I'm fed up with you coming home from the pub blind drunk when your dinner's in the oven ruined. Now you're seeing tigers, either you see a doctor or I'm going home to mother." She didn't go, more's the pity.'

The factory was like a bad dream of hell. After the high, wide skies, the larks in their heaven above, green trees heavy with leaf and graceful, elegant wild creatures in the eye, it was too much to take.

After my lifestyle, it was such a traumatic experience that I can never raise an ounce of indignation when the whole nation goes into a state of paranoia over the latest British Leyland strike. As I see it, they have gone out for a breath of fresh air.

One day, when my feet are itching enough and somebody has crossed my palm with silver, I will take a troupe of elephants over the Alps in Hannibal's footsteps for no other purpose than the pursuit of knowledge. I will take them at the same time of the year, by the same route and in the same time marching the length of Spain and over the mountains to Italy.

Every schoolboy knows about Hannibal's feats but a lot of new light could be thrown on the subject by repeating the journey in the way that Thor Heyerdahl's epic voyages have enlightened the world about the spread of cultures.

To an elephant man, Hannibal's achievements were prodigious, the equivalent in modern warfare of fighting a major tank battle in terrain like the Everglades swamps. The wrong weapons in the wrong conditions at the wrong time: the logistics of the operations suggest that great squadrons of the mighty Carthaginian Army would be needed to support the elephants in the Alps crossing without thinking about fighting them at the end of the journey; they would be a hindrance, a massive albatross round the army's over-extended neck and not a tactical advantage.

A lot could be learned from following Hannibal's footsteps; not for commercial purposes, not for anything special except the fun of knowing. And on that long, shuffling trek across populous Spain, and up those foothills, and along those precipitous Alpine passes, under the glare of television lights and flashing of press photographers' cameras, I would have each elephant carry a huge slogan:

'SAVE THE ANIMALS FROM MANKIND FOR MANKIND.'

'But first, save them from fanatics and conservationists!'